The Heinemann English
Wordbuilder

The Heinemann English
Wordbuilder

Guy Wellman

Heinemann International
A division of Heinemann Educational Books Ltd
Halley Court, Jordan Hill, Oxford OX2 8EJ

OXFORD LONDON EDINBURGH
MADRID ATHENS BOLOGNA PARIS
MELBOURNE SYDNEY AUCKLAND SINGAPORE TOKYO
IBADAN NAIROBI HARARE GABORONE
PORTSMOUTH (NH)

ISBN 0 435 28556 4

First published 1989

Design by Arc Design
Illustrations by Laura Potter and Richard Wileman

Printed in Great Britain by
Butler & Tanner Ltd, Frome and London

91 92 93 94 10 9 8 7 6 5 4 3

Contents

Introduction

Why

This book is designed to help the student of English whose only weapons in the battle against vocabulary have, until now, been a dictionary and a dog-eared note-book with lists of unconnected words, approximate translations alongside. I felt a book which would help students to build their active vocabulary, while at the same time helping with the recognition of less common or important words, would be a useful tool with which they could work their way deeper into the language.

Who

The book is designed to be used by a class of students, a couple of friends or an individual working alone. It is particularly useful for students who are not living in an English-speaking country, and so are not exposed to the everyday expressions that are presented and practised in this book.

The level is post-intermediate, which means it should be useful for students who have met the basic structures of English at least once, but have a relatively narrow vocabulary range. It is particularly good practice for users who wish to improve their speaking or writing, or for those who are preparing for a national exam or for the Cambridge First Certificate. Even Cambridge Proficiency exam candidates and other advanced users and students of English will find that there is a lot they can learn in the Heinemann English Wordbuilder.

Because this is a book about language, some of the sections will be most beneficial if the user can argue, experiment and practise with someone else, but users working alone at home can greatly improve and broaden their use of English through the presentation and written practice provided.

What

The Heinemann English Wordbuilder is made up of 60 units. Each unit focusses on one vocabulary area. It starts with a reference section which shows you the words (in bold print) at work, that is to say in context. This is followed by a practice section of exercises and ideas for further written or spoken practice with space for you to add any other expressions you know or meet. The Index at the end of the book contains every word and phrase and so acts as a quick reference guide for you. Some words have a star beside them. You should be careful how you use these. A brief note on each is included in the Key at the back of the book.

You will find there are passages to read, some long, a few quite difficult, and many full to the brim with the target vocabulary. There are often checking exercises after them to make sure the words have 'gone in', that is to say that you have remembered them. There are other exercises, too: matching, gap-filling, defining, ordering, etc. many of which have the answers on the page, which you are asked to cover. The advantage of this is that you can do the exercises again and again if you like, to check how your vocabulary is growing. There are games and quizzes, not really to test your general knowledge but rather to motivate you to study the language under review. (I, personally, would rather be asked to guess – or work out from given data – when, why or in what order certain things happened in Siberia than just read a page of historical facts, for instance. Wouldn't you?)

None of the material is 'authentic' English. You would have to read hundreds of extracts from other sources before you met the thirty or forty words and expressions that you will find grouped in each section here. You should, of course, read widely in addition to this book, to improve your reading skills and to see the vocabulary you have learnt in this book at work.

How

There are three main ways in which you can use the Heinemann English Wordbuilder in class or on your own: by looking up a particular word or expression in the Index and then working on that particular unit; by finding a unit of interest and working through it systematically; by working through all the units one by one.

If you are working alone, and you wish to use the book to increase your vocabulary range, work through at a reasonable pace. If you come across a section which you think is of no importance to you or in which you feel your vocabulary is already very strong, leave it out, perhaps returning to it later. Some parts are easier than others. Never spend too long on one particular section. Treat the book as a cross between a manual and a collection of short stories, not as a novel which you want to read quite quickly from cover to cover. Sometimes refer to it to check a word you're not sure of or need to use; sometimes browse through it and pick a section to read and study, just because it's of interest or perhaps an area of English you have never really considered before. And keep coming back to it, as you would a story you have just enjoyed. Each time you look at a particular section, you will find your vocabulary seems stronger, more refined, more elastic than the time before.

At the end of nearly every unit, there is a Practice section which asks you to incorporate the new and old vocabulary you have studied in a series of speaking or writing activities. They are an important part of the book. There is little point in having thirty thousand words in your head if you are only able to call up about five hundred when you find yourself in a particular situation. The Practice sections will help you to start using the vocabulary more or less automatically and without too much hesitation. These sections will also help your speaking and writing skills in general. There is enough here to give Examiners quite a surprise when they read your compositions and hear your answers to Interview questions.

The book contains a lot, we hope most, of the essential vocabulary within the topics covered. However, if you are a keen reader of or listener to English, you will occasionally come across items that are not included here. You might like to use the 'Add more words ...' sections in each unit to note these down and to make the Wordbuilder very much your own book.

The Key
At the end of the book, you will find a Key. Here we have given the answers to exercises. Look at the title of the unit you are working on and the page number. Then find these in the Key in order to check your work or find words you didn't know. When the answers depend on general knowledge or are particularly difficult, you will find them in the unit itself. Only refer to the Key when you have done a task. No cheating!

Note that in the practice sections there are some activities suggested which are better done with other students, so that you can speak together in small groups. You have been given the choice between speaking and writing, however, in case you are working on your own.

I hope you enjoy using the book. Writing it made me realise again what an interesting language English is. I hope you'll find you agree.

Guy Wellman

Names

Quiz

See how easily and quickly you can find the missing names in the sentences below. The answers are printed after the exercise to help you.

1 William F. Cody (1846 – 1917) was **nicknamed** ... .
2 Mozart's **Christian names** were ... .
3 Queen Elizabeth's youngest son **is called** ... .
4 The Idlewild Airport in New York **was renamed** ... after this man's death.
5 ...'s **real name** is Richard Starkey.
6 A Swedish actress **by the name of** Greta Gustaffson adopted the screen **pseudonym** of ... .
7 Bach's **initials**, J.S., **stand for** ... .
8 Mrs Mark Phillips' **maiden name** was ... .
9 The newest airport in Paris is **named after** ... .
10 Most Englishmen have pretended at some time in their life to be William Younger, **alias** ... .
11 Samuel Clemens' **pen-name** was ... .
12 The stretch of coastland between Toulon in France and Spezia in Italy **is known as** ... .
13 The tallest building in Paris **takes its name from** the engineer, ...
14 Someone **christened** Adolph Schickelgruber became world-famous **under the name of** ... .
15 The film recognised as the first 'talking picture' **was entitled** ... .
16 During the seventies **a certain** Cassius Clay **changed his name** to ... .

Answers
1 Buffalo Bill   2 Wolfgang Amadeus   3 Prince Edward   4 Kennedy International Airport   5 Ringo Starr   6 Greta Garbo   7 Johann Sebastian
8 Princess Anne (Windsor)   9 Charles de Gaulle   10 Billy the Kid   11 Mark Twain   12 The Riviera   13 (Alexandre Gustave) Eiffel   14 Adolf Hitler – the best known **false name** in the world?   15 The Jazz Singer   16 Mohammed Ali

Practice

1 Discuss or write the answers to these questions.

1 What nicknames have you had, if any? Why did people choose them?
2 What will you call or have you called your children? Why?
3 What's the **derivation** of the most popular surnames in your country?
4 How has the fashion in first names changed in your lifetime?
5 How important do you think a good name is for pop and film stars?
6 How important is a good name for commercial products like shampoo, soap, cars or cigars? Can you think of any examples of names which have ruined a product's success?

2 Write a dialogue between a husband and wife as they try to agree on names for their expected child.

■ Add any other expressions about names as you meet them.

....

....

....

....

....

....

....

....

....

Age

Reading

Read through these expressions relating to how old we are and what age does to us.

1900
> a **new-born baby**, 10 lbs. 3 ozs. at birth
> **ten months old**
> **nearly eighteen months old**
> a **toddler**
> **four next birthday**
> **coming up to school age**
> at **infants'** school
> a **schoolgirl**

1910
> all those in the 9 – 11 **age group**
> he had a happy **childhood**
> he's a nice **kid**
> a **teenager**
> **in his youth**
> the agonies of **adolescence**
> still a **minor**, legally speaking
> a **juvenile delinquent**
> congratulations on your **coming of age**

1920
> you have to be **over 21**
> Miss June Hoskins, **aged** 22, of 35 Stanfield Road
> **in his mid-twenties**
> **in his prime**
> **at the age of** 26 she got married
> **by the age of** 26 she had lived in five different countries
> an **adult**
> a **grown-up**

1930
> don't be so **childish**
> he's **turned thirty**
> **thirtyish**
> not a **youngster** any more
> **not as young as she was**
> 36 **years of age**
> **approaching middle-age**
> the **Under 40s** Social Club

1940
> **on the wrong side of** forty
> beginning to **look his age**
> an **ageing** playboy
> beginning **to feel her age**
> I prefer **mature** people

she's still got her **girlish** sense of humour
in his late forties
she's **older than she looks**

1950
still playing his **schoolboy** tricks
in her early fifties
he's **aged a lot** lately
he**'s getting on** (**in years**)
one of the **older generation**
I'm **twice your age**, young man!
the same age as her husband
heading for retirement

1960
he's **over the hill** *
Sunday Excursion for the **Over 60s**
growing old gracefully
a **pensioner (an old age pensioner, OAP)**
he's **coming up to seventy**
you're **old enough to know better**
you're **as old as you feel**
an **elderly** lady

1970
a **septuagenerian**
Help the **Aged**
she's **still going strong**
in her seventy-fifth year
his **elder** brother's death
her **eldest** sister's death
becoming **senile**
old age comes to all of us

1980
his **eightieth birthday**
an **octogenarian**
he's **as old as the hills***
in her **second childhood**
he's **got one foot in the grave***
he'll soon **be pushing up the daisies***
she's **kicked the bucket***
she's **passed away / on**

Practice

1 Discuss or write the answers to these questions.

1 How has your relationship with your parents and other members of your family changed as you have grown older?
2 At which age would you most like to stop the world for ten years so you could enjoy it? Has that age passed or is it still to come?
3 Some people say there are a lot of similarities between childhood and old age. Do you agree?
4 Do you think young people are growing up faster these days? If so, give examples.
5 Do you agree or partly agree with the saying **'Life begins at forty'**?

2   Write on one or more of the following topics.

1 a dialogue between a psychiatrist and a middle-aged man who is worried about his age and getting old.
2 a section of your speech at a public meeting in support of the vote for teenagers.
3 the approximate age at which you normally think of or remember these people, as in the examples.

Winston Churchill   *in his mid- to late sixties*
Olga Korbut   *in her early teens, just after adolescence*

1 James Dean	5 Marilyn Monroe
2 Ronald Reagan	6 Marlon Brando
3 Elvis Presley	7 Joan Collins
4 Mahatma Gandhi	8 Mozart

■   Add any other expressions about age as you meet them.

. . . .
. . . .
. . . .
. . . .
. . . .
. . . .
. . . .
. . . .
. . . .
. . . .

Family relationships

Next of kin . . . .

Brain teaser

Try this little brain-teaser when you have five or ten minutes to spare. Alternatively, just note the names we give to the various **members of our family**.
Each of the fourteen people below **is married to** one of the others. From the information you are given, find out who is married to whom. Note there are three generations here. The answers are on page 14.

Alan is Caroline's **nephew** and Larry's **cousin**.
Barbara is Larry's **mother** and Maggie's **sister-in-law**.
Caroline is Edward's **daughter** and Maggie's sister-in-law.
David is Gordon's **brother-in-law** and Alan's **uncle**.
Edward is Ingrid's **grandfather** and Maggie's **father-in-law**.
Fanny is Caroline's mother and Alan's **grandmother**.
Gordon is Helen's **son-in-law** and Nigel's brother-in-law.
Helen is Barbara's **mother-in-law** and Larry's grandmother.
Ingrid is Gordon's **niece** and David's **daughter-in-law**.
John is David's **father** and Gordon's father-in-law.
Karen is Gordon's daughter-in-law and Maggie's daughter-in-law.
Larry is John's **grandson** and David's **son**.
Maggie is Larry's **aunt** and Fanny's daughter-in-law.
Nigel is Ingrid's father and Fanny's **son-in-law**.

Practice

1 Choose the most suitable word or phrase to complete the sentences below. The answers are on page 14.

  1 Mrs Jones had ... .
    a a trio **b** a treble **c** triplets
  2 Mrs Vine had had ... the week before.
    a quarts **b** quads **c** a quartet
  3 Twins often seem to ... a generation.
    a hop **b** skip **c** jump
  4 There was a case of ... twins in our town recently.
    a Japanese **b** Chinese **c** Siamese
  5 There's a ... of twins in our family – on my father's ... .
    a story   **b** geography   **c** history
    d tree   **e** side   **f** line
  6 I was ... child, though.
    a an only **b** a missing **c** a single
  7 All the members of our football team are **related** ... marriage.
    a by **b** to **c** on
  8 When Mother **remarried**, her second husband, my ..., gave me a new bicycle.
    a forefather **b** stepfather **c** grandfather
  9 He said to me, 'Look, I know you're not my own ..., but let's be friends.'
    a flesh and blood **b** blood and guts **c** skin and bones
  10 My ... **originated** from a tribe of Red Indians.
    a ancestors **b** ancients **c** antiques
  11 Not many of my own ... relatives are still alive.
    a blood **b** skin **c** heart

12 My ... -grandfather fought at the Battle of Waterloo.
  a grand grand grand   **b** great grand grand   **c** great-great-great
13 My brother-in-law **inherited** £500,000 in his uncle's ... .
  a will   **b** testament   **c** wishes.
14 I was left £50 and a cat by ... relative; I believe it was a ... cousin – or perhaps it was a ... -aunt.
  a a distant   **b** an unclear   **c** a long-distance
  d double   **e** second   **f** dual
  g grand   **h** great   **i** large
15 Peter is an **orphan**; he was ... at the age of two.
  a adjusted   **b** adapted   **c** adopted
16 Paul comes from a **broken home**; he has lived with a number of ... parents.
  a loan   **b** foster   **c** second-hand
17 Mary was from a **single-parent family**; now she's **looked after** by her ... .
  a keeper   **b** warden   **c** guardian.
18 I'm off to have Sunday lunch with my ... now.
  a outlaws   **b** by-laws   **c** in-laws

2 Discuss or write the answers to these questions.

1 In what ways do you take after members of your family, in appearance and character?
2 How **close** are you to the various members of your family?
3 What sort of presents do you normally receive from your relatives?
4 Do most people you know get on with their in-laws?
5 What is the system of adopting and fostering in your country?
6 I wouldn't like to be / have been an only child. Do you agree?

3 Write on one or more of the following topics.

1 Write a paragraph from a short story describing a wedding or a funeral.
2 Write an imaginary page from the diary of a foster-parent whose foster-child is leaving tomorrow.

■ Add any other expressions about family relationships as you meet them.

. . . .

Answers
The married couple are: Ingrid and Larry, Edward and Fanny, Helen and John, Alan and Karen, Gordon and Maggie, David and Barbara, Caroline and Nigel.

1 triplets   2 quads   3 skip   4 Siamese   5 history   my father's side   6 an only child   7 by marriage   8 stepfather   9 flesh and blood   10 ancestors   11 blood relatives   12 great-great-great-grandfather   13 will   14 a distant relative, second cousin, great-aunt   15 adopted   16 foster-parents   17 guardian   18 in-laws

Marital status

Reading

Note how various relationships are described in the letter from Hollywood below.

185 Beverley Hills,
Hollywood,
Nr. Los Angeles,
California

13th July 1985

Dear Fiona,
Thanks for all your news. Things are very much as normal here. Harry and I have **split up** – we both felt we had had enough of each other. He's **dating** a girl who was **going steady with** Paul when you were here – I think they're quite **serious** – and I'm seeing a film producer called Harvey who's waiting for his **divorce** to come through. We're more than '**just good friends**' but I don't know how long it will last. My **late husband's former mistress is marrying his first wife's third husband** on Saturday. In fact, it's going to be a **double wedding** because her **second son by her first marriage** is **getting married** to the girl he's been **sharing a flat with** for the past six months. You remember? That's her **half-brother's ex-fiancée**, the one who was **going out with** Jason back in January.
Anyway, how are you? Still the ideal couple over there in Eastbourne, are you? Do I hear **wedding bells**?
Lots of love for now,
Mandy

Practice

1.   Choose the best words to complete the short conversations below.

   1 A Excuse me, ... , can I see your driving licence?
        a Mr **b** sir **c** mate
    B I'm sorry, ... , I don't seem to have it on me.
        a sir **b** policeman **c** constable
   2 A ...! Can I have a menu, please?
        a Sir **b** Mister **c** Waiter
    B Here you are, ...
        a madam **b** Ms **c** Mrs
   3 A Did you understand the question, ... Smith?
        a Sir **b** Madam **c** Miss
    B Yes, I did, my ... .
        a master **b** lord **c** majesty

2 Discuss or write the answers to these questions.

1 Do you think the idea of getting engaged is old-fashioned?
2 Why do you think divorce is nearly as popular as marriage in some countries but not others?

3 Write on one or both of the following topics.

1 Write, and act out if you wish, a typical conversation between a middle-aged married couple who are planning their typical weekday evening at home.
2 Write part of the letter that you write, angrily or sadly, to a newspaper, after reading the headline 'Hollywood Movie Star's Sixth Marriage Ends'.

■ Add any other expressions about marital status as you meet them.

. . . .

. . . .

. . . .

. . . .

. . . .

. . . .

. . . .

. . . .

. . . .

. . . .

. . . .

. . . .

. . . .

Countries, Nationalities

> Country of origin............................
> Nationality......................................

Quiz

Below is a series of competitions for you to try in groups. Its main aim is not to test your **geography**, but to help you study and practise your English.
Only look at the left-hand column. Cover the words on the right.Try to answer the questions. Then check your answers by looking at the words in the right-hand column.

1 Which countries have **borders** with the following groups of countries given below?

1 Guatemala
  El Salvador
  Nicaragua
	Honduras

2 Algeria
  Niger
  Chad
  Sudan
  Egypt
	Libya

3 Colombia Costa Rica	Panama

2 Now, the reverse: which countries border those on the left below? And what nationality are most of the people in them?

1 **Switzerland** (five)		**Swiss**
	Italy	Italian
	Liechtenstein	Liechtensteiner
	France	French
	Austria	Austrian
	West Germany	German
2 **Bolivia** (five)		**Bolivian**
	Brazil	Brazilian
	Peru	Peruvian
	Argentina	Argentinian
	Paraguay	Paraguayan
	Chile	Chilean
3 **England** (two)		**English**
	Scotland	Scottish
	Wales	Welsh

3 Travelling between the cities below, by the shortest possible land route, which countries would you pass through? And what nationality of people would you see most of? Name four countries for each journey.

1 From Tel Aviv to Ankara	Israel	Israeli
	The Lebanon	Lebanese

		Syria	Syrian
		Turkey	Turkish
2	From Kabul to Katmandu	Afghanistan	Afghan
		Pakistan	Pakistani
		India	Indian
		Nepal	Nepalese
3	From Bucharest to Dresden	Romania	Romanian
		Hungary	Hungarian
		Czechoslovakia	Czech(oslovakian)
		East Germany	East German
4	From Lusaka to Entebbe	Zambia	Zambian
		Zaire	Zairean
		Tanzania	Tanzanian
		Uganda	Ugandan

4 Which countries have the **currencies** listed below? And what nationality are most of the people who have that kind of money in their pockets?

1	rand	South Africa	South African
2	yen	Japan	Japanese
3	renminbi	China	Chinese
4	rial	Iran	Iranian
5	markka	Finland	Finnish
6	zloty	Poland	Polish
7	drachma	Greece	Greek
8	baht	Thailand	Thai
9	guilder	Holland	Dutch
		(The Netherlands)	
10	rouble	Russia	Russian
		(The Soviet Union)	
		(The USSR)	

5 Don't worry if you're finding them difficult; the idea is not to get them all right. I had the advantage of an **atlas** and **encyclopedia**.
Which countries have these cities as the **capital**? And what nationality are most of the people living in them?

1	Caracas	Venezuela	Venezuelan
2	Sofia	Bulgaria	Bulgarian
3	Nairobi	Kenya	Kenyan
4	Seoul	South Korea	South Korean
5	Montevideo	Uruguay	Uruguayan
6	Lagos	Nigeria	Nigerian
7	Addis Ababa	Ethiopia	Ethiopian
8	Amman	Jordan	Jordanian
9	Harare	Zimbabwe	Zimbabwean
10	Riyadh	Saudi Arabia	Saudi (Arabian)
11	Baghdad	Iraq	Iraqi
12	Reykjavic	Iceland	Icelandic

6 In which countries do cars with these signs on them probably start their journeys? And what nationality are their drivers likely to be?

1	CDN	Canada	Canadian
2	MEX	Mexico	Mexican
3	MA	Morocco	Moroccan
4	L	Luxembourg	Luxembourger
5	E	Spain	Spanish
6	YU	Yugoslavia	Yugoslavian

7 IRL	Ireland / Eire	Irish
8 USA	The USA (The United States)	American
9 NZ	New Zealand	New Zealander

7 In which countries would you find these dishes most often? And what nationality would most of the people eating them be?

1 satay sauce	**Indonesia**	**Indonesian**
2 couscous	**Morocco**	**Moroccan**
3 kebabs	**Turkey**	**Turkish**
4 smörgos	**Sweden**	**Swedish**
5 white chocolates	**Belgium**	**Belgian (Flemish)**
6 brown cheese	**Norway**	**Norwegian**
7 kangaroo-tail soup	**Australia**	**Australian**
8 chicken livers in port	**Portugal**	**Portuguese**
9 pastries with nuts and dried fruit	**Denmark**	**Danish**

8 English is an easy language, so most of the words in the third columns above, except those ending -*ish* or -*ese* can be used as an adjective or as a noun: *She's Italian* or *She's an Italian* – *He's Israeli* or *He's an Israeli*. This is always true of those words ending -*an* or -*i*.

But there are some special cases, such as the form a **Dutchman**, an **Irishman**, an **Englishman**, a **Frenchman**, a **Welshman**. People from Scotland can be rather complicated. We can call them **Scottish** or **Scotsmen**. If you want to make them angry, you can call them *Scotch*. Alternatively, we can say **He's (She's) a Scot**. Using *He's a …*, see if you can give the nationality of the following people:

1 Alan Wells, sprinter	a **Scot**
2 Lasse Viren, long-distance runner	a **Finn**
3 Bjorn Borg, tennis player	a **Swede**
4 Hans Christian Andersen, story-teller	a **Dane**
5 Lech Walesa, trade union leader	a **Pole**
6 Kemal Attaturk, national hero	a **Turk**
7 Pablo Picasso, artist	a **Spaniard**
8 Alexander Dubcek, one-time party leader	a **Czech**
9 John Walker, middle-distance runner	a **New Zealander**

Game

To finish, a word-association game. What do you think of when you hear the word *Danish?* Danish bacon? Danish butter? Danish cheese?

1 Write or say the word you think of first to go with each of the words below. Possible answers are given on the right. See how often you think of the same word as the one printed in the book.

1 Danish	bacon
2 German	beer
3 French	perfume
4 Irish	whiskey
5 Japanese	motor bikes
6 American	football
7 Greek	islands
8 New Zealand	butter
9 English	weather
10 Russian	dolls

11 Argentinian	beef
12 Egyptian	pyramids

2 Now, play the game the other way round. Write or say the nationality you associate with the things listed below. Are they the same as those in the book?

1	cigarettes	Turkish
2	cheese	Swiss
3	carpets	**Persian**
4	coffee	Brazilian
5	tortillas	Mexican
6	silk	Thai
7	shoes	Italian
8	rugby	Welsh
9	goulash	Hungarian
10	tulips	Dutch
11	cigars	Cuban (Havana)
12	guitar	Spanish
13	restaurants	Chinese

■ Add any other words or expressions about countries and nationalities as you meet them.

. . . .

. . . .

. . . .

. . . .

. . . .

. . . .

. . . .

. . . .

. . . .

. . . .

. . . .

Location

Address ....(**number**, **road**)
................(**town**)
................(**county**)
................(**post-code**)

Reading

1 Here are some typical English and American addresses. Which do you like – or dislike – the sound of?

Apartment 2, Marigold **Mansions**
The Grange, West Hill **Drive**
21 Wellington **Gardens**
10 Rillington **Place**
365 Churchill **Avenue**
18 Newtown **Crescent**
33 Sunset **Boulevard**
28 Poplar **Terrace**
12A The **Promenade**
322A Waite's **Walk**
1 The High **Street**
8 Chestnut **Grove**
1 Tin Pan **Alley**
24 Lincoln **Lane**
130 Hovis **Hill**
48 Cannery **Row**
21 The **Arcade**
4 The **Square**
8 Park **Close**

Dear Santa Claus,
Could you please bring me a
map of the world for Christmas?
My address is
Flat 3
42 Osbourne Street
Southampton Hampshire
England Great Britain
The United Kingdom
The British Isles W. Europe
The Northern Hemisphere
The World The Universe.
Thank you. Love Jason ×
P.S. It's the fourth house on the
left, just past the third lamp-post,
and my room is on the first floor
facing the street, or if you come
the back way, the second door on the
right along the landing from the bathroom.

2 Look at the letter to Santa Claus. How would you write your address?

3 Cover the right-hand column. Then read and become familiar with the directions in the left-hand column. When you can use the phrases on the left with ease, study the right-hand column. It contains expressions of location and the names of places associated with each line on the left. Learn to use a few at a time.

Well, it's **situated in**
central Germany –
or rather,
the centre of
West Germany.
It's almost exactly
due west of Prague,
mid-way between
Luxembourg and
East Germany.
It's **about 100 miles**
from the Belgian
and French
borders.
It's **roughly**

in the **Far East,** in the **Middle East**
in the **North of** Spain, in **southern** Portugal
inside the **Arctic Circle**, in **S.E. Asia**
near the **Antarctic**, within **the tropics**
at the **South Pole**, on the **Equator**
on the same line of latitude as Peking
longitude 8 degrees East
on the other side of the Andes from Lima
50 miles to the north of Oslo
just over the border from El Paso
approximately 40 kilometres from the coast
some 30 miles from the nearest big town
10 miles along the coast from Valencia
100 miles down river from Khartoum
three hours by car from Rio

half an hour's
drive from Frankfurt,
which is in
turn **an hour's**
flight from
Berlin.

a **three-day journey by train from** Algiers
a **five-day voyage from** Perth
four hours by plane from Singapore
eight hours by air
two days by ship
twenty-four hours by sea

It **stands on**
the Rhine, **just**
above where the
Rhine **meets** the
Main, **at the**
southern tip
of the most
picturesque **stretch**
of the river.
It is **set in**
the middle of
one of the world's
finest wine-producing
areas.
It **is built on the**
edge of the Taunus
forests and **is surrounded**
to the north and west
by trees.

it **lies on the coast**
near the mouth of the Ganges
on the banks of the Nile
deep in the interior
in the Loire **valley**
miles from anywhere
in the most northerly part of Sweden
the **southernmost** London **district**
the **furthest point west**
the **south-east corner of** Switzerland
on the fringe of the agricultural region
just below the industrial heartland
in the centre of a holiday resort area
on the slopes of the Himalayas
at the foot of the mountains
on the side of a hill
on a long, thin peninsula
on an island
beside a lake

It **lies on the other**
side of the river from
the city of Mainz and
stretches several miles
in the direction
of Koblenz.
Approaching it from
the north, by car
or by train,
I always used
to travel **down**
the west bank
of the river

a **few miles from the mainland**
directly opposite the port of Southampton

extends over an area of 80 square
kilometres

it can be reached by road or rail
coming from the highlands

drive down the motorway
travel cross-country
keep to the minor roads
go via Lyons

The **district**
is **some**
distance
from the
city centre,
in one of
suburbs lying
to the south and
running adjacent
to the Rhine.

on the far side of town from the beach
quite a long way from the bus station
a bus journey from the town centre
just a stone's throw from the airport
quite a way out of town
on the outskirts of the town
in one of the outlying villages
in a very remote part
parallel to the canal
a few miles inland

To find it from the
Centre Station, you
turn left out of the
main gate, **follow the**
main road up the hill,
across the traffic
lights, over the next
crossroads and then
through a long tunnel.

to get to it **from the ferry terminal**
bear right
go straight on
cross over
follow the pavement round
through a pedestrian precinct
up and down the hill
across the fields
along a country lane

To get to the street,
it's **left at the next
lights**, under the
railway bridge, second
turning on the right
then **third left**.

take the left fork at the junction
over a railway crossing
through a little wood
leave the cathedral on your right
follow the signs to Endgate
head for the spire in the distance

There is a **short
cut** through
the **back streets**
but **the long
way round**
is easier.

it's **about two miles as the crow flies**
quite a lot further by road
half-an-hour's walk
about forty minutes on foot
a **ten-minute bus ride**
quarter-of-an-hour on the underground
twenty minutes by taxi

The street is
**one of the
turnings off
to the right.**
You can't miss it.

two blocks away from the hospital
the **third exit off the roundabout**
a **sharp turning to your left**
a **one-way street**
a **no-through road**
a **cul-de-sac**

The **house** is
at the far end
of the street,
**the third or
fourth from the
end on the right,**
just down from
a little pizzeria.

halfway along on the left
towards the end of the street
on a bend in the road
the **last one in the street**
on a corner, opposite a florist's
just across the road from a telephone kiosk
next to an Indian restaurant
just past a pillar box
with a bus-stop right outside

It's a **five-storey
building** and the
flat is **on the
second floor.**
It's **self-contained**
and has
**its own entrance
down a little
alley** that
**runs along the
side of the
building.**

a **(semi-) detached house**
a **terraced house**
a **skyscraper**
a **tower block**
a **bungalow**
a **maisonette**
a **bed-sitter (bed-sitting room)**

a **long drive leading up to the house**
parking space at the front
a green **front door**
a **side entrance**
over a shop

Ignore the **steps
leading down to
the basement** and
go up **the first
flight of stairs,**
through the door
at the top, a
few yards **along
the passage,** then
**up the staircase
to your right.**
Go **through the hall.**
To your left is
the second **bedroom.**
The **kitchen's**

take the lift up to the third floor
a **spiral staircase leading to the attic**

a **revolving door**
a **sliding door**

a **few steps along the landing**
through the French windows
out on to the balcony

the **master bedroom**
the **spare room**
the **bathroom**

on your right.
Then go **along
another passage
leading off to**
the left.
The **lounge**,
which **looks out
on to** the street,
is **the second
door on the
left**.

the **toilet**
the **lavatory**
the **WC**
the **loo**
the **larder (a food cupboard)**
the **living room**
the **sitting room**
the **dining room**

it **faces south**

**On your right
as you go in,
behind the door,**
there's an armchair;
at least there
was ten years ago.

**just inside on the left
to the left of the fireplace
along the wall opposite
on the right as you look at it
directly in front of you
under the window
next to the piano**

That was where she was
sitting when I left the
room ten years ago. If
she's still there, give
her my regards, will you?

Practice

1. Look at the map of the world. Plan your ideal journey round the world.

2. Describe the layout of your home and where the furniture is in each room.

3. Explain how to get from your house to the nearest railway station.

■ Add any other words or expressions about locations you meet.

. . . .
. . . .
. . . .
. . . .
. . . .
. . . .
. . . .
. . . .
. . . .
. . . .
. . . .

Build

Reading

Where do you belong below?

he's a **giant** (of a man)
she's an **Amazon**
extremely tall
tallish
above average height

medium build
he's / she's got a **good figure**
he's / she's **well-built**

stocky   **petite**
plump   **thin**
corpulent   **skinny***
built like a barrel*   **like a pipe cleaner***
he's **as square / big round as he's tall**   **there's nothing of her**
obese*   **like a lamp-post***
overweight   **puny-looking***
squat   **slight and slender**
muscular   **slim**
below average height
on the short side
short
tiny
a **midget**
knee-high to a grasshopper / an ant

Practice

1. Discuss or write the answers to these questions.

   1 Which of the above adjectives and phrases would suit a student in your class or a member of your family?
   2 Do you think your build sometimes determines your character? If so, how?
   3 What sort of build should gymnasts, footballers and weight-lifters have?
   4 Which word in each pair of words would you prefer people to use about you? Why?

   1 skinny / slim
   2 well- built / corpulent
   3 overweight / obese
   4 **all skin and bones / there's more fat on a chip**

   5 plump / stocky
   6 short / below average height
   7 a midget / knee-high to an ant

■ Add any other expressions about your or other people's build as you meet them.

....
....
....

From the neck up

Reading

Think about hair first. Notice the different descriptions of hair in the two life stories below. Then read the advertisements.

	Him	Her
at birth:	**thick (jet) black hair**	**a few mousy strands**
aged 3:	**curly brown** hair	**hair in bunches** fastened with **slides, grips** and **ribbons**
at 13:	a **crew cut** – an early **skinhead**	**hair in plaits**, otherwise completely **straight**
at 16:	long **sideboards, spikey**	**in a bun**
at 19:	**shoulder-length** hair	**back-combed**, with a **ponytail**
at 23:	**wavy, swept back**, with a **side parting**	January: she's a **blonde** March: she's a **brunette** May: she's a **redhead** (she's got **auburn** hair) July: she's **ash-blonde** October: she's **dyed** it pink
at 28:	**neat style** with **a fringe**	**frizzy**, slightly **streaked**
at 35:	**a few grey hairs**	**combed forward**, a few **highlights**
at 40:	his hair's **receding**	she's **greying**
at 45:	**distinguished**, but he's **balding**	her hair's **thinning**, so she's experimenting with a **wig**
at 50:	he's trying a **toupee**	her hair's **going white** fast
at 55:	completely **bald**	the wig's **matted, unmanageable**, so she has a blue **rinse**

CLOVER
SHAMPOO
for **dry, normal** and **greasy** hair
gets rid of **split ends**
flyaway hair will be a thing of the past
fights dandruff
gives your hair **body**
5 good reasons to start using CLOVER!

AHEAD OF TIME
Unisex Hair Salon

Trim	£6.50
Cut and **Blow Dry**	£15.00
Perm(anent Waving)	£27.50
Razor cutting	£2.50 extra
Highlights from	£25.00

Practice

1 Now look at facial features. On the left are some adjectives often used to describe a particular part of the face or head. Cover the right-hand column and see if you can tell which part in each case.

1 **high, lined**	forehead
2 **rosy, hollow**	cheeks
3 **double, pointed**	chin
4 **false, long**	eyelashes
5 **bushy, pencil-thin**	eyebrows
6 **snub, hook** (or **Roman**)	nose

7 **cauliflower, pierced**	**ears**
8 **piercing, hazel**	**eyes**
9 **square, upper**	**jaw**
10 **thick, cherry**	**lips**
11 **wide, mean**	**mouth**

And here you can see most of these features in these two pictures.

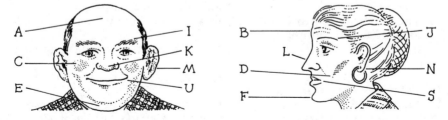

2 Demonstrate the actions listed below and explain when you would use them.

1 **smack your lips**
2 **raise your eyebrows**
3 **prick up your ears**
4 **mouth something**
5 **flutter your eyelashes**
6 **purse your lips**
7 **blow your nose**
8 **puff out your cheeks**
9 **turn your nose up**

3 Keep the right-hand column covered. On the left are some definitions of facial features. Write or say what they are. Then find the appropriate word on the right.

1 openings in the nose	the **tongue**
2 the soft lower parts of the ears	**eyelids**
3 flat parts on the side of the face above the cheek-bones	a **moustache**
4 hair that grows on the chin and jaw	the **complexion**
5 the bony case that protects the brain	**nostrils**
6 the tissue our teeth are in	the **brow**
7 the passage from the mouth towards the stomach	a **beard**
8 the semi-poetic name for the forehead	**gums**
9 the colour and state of the skin on the face	**lobes**
10 hair that grows above the upper lip	**temples**
11 the movable skin which opens and closes the eyes	the **throat**
12 the organ used for tasting, swallowing and speech	the **skull**

4 Study the words and the picture. Then cover the words and test your memory while looking at the picture.

1 **lines, wrinkles**
2 a **wart**
3 **bags under the eyes**
4 a **beauty spot**
5 **freckles**
6 a **mole (a birthmark)**
7 a **(cold) sore**
8 a **stye**
9 **spots, pimples**
10 **dimples**
11 a **boil**
12 a **scar**

5 When do you get problems with your head, neck and face? Match the accidents 1 – 13 below with their causes in the right-hand column.
You can still have all sorts of problems even when you are enjoying yourself.

1	a **stiff neck**	from swimming underwater a lot
2	a **sore throat**	from diving headfirst into an empty pool
3	**bloodshot eyes**	from eating too many sweets
4	**eyestrain**	after that early morning swim
5	a **headache** or **migraine**	from watching the Wimbledon doubles final
6	**toothache, sore gums** or	
7	an **ulcer** in the mouth	after refusing to leave the night-club
8	a **runny nose** or	
9	a **blocked-up nose**	from trying to read in the dark
10	a **black eye**, **swollen lips** and	
11	a **nosebleed**	from staying too long in the disco
12	feeling **giddy** or **dizzy**	from shouting too much at the football match
13	**concussion**	from dancing too many Viennese waltzes

I had a pretty bad week myself last week. (These columns are in the right order.)

On Monday, I **singed my eyebrows**	while trying to light the gas-cooker.
On Tuesday, I **grazed my chin** and **scratched**	
my cheek	on a revolving door.
On Wednesday, I **banged my head**	when I walked into a door,
On Thursday, I **chipped one of my front teeth**	when I fell on the ice.
On Friday, I **knocked the other front tooth out**	when I fell on the ice again.
On Sunday, I **scalded my face**	with my shaving water,
split my lip open	eating one of my wife's rock-cakes,
came out in a rash	because of something I'd eaten
and **had earache**	for some reason or other.

6 Find and cut out photos of people from newspapers and magazines. Label the facial features which stand out.

7 Describe the face that comes to mind when you imagine a typical:

1 headmaster / headmistress
2 boxer
3 second-hand car salesman
4 air-force officer
5 English king
6 Chinese girl
7 pop drummer.

8 Write a short police 'Wanted' notice regarding one of the 'criminals' in your class or family. Draw an accompanying picture if you can.

■ Add any other expressions about these parts of the body as you meet them.

. . . .
. . . .
. . . .
. . . .
. . . .

From shoulder to fingertips

Game

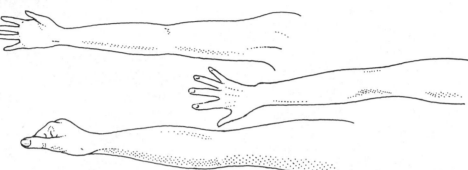

Cover the right-hand column. Which parts of the picture above – or things associated with a particular part of the picture – would these people be most concerned with?

1	a fortune teller	the client's **palm**
2	a bridegroom	his bride's **ring finger**
3	a driver who notices a student hitching a lift	the student's **thumb**
4	a karate expert	his opponent's **forearm**
5	a boxer	his opponent's **fists**
6	a detective searching for clues	some **fingerprints**
7	a policeman carrying handcuffs	the suspect's **wrists**
8	a manicurist	the client's **fingernails**
9	a soldier on rifle parade	his **shoulder**
10	passengers on a crowded tube train	other people's **elbows**
11	someone keen to see if you're ticklish	your **armpit**
12	a mother whose son has been in a fight	his **knuckles**
13	a Mr Universe judge	the contestants' **biceps**
14	someone trying to see what you're pointing at	your **index finger** (**forefinger**)
15	a pianist playing top notes	the **little finger** on the right **hand**

Practice

1. Many parts of the body are verbs as well as nouns. Demonstrate or write a description of these actions.

   1. **thumb through** a book
   2. **thumb a lift**
   3. **hand someone** a pen
   4. **palm someone off with something** second-rate
   5. **elbow your way** through the crowd
   6. **shoulder responsibility**
   7. **finger** a document

2 Act or write an interview in the doctor's surgery. The patient describes the pains he or she keeps getting in his/her arm. The doctor does some tests, tries to decide what's wrong and suggests what should be done.

■ Add any other expressions about these parts of the body as you meet them.

. . . .

. . . .

. . . .

. . . .

. . . .

. . . .

. . . .

. . . .

. . . .

. . . .

. . . .

From the bottom down

Reading

Read the excerpts from little Johnny's composition below. Make sure you know which sections of the diagram he is referring to.

13.1.90   My Christmas Holiday

As a special treat, my Mummy and Daddy took me on a winter sports holiday this year. We all went to the Swiss Alps for a fortnight. I enjoyed the first few days, but skiing was more difficult than I thought. On the third day, I twisted my **knee**, bruised my **shin**, sprained my **ankle**, damaged a **tendon** in the back of my **foo**t – my **Achilles tendon**, I think it's called – got cramp in my **calf**, squashed my **big toe**, got corns on my **heels** and hard patches of skin on the **soles** of my feet, pulled a muscle in my **thigh**, and rubbed all the skin off my **instep**. On the fourth day, I was unfortunate ... as we were getting on the bus to the airport, I tore a **hamstring**. (My broken **leg** and fractured **pelvis** happened after I got home.)

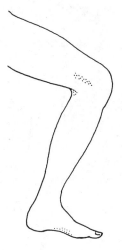

Practice

1 Make sure you understand the idiom in each of these questions, then think of a possible answer. Write it down or compare your ideas with a partner.

   1 Why was the teacher **rocked back on his heels**?
   2 How did you **put your foot in it** with your neighbour?
   3 Why was the teacher **on her knees** after the lesson?
   4 In what ways do students have to **toe the line**?
   5 Why **haven't you got a leg to stand on** concerning your homework?
   6 Why have you got to **be on your toes** in that teacher's lesson?
   7 How did your parents **cramp your style** at the disco?
   8 When should parents make children **stand on their own two feet**?

2 Discuss or write the answers to these two questions.

   1 What exercises do you know of that are designed to keep the different parts of the leg in good shape? Explain how to do them.
   2 What problems do people have with the different parts of their legs, through accidents, age or lifestyle? What can they do about them?

■ Add any other expressions about these parts of the body as you meet them.

. . . .
. . . .

Inside and outside the torso

Reading

Look carefully at the two pictures below and the list of words under each of them. Then test yourself on the names of things by covering the lists of words and trying to identify each number and letter in the pictures.

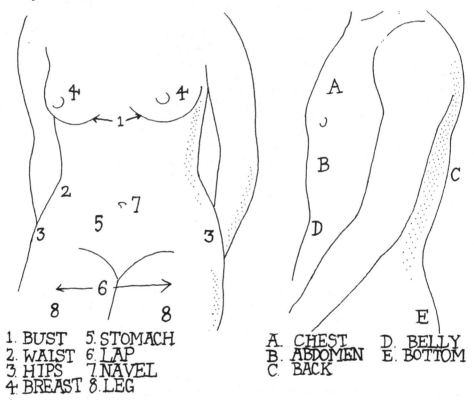

1. BUST   5. STOMACH
2. WAIST 6. LAP
3. HIPS   7. NAVEL
4. BREAST 8. LEG

A. CHEST   D. BELLY
B. ABDOMEN E. BOTTOM
C. BACK

Note the following.

1 Her **bust** is 38", his **chest** is 40".
2 She's got a 24" **waist**. His **waist** is 32".
3 She measures 40" round the **hips**. His **inside leg** measurement is 32".
4 I've got a **stomach-ache**,
5 a **bad back**,
6 and a **pain in my abdomen**.
7 Hasn't he got a **fat belly**?*
8 Were you **breast-fed** as a baby?
9 Let the baby sit on my **lap**.
10 My **bottom** aches from sitting down all day.
11 The belly-dancer had a bare stomach except for the pearl in her **navel** (**tummy button**).

Practice

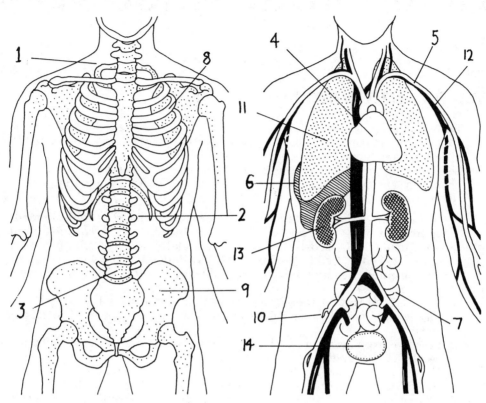

1. What's where inside us? Study the words below, then test yourself with the help of the picture.

1 **collar bone**	8 **ribs**
2 **spine** or **backbone**	9 **pelvis**
3 a **vertebra (vertebrae)**	10 **appendix**
4 **heart**	11 **lungs**
5 **arteries**	12 **veins**
6 **liver**	13 **kidneys**
7 **intestines**	14 **bladder**

2. Now describe where each organ or bone in Exercise 1 is found in the body.

3. Write a simple description of the function of each of the items in Exercise 1.

■ Add any other words or phrases about these parts of the body you meet here. (If you are still curious, you can consult a bi-lingual dictionary for further organs.)

. . . .

. . . .

. . . .

. . . .

. . . .

. . . .

Compound adjectives

Study and practice

There a lot of compound adjectives in English. Here are some common ones which are formed from parts of the body. For example, *heart* gives us **warm-hearted**, **kind-hearted**, **hard-hearted** etc.

Look at the list of similar compound adjectives below and guess what they mean. Then read sentences 1 – 10. Complete each sentence with the appropriate adjective(s).

left-handed	**double-breasted**	**narrow-waisted**	**cold-blooded**
big-headed	**pot-bellied**	**red-faced**	**round-shouldered**
sour-faced	**cross-eyed**	**knock-kneed**	**slim-hipped**
light-fingered	**strong-willed**	**bow-legged**	**empty-handed**
dark-skinned	**fair-haired**	**broad-minded**	**right-footed**

1 My boss is terribly ... , walking around as if he were holding his salary cheque between his knees. His wife's quite the opposite: ... , as if she had just got off a horse.
2 I used to wear ... suits until I decided that one button was far more suitable for ... people such as myself.
3 My sister is so ... and ... she reminds me of one of those long thin wine bottles.
4 He's Scandinavian, so he's ... and ... , and looks far better in jeans than I do.
5 It looked as if United were going to return home ... until Bradfield scored with an incredibly powerful ... shot from outside the penalty area.
6 Off we go on holiday with visions of returning ... and beautiful, forgetting that we always come back ... and with peeling backs.
7 Hoskins, if you go on staring at that magazine any longer, you'll go ... . Now either be ..., dear boy, and put it away or give it to me until the end of the lesson.
8 My boss is so ..., always looking as if he knew tomorrow was going to be the end of the world. And his wife is so ... ; I have to keep a careful eye on my things when they come round to the house, or they just disappear.
9 Most ... tennis players seem to win more easily against right-handers. Talking of tennis players, aren't those professionals a ... bunch, shouting all the time about how great they are?
10 A lot of liberal, ... people find it difficult to accept that there is such a thing as ... murder.

Practice

1 Complete each sentence with the appropriate word from the list below. Note that they are all adjectives made from parts of the body, and that *bloody* is a frequently used and not very rude swear word.

hairy	**cheeky**	**bloody**	**leggy**	**handy**
nosey	**hearty**	**skinny**	**heady**	**chesty**

1 ... congratulations on your success!
2 I could watch those ... women high jumpers for hours.
3 That sounds like a rather ... cough you've got.
4 The shops are quite ... – only two minutes' walk.
5 No, you can't borrow my girlfriend for the evening! Don't be so ...!
6 It's nothing to do with you what we're doing tonight! Don't be so ...!
7 She's so ... that when she turns sideways, she's almost invisible!

8 Did you know he's got a ... chest? Like a doormat, it is!
9 I reckon you'd have to be a ... fool to want to learn this ... stupid language!
10 I feel quite ... after getting all those right. Or perhaps it's the champagne.

2 Discuss or write the answers to these questions.

1 Which elements of your body – from **split ends** to **toenails** – do you wish were different in some way?
2 What are the necessary **physical attributes** of the following types of athlete? Use the phrases: *You have to be / have ...; You need ...; You can't ... without ...* .
   1 a swimmer
   2 a skier
   3 a tennis player
   4 a footballer
   5 a sprinter
3 How important do you think **physical appearance** is for a happy or successful life?

3 Write a paragraph on one of the following topics.

1 A description in your diary of how your body felt when you suffered from and slowly recovered from frost-bite or bad sunburn.
2 Continue this paragraph: 'Suddenly the door opened and the strangest-looking man I have ever seen seen came into the room. ...'
3 A description from your short story of the people in the waiting room of a marriage guidance bureau.

■ Add any other adjectival expressions about the body as you meet them.

. . . .
. . . .
. . . .
. . . .
. . . .
. . . .
. . . .
. . . .
. . . .
. . . .
. . . .
. . . .
. . . .

The senses

Dialogue

1 Read the conversations below. Note these patterns used to talk about the five basic senses.

A Look at that!
B I can't **see** anything.
A It **looks like** a boat.
B Where?
A Over there! It's clearly **visible**.
It's just come **in sight**
It's just come **into view**.
B You must have good **eyesight**.
You must have sharp eyes.

A Listen to that!
B I can't **hear** anything.
A It **sounds like** a cry for help.
B Where's it coming from?
A Over there! It's clearly **audible**.
It's a very clear sound.
B Your **hearing** must be good.
You must have good ears.

A Smell this!
B I can't **smell** anything.
A It **smells like** stale fish.
B Does it?
A Yes, it's quite a strong **smell**.
You must have a very sensitive nose.
You must have a keen **sense of smell**.

A Taste this!
B I can't taste anything wrong.
A It **tastes like** vinegar.
B Really?
A Yes, it's got quite a strong
(after-)taste.
B You must have a very sensitive
palate.
Your **sense of taste** must be very good.

A Touch (Feel) this!
B I can't **feel** anything.
A It **feels as if** it's vibrating.
B Where?
A Here. It's quite a strong
sensation.
It's a very funny **feeling**.
B You must have very sensitive
fingers.
You must have a special **sense
of touch**.

Remember: taste can also relate to artistic and social life.

Is your bedroom **tastefully** decorated?
Don't you think that joke you told at the party was **in rather poor (bad) taste**?
The vicar certainly thought it was **tasteless**.

Note too:

That darts player has **a good eye**.
That musician has **a good ear**.

And also:

It's **out of sight, out of earshot**, and **out of reach**.

2 There are more than five senses, aren't there? Have a look at this short conversation.

A Something tells me you could do with another drink.
B You must be **psychic**. Thanks.
A I can **sense** that you probably love tea. Is that so?
B Great. You must have **extra-sensory perception**.
A And I **feel it in my bones** that it's China tea. Am I right?
B Fantastic. We must be **telepathic**.
A My **intuition** says it's green tea.
B What an **instinct** you have!
  A small cup, is it?
A No, a large one, please.

Practice

1 Often our five senses don't work as well as they might.
Cover the right column, and then the left, and try to recall the equivalent expression from the other column.

to be **short-sighted / long-sighted**	to be **hard of hearing**
to **go blind**	to **go deaf**
to **wear glasses / contact lenses**	to **wear a hearing aid**
to be **as blind as a bat**	to be **deaf as a post**
to **read Braille**	to **lip-read**
	to use **sign language**
to be **colour blind**	to be **tone-deaf** (of music)
to visit **an oculist**	to go to an **ear specialist**

2 Look at the list of words formed from the word *sense*. Complete the sentences with an appropriate word from the list or the word *sense,* which you will use three times.

**sensible   sensitive   sensation   sensational   sensual   sensuous
senseless**

1 What should you say? You'll just have to use your common ... .
2 The news of the scandal caused a ... .
3 I've always found the buzzing of bees has a very ... attraction.
4 I think the ... thing to do would be to stop now and get a good night's sleep.
5 In one ... I think you're right, but not completely.
6 Kleindorf's defeat of Real Madrid in the European Cup was ... .
7 It's ... trying to argue with him; he never listens to a word anybody says.
8 She's very ... on the subject of divorce, so be careful what you say.
9 I felt a ... of 'deja vu' when I was turned down for the job the second time.
10 The cashier at the bank has incredibly ... hands.

3 A hundred British people were asked to complete the phrase *a sense of*. These were the most popular choices. Do they tell you anything about the British?
Complete each sentence 1 – 9 with an appropriate phrase.

a **sense of humour**	a **sense of duty**	a **sense of power**
a **sense of fairness**	a **sense of adventure**	a **sense of timing**
a **sense of discipline**	a **sense of fun**	a **sense of balance**

1 Having a little red button not far from his desk must give a President an enormous ... .

2 Without a ... you'll never be able to hit the ball correctly.

3 Some people say that a ... is the only thing that makes difficult situations bearable.
4 He went ahead and arrested his uncle through a ... .
5 One of the major tasks of parents should be to give their children a ... .
6 His inborn ... led him to the slopes of the Himalayas.
7 At high altitudes one is apt to lose one's ... .
8 His ... is so strong, he protests to umpires on behalf of his opponent.
9 Personally, I don't call putting dead fish in friends' beds a sign of a healthy ... .

4 Discuss or write the answers to these questions.

1 What ten things would you miss most if you were blind or deaf? In other words, what are your favourite sights and sounds?
2 What evidence have you heard of people who are deprived of one sense having unusually well-developed other senses?
3 Do you believe in a sixth sense? Have you heard of any cases of ESP (extra-sensory perception)?
4 Goethe said that a meal should please the eye before it pleases the stomach. How important do you think this is?

5 Write a paragraph on one or all of the following subjects.

1 Your sensations (visual, aural and personal) while watching a forest fire. This will be part of your short story.
2 A page from your diary, recording your feelings and sensations as you looked at a room the morning after a party.
3 Part of a letter to a friend telling him or her about a lovely long walk you had one spring morning.

■ Add any other words about the senses as you meet them.

. . . .
. . . .
. . . .
. . . .
. . . .
. . . .
. . . .
. . . .
. . . .
. . . .
. . . .
. . . .
. . . .

Character and personality

Game

Are we the kind of people we are because of the time of the year we were born? See if you can complete the adjectives below at home over the next day or so. Each one has a clue beside it to help you and a dot for each letter that you need to add.

ARIES (Mar 21 – Apr 20)
You won't find him in the corner at the party.   o.tg.i.g
That's her doing the can-can on the table.   ex...v.rt
She has no problems.   c.. ef.ee
He never frowns.   l...t-h.a.t.d
She tells no lies.   t.u.hf..
He has few secrets.   o..n
He'll tell you if he doesn't like your make-up.   c.n.id
She'll tell you if she doesn't like your after-shave.   f...k
He's the person to ask for that five pounds you are owed.   e..y-g...g

TAURUS (Apr 21 – May 20)
He knows what he wants and he usually gets it.   s.r.n.-wi..ed
She never gives up without a fight.   d.t.r.i.ed
He knows he's good.   s.l.-as.u..d
She knows she's as good.   s.l.-co..i..nt
She likes to be the boss, the one on top.   d.m.n.nt
He wants to be even bigger, even better – the best   am..t.o.s
and expects high standards of performance from others.   d.m.n.i.g
He works 18 hours a day, jogs,and plays squash.   e.e.ge..c
She hates to lose, in business or at tiddlywinks.   c.mp...t..e

GEMINI (May 21 – Jun 20)
She thinks she's good.   p.o.d
He thinks he's superior to everyone.   a.r.g..t
'As the most experienced and sensible person
present, I ...'   p.mp..s
'Of course, I could have beaten him even more
easily, but I wanted to give him a chance.'   b..stf.l
She won't share her presents with her sister.   s..f..h
He spends half the day in front of the mirror.   v..n
She thinks the whole world revolves around her.   s..f-c.n.r.d
He thinks he's the centre of the universe.   e.oc..t..c
She looks down on anyone who hasn't got a
heated indoor swimming pool at home.   s.o.b..h

CANCER (Jun 21 – Jul 20)
She seems to enjoy finding fault with others.   c.it...l
He'll take off marks if you don't dot your i's.   p.t.y
She can only ever see one side of things.   na...w-m.n..d
He always likes the fat taken off his bacon.   f.s.y
He's like a donkey.   s.u.b.r.
She's like a mule.   o.s.in.t.
He loves money, loves having 'things'.   m.t.r.a.i.t.c

Oh yes, he'll help you – if you make it worth his while.   m.r.en.ry
She never lets her husband out of her sight.   p.ss.ss..e

LEO (Jul 21 – Aug 21)
You never know what he's going to do.   u.p.ed.ct..le
He never knows what he's going to do.   i.d.c.s.ve
There are two things I don't like about her – her face!   t.o-f...d
Be careful what he's saying about you behind your back.   h.po.r.t.c.l
Be careful what she's doing while your back is turned.   d.sh.n..t
He behaves like the weather in April.   cha.g.a.le
She behaves like the proverbial primadonna.   t.mp.r.m..t.l
He says what I want to hear, not what he thinks.   i.s.nc.r.
He never does all the things he says he'll do.   u.r.l.a.l.

VIRGO (Aug 22 – Sep 22)
Other people's points of view always impress him.   i.p.e.s.on..le
She'd believe you if you told her pizzas grew on trees.   g.ll.ble
She lacks will-power.   w..k-w....d
He lacks courage.   c.w..d.y
He doesn't do much – he just sits back and watches.   p.s..v.
She'll do what she's told.   ob.d...t
You never know what he's thinking.   s.cr.t..e
'It was an honour just to be on the same court as McEnroe.   h.mb.e
How I beat him 6-0, 6-0, 6-0? It was just luck.'   m.d..t

LIBRA (Sep 23 – Oct 22)
He uses his common sense.   s.n.i.le
She never does silly things under pressure.   l.v.l-h..d.d
She's like the Libran symbol of the scales.   w..l-b.l.n.ed
She'd solve all the problems on a desert island,   p.ac..l
and nothing would upset her.   c..m
He'd be a good judge or referee.   f..r-m..d.d
She's got both feet on the ground and is really down-to-earth.   r.al..t.c
His heart rarely rules his head.   r.t..n.l
I think, therefore I am. That's my approach.   l.g.c.l

SCORPIO (Oct 23 – Nov 22)
Keep out of her way when she loses her temper.   a.gr..s.v.
He's always the first one to put his fists up,   v..l.nt
and he's quick to use them – to the full.   b.u.al
He may even add a boot or two for good measure.   v.c.o.s
She won't let anything stand in her way.   r..hl..s
He has no principles about hurting other people.   u.sc.u.u.ous
He almost seems to enjoy causing trouble.   m.l.c.ous
She's a strong believer in an eye for an eye,   sp.t...l
and a tooth – or, in her case, teeth – for a tooth.   v.n.i.t.ve

SAGITTARIUS (Nov 23 – Dec 20)
Those with some Latin blood in their veins.   p.s.i.n.t.
They are fiery and emotional.   h..- bl..d.d
She's not afraid to go mountain climbing,   b.a.e
or to join a mountain rescue team.   c.ur.g...s
He wants to go to wild and unexplored places.   a.v.nt.r..s
They're vivacious, like champagne bubbles.   l.v.l.
She puts her heart and soul into her profession.   d.d.c.t.d
On the sinking ship, the dog never left its master's side.   d.v.t.d
These friends do not desert you in a crisis.   l.y.l

CAPRICORN (Dec 21 – Jan 19)
He'd always stop to help a disabled person across the road.   c.ns.d....e
That's her on the beach wiping oil off the sea-birds' feathers.   t.nd..

She wouldn't hurt a fly.	**g.nt..**
He leaves £10 tips.	**g.n.r..s**
He wouldn't mind if she dyed her hair green.	**t.lr..t**
She lets him sleep when he gets back from a hard day's work.	**u.d.rst.n.i.g**
He defends her in any argument.	**p.o.ect.ve**
She kisses him on the cheek every minute or so.	**a.f.c.i.n.te**
She always sends a card on her parents' anniversary.	**th..g.tf.l**

AQUARIUS (Jan 20 – Feb 18)

If she likes you, she'll fling her arms around you and say so.	**i.p.l.i.e**
He jumps into the bath without testing the water.	**i.p.t.ous**
Lose your way with *her* in the car? You'd better not!	**i.p.t.e.t**
He's constantly like a child on Christmas Eve.	**ex.i.abl.**
He's a typical 'angry young man'.	**r.b.l.i.us**
She's Trotsky, Castro and Guevara all rolled into one.	**r...lut.o..ry**
He's got a memory like a sieve.	**f..g.tf..**
He thought a double brandy would help the baby sleep.	**i.res...s.ble**
If she gets an idea in her head, there's no stopping her.	**u.c.n.r.l.a.l.**

PISCES (Feb 19 – Mar 20)

There she is, over there, on her own in the corner.	**s.y**
He's afraid that the whole world is looking at him.	**s.l.-c..s..ous**
She peeps round her front door like a mouse.	**t.m.d**
He's always the last to introduce himself.	**r.s..ved**
Be careful not to upset her. It's easily done.	**s.n.i..ve**
He can see beauty in a pile of rubbish.	**i..gin....e**
He can then turn the pile of rubbish into a work of art.	**c.e.t.v.**
I was moved to tears by the beauty of his sculpture.	**em.t.... l**
He doesn't know who he is, where he is, what to do or why.	**u.sta.le**

Practice

1 Ladies and gentlemen, which of these traits of character do you most dislike in a partner? Place them in order.

vanity	**hypocrisy**	**pomposity**	**stubbornness**
obstinacy	**selfishness**	**dishonesty**	**pettiness**
arrogance	**snobbishness**	**timidity**	**possessiveness**
shyness	**meanness**	**rashness**	**aggressiveness**

Ladies and gentlemen, which of these qualities is most important for you in a partner? Place them in order of importance.

compassion	**vivacity**	**frankness**	**self-assurance**
tolerance	**patience**	**generosity**	**ambition**
sincerity	**imagination**	**passion**	**humility**
modesty	**sensitivity**	**courage**	**creativity**

2 Discuss or write down the personal characteristics (good and bad) that you would expect to find in these people.

1 a nurse
2 the chairman of a multinational company
3 an actor
4 a politician
5 a teacher

3 Discuss or write answers to these questions.

1 How would you say your **national character** is different from that of people in the immediately neighbouring countries?
2 How do you think your character has changed or developed over the years? Are there any aspects of your personality you still don't like?
3 Write a sentence to describe the character of each of your fellow students or family. Then read the sentences to them. See if they can identify each person.
4 Choose two of the star-signs and write a paragraph for each, as if for a magazine, analysing personality. Use the adjectives in those sections to give you some ideas.
5 'The weaker sex? The fairer sex? Not any more!' Write an article of 250 – 300 words contrasting the image of women today with that of a few hundred years ago.

■ Add any other expressions about personality and character as you meet them.

. . . .

. . . .

. . . .

. . . .

. . . .

. . . .

. . . .

. . . .

. . . .

. . . .

. . . .

Attitudes and beliefs

Reading

Read the text that follows in stages – it's rather long – and note the language it offers you in the area of opinions, beliefs and attitudes.

Fifties people wore pointed shoes. Sixties people wore flowers in their hair. Seventies people dyed their hair pink. So what about the Eighties? Is this a fair picture of an Eighties couple or not? If not, why not?

A 1980s Couple

They are **passionate believers in** vegetarianism and **regard** people who eat meat as worse than criminals. (**In their view**, egg-eaters are really no better, as eggs are baby chickens.)

> I **suspect**, though, that part of them is sometime**s dying for** a nice big juicy steak.

They are **suspicious** of all frozen food, **despise** any product that contains additives, **wholly disapprove of** white bread, and **reckon** that consumers of 'poisonous' white sugar will nearly all die young.

> I **hope** they're wrong.

They **view** things like whaling and seal-hunting with disgust, and **find** vivisection extremely distasteful. They are **fierce opponents of** fox-hunting and are also **opposed to** women accepting presents of fur-coats.

> I **dread to think** what their **views** would be on those cosmetic firms which try out their products on poor, defenceless little rabbits.

For them, zoos are degrading; they **refuse to accept** that they serve any useful purpose whatsoever. On the other hand, they **welcome** the growth of wild-life parks and reserves.

> I can't **make up my mind** where I **stand** on this. **They know their own minds**, as usual.

They **feel strongly** that most doctors are little better than drug-pushers, and **are convinced** that acupuncture is the medicine of the future.

> I **suppose** they might **have a point** there.

They **recommend** natural childbirth for all mothers-to-be and **reject** the need for such things as induction, drips and painkillers, except in special circumstances.

> I **expect** one or two of you mothers would **disagree.**

They are **in favour of** abortion being freely available, and I **guess** you don't need me to tell you their **feelings** on women's equality. They are **against** corporal punishment of any kind – I **would imagine** their **attitude towards** capital punishment is fairly predictable – and **is pro** voluntary euthanasia.

They **take a keen interest in** the fortunes of the Third World, and doubt whether any of the Western powers really **care**.

They are **supporters of** conservation in its broadest sense, **back** all tree-planting projects, and **strongly approve of** recycling waste paper and other rubbish.

> I **presume** most people would **share** that particular **viewpoint.**

They **would like to see** solar energy **taken more seriously** and **are fiercely anti**-nuclear power.

> **My own feeling is** that solar energy in Britain is rather a contradiction in terms.

They are **under the impression that** all politicians are either gangsters or fools.

> **I must admit, I'm afraid I'm tempted to agree**.

They **advocate** prisons without bars and **are of the opinion that** 99% of serious criminals are in need of psychiatric help.

> **To my mind**, pleas of insanity have become suspiciously common.

They are **prepared to accept** that UFOs probably do exist, and they **have no time for** people who **dismiss** reincarnation **out of hand**.

It all **seems** a bit improbable **to me**.

They **adore** punk clothes, but **can't stand** the people. They **rate** Lennon above McCartney and are **great fans of** Stevie Wonder.

I**'ve never understood** their **taste** in clothes or **trusted** their **judgement** when it comes to music.

As far as they are concerned, tobacco is an unspeakable evil, but they **support** the movement for the legalisation of soft drugs. They **are** also **for** restrictions regarding the sale of alcohol.

Me? I **don't mind** much about the drugs thing, but I**'m quite fond of** my old pipe and rather **keen on** my brandy after dinner.

They **consider** that marriage should be a loose arrangement that ensures security for children, but **maintain – insist** even – that one balanced parent is **preferable to** two who are always at each other's throats.

They're the sort of people who **believe in** the freedom of all people at all times, and **think** anyone with a different **point of view** must be crazy.

I **wouldn't have thought** that was a very liberal **approach**, but never mind.**If you ask me**, nobody's totally **open-minded**.

Oh yes, and they jog.

OK, so you may **see eye to eye with** them on some of those **issues**, but you should try being related to one of them, that's all!

Practice

1 Here are some names we give to people who have quite definite attitudes, views of behaviour:

a sadist	**h** romantic	**o** anarchist
b agnostic	**i** optimist	**p** perfectionist
c racist	**j** nationalist	**q** disciplinarian
d patriot	**k** activist	**r** philanthropist
e cynic	**l** atheist	**s** fanatic
f idealist	**m** pessimist	**t** realist
g fatalist	**n** masochist	**u** nonconformist

Now, who might say which of the following statements?

1 I don't believe in God.

2 I don't think I believe in God.

3 I don't believe that anyone really believes in anything.

4 Love makes the world go round.

5 Face facts: love doesn't make the world go round – the sun does.

6 Any player not on time for training will be fined £10 for every minute he's late.

7 Me, emigrate? You must be joking. It would break my heart.

8 I'm not a bad sort of person. I just happen to believe that my country is superior to and more important than any other.

9 I'll **concede** that 99.9% is a good examination result. I just want to know why you failed to get 100%.

10 Honestly, I**'ve nothing against** foreigners, as long as they don't come and live next door to me or try and marry my daughter.

11 What will be will be.

12 I don't know why you bother to talk about the next World Cup. There will probably have been a nuclear war by then.

13 It's no good just sitting and talking about social injustice. The time has come to do something about it.

14 We shall achieve our aims by any means available; if that includes bloodshed and suffering for innocent people, that's the way it'll have to be.

15 I ran fifty kilometres in the midday sun today. Every kilometre hurt more than the last, so I feel really good about it. It must have done me good.
16 You might not enjoy this, but I'm certainly going to enjoy watching you suffer.
17 What did those politicians, lawyers and priests ever do for me? We should all follow our own ideas on government, law and the church.
18 Just because you're losing 0-6, 0-6, 0-5 and 0-40 doesn't mean you're necessarily going to lose.
19 I don't **care** what they say – palace or not, royalty or not, hundredth anniversary or not, I am not going to wear a tie.
20 It's the moral duty of all of us to do what we can to reduce the amount of human suffering in the world. At least, **that's the way I look at things**.
21 I **am convinced** that we are capable of creating paradise here on earth.

2 Discuss or write answers to the following questions.
1 What is your attitude to the issues mentioned in 'A 1980s Couple?
2 What is your opinion on a controversial issue in the news at the moment?

3 Act or write out short arguments between the pairs of people below, who are attacking each other's standpoints and attitudes. Start: *The trouble with people like you is ... .*

1 a vegetarian and a cattle farmer
2 a doctor and a teacher
3 a 'green' supporter and the director of a firm producing chemicals
4 a fourteen-year-old and an eighteen-year-old

4 Write part of your speech as a politician, in which you outline your views on defence spending, taxation, law and order and foreign policy.

5 Write in dialogue form the middle of an interview between a headmaster and a candidate for a job as a teacher. The questions are getting difficult. Start: *So, Mr Brown, what is your attitude towards pupil power in schools? And how do you view the recent trend towards ...?*

■ Add here any other expressions about attitudes and beliefs as you meet them.

. . . .
. . . .
. . . .
. . . .
. . . .
. . . .
. . . .
. . . .
. . . .
. . . .
. . . .

Thinking, wanting and knowing

Reading

In this excerpt from a Scandinavian film script, note the variations we have on the work *think*.

Read the script silently or act it out in threes, taking the parts of Haro, Leni and the director.

Scene 246 from 'Brakbordsma' *(Breakfast)* by Ingmar Pintman.

Leni stares into her coffee cup, **contemplating** her life in the bottom of it.

Leni: Can you **picture** us in ...?

She breaks off. Haro looks up from his paper; their eyes meet briefly.

Leni: Do you envisage us doing this for the rest of ...?

Long pause. Haro **is lost in thought, in a world of his own.** He gazes out of the window, reflecting on the chances they have missed.

Leni: I can't **imagine** anything any more that will break the routine of ...

The camera passes over Haro's **meditating** face.

Leni: It's become impossible to **visualise** a time or place in which we won't ...

Pause. Suddenly she **collects her thoughts, pulls herself together.**

Leni: How's breakfast?

Haro is not **concentrating, pre-occupied with** the falling snowflakes.

Haro: Cold. (Pause) Cold bacon.

Leni **is dreaming of** her childhood.

Leni: I **wasn't aware** you liked it hot.

Haro continues to **speculate** on what might have been.

Haro: I don't.

Long pause. They both **have a lot on their mind.**

Haro: If you **weigh up** both sides, **balance the pros and cons,** consider it **from each angle, bear in mind** every little detail, you begin to **realize** that the importance of hot bacon can be greatly **exaggerated in one's mind.**

Leni is **inventing an excuse** for not going with him this evening, **making up a story** on which to **improvise** later.

Leni: I **was day-dreaming.**

Pause. She **has a sudden brainwave.**

Leni: **Suppose** ... just suppose that there was another opportunity, another chance to ...

Haro: I've been **toying with the idea of** cutting out the bacon ... at breakfast.

Pause.

Leni: This evening ... you know, this evening, I'm sorry, but I'm ...

Haro: I'm **seriously thinking of** doing without it.

The word **is going over and over** in Leni's brain until she whispers it, almost inaudibly.

Leni: That's just **make-believe.**

Haro **pretends** not to have heard.

Haro: I've **come to a decision.** (Pause) This **conclusion** I've **reached** ... it's that ...

His **mind begins to wander.** She is trying to **guess** what is **going on in his head.**

Haro: I've **discovered** certain things about myself in the last few weeks, you see ... and I've **decided** ...

He is suddenly **miles away,** his **mind is a blank.**(Pause) He tries again.

Haro: Yes, I've **resolved** ...

Leni **thinks** she **understands**; her **mind is racing**.
Haro: **Made up my mind**, you know ... I'm **going to** try sausages.
Leni: Why don't you **sleep on it, think it over**?
Haro: I never **change my mind** after breakfast. (Pause) **On second thoughts**, ...
A flash of inspiration from Leni:
Leni: It **strikes** me that ... they've been very foolish. Has it **occurred to** you that they might ... **reconsider**?
She **is confused**.
Haro: What do you mean?
The camera tracks to the window and the falling snow.
Leni: Nothing.

Jigsaw Reading

Here are some comments made by two people at various times in their working life – when they were 16, 26, 36, 46 and 56. Unfortunately, they have become mixed up. Read them and try to decide at which age each was spoken. Notice how many **feelings**, **desires**, **hopes** and **fears** are expressed. Which paragraph do you identify with most? Which person do you envy less, feel more sorry for?

My twelfth job in ten years; it was **the last thing I wanted**. **All I've ever asked for** is a bit of security. I'm **determined to** keep this job with Sutton and Co. longer than the others, so I'm **keen to** make a good impression.

I'**d love to** do something like teaching for a while, as a change from book-keeping. Teaching English to foreign students **appeals to** me; I really **like the sound of** it. **For two pins, I'd leave** James, James and James and try a summer course at the Sunshine School of English just down the road. **To be quite honest**, I just **don't feel like** going into the office today – or ever again. I'm **in the mood for** something completely different.

I'm between jobs again at the moment. I'**ve forced myself to stop worrying** about it. I'll **be glad if** I can keep finding work until I'm old enough to stop. I **could do with** three or four more long term temporary contracts. Of course, I **wouldn't say no to** a permanent one, but ... . Quite frankly, I **wouldn't mind** going abroad, but I should think foreign employers would be a bit **reluctant** to take on someone my age.

I'm **undecided as to** whether to go on to university or leave school now. I **feel quite tempted to** start work in the real world, but on the other hand I'**d quite like** three years doing nothing very much and give myself time to **make a choice** of career. To tell the truth, I **don't really fancy** getting tied down to one profession just yet.

I'**d rather not think** about how many jobs I've had. I used to **dream of** making my way up to the top of some firm or other – a firm of accountants, perhaps. Instead, I've **settled for** odd jobs here and there, **aimed for** posts they didn't even **consider** me for, **compromised** left, right and centre and **made do with** what came my way. At times I **would have given my right arm for**

I suppose I'**m resigned to** being an accountant with J, J and J until I'm 65. I know it's too late to **have regrets**, but I do **wish** I had tried harder to make the break. I **had every intention of** doing so. There seemed to be so many **options** open once, so many **alternatives** to pick from, so many possibilities from which to **choose**. I recall how I **flirted with** journalism, how I

a comfortable job, regular salary, some sort of prospects. And each time I **accepted** second or third best. I do so **yearn** for a second chance. Silly, isn't it?

I've just had my notice from Smith Bros. Ltd. **I'm dreading** having to look round for work again. **I've given up** being choosy. **I'd be more than happy just to** have any sort of job now. **I'm desperate to** find anything that's reasonable. I really **have no strong preference** any more.

I **can't wait to** leave school. **I'm dying to** start work. **I mean to** find a nice steady job in a well-established firm, and **intend to** work my way up from the bottom. **I'm anxious to** learn about all sides of the business, because I **hope to** be on the management side by the time I'm 40.

was once quite **committed to** becoming a social worker, how I **turned my back on** a teaching career. I hate **to admit** it, but I **fear** it's true. **I'm longing** for my retirement.

Well, **I've made a resolution to** leave the old firm within the next eighteen months. **I'm really looking forward to** a change. **I couldn't face** going on in accountancy until I retire. **I feel inclined** to try publishing; **I've got my eye on** a company just down the road. I **have half a mind to** write to them today.

I didn't really **plan to** get into accountancy. **I'm not sure I ever really wanted to** work in the world of business, but there it is, here I am. I suppose I **was just drawn** to it somehow, **attracted to** it like a magnet. **I'm going to give it** a few more years and then change. I rather **like the idea of** being a journalist; there is a newspaper office just down the road.

Practice

1   Rewrite the sentence given in each item four times, using each of the four words below it. For example:

> I wouldn't like to be a millionaire.
> fancy / hate / pleasure / last
> I *wouldn't fancy being* a millionaire.
> I *would hate to be* a millionaire.
> *Being* a millionaire *would give me no pleasure at all.*
> A millionaire *is the last thing I would want to be.*

1 I want to see him again very much.
  forward / dying / wait / longing
2 I didn't intend to spend so long there.
  planned / mean / planning / intention
3 I would like a holiday.
  could / feel / mind / say no
4 I want to go to London on Saturday, not Sunday.
  rather / prefer / preferable / preference
5 I don't really want to move away from the coast.
  keen / reluctant / fancy / idea

2   Discuss or write the answer to this question.
How have your ideas, plans, feelings on the following subjects changed in the past five or ten years?

1 marriage
2 career
3 bringing up children (present or future)
4 money

3 Act or write conversations in which each of the people below is interviewed about their attitude to their work.

1 a young reporter recently taken on by a national newspaper
2 a worker on an assembly line
3 a pilot who has recently retired
4 a 45-year-old actor or actress who is past his or her best
5 an English teacher who's been teaching beginners for twenty-five years

4 Act or write out a conversation in which you discuss your holiday plans for next summer with two friends. See if you can agree on a holiday together, although you have very different ideas about what you would really like to do.

5 Write a goodbye note left by a runaway teenager for his parents.

6 Write, in dialogue form, a conversation which took place eighty years ago between a young man and his future father-in-law. The young man is trying to prove he will be a worthy husband for the other's daughter.

■ Add here any other words or expressions about thinking, wanting and knowing you may meet.

. . . .
. . . .
. . . .
. . . .
. . . .
. . . .
. . . .
. . . .
. . . .
. . . .
. . . .
. . . .
. . . .
. . . .
. . . .

Moods

Reading

Here are some of the most common adjectives we use to describe the way we feel. Each one has a clue with it, to help you understand the **mood**, and to allow you to test yourself later. Some of the clues contain useful phrases about the **weather**. Have you ever had a year like this? Read on.

JAN

1	Another year gone, never to return.	**melancholic**
7	I suppose none of us is getting any younger.	**pensive**
10	To think nearly half the world is white with snow today.	**thoughtful**
16	The **snow** never seems as white as it used to be.	**nostalgic**
23	Oh, for the spring!	**full of longing**
31	*Love Story* on TV again tonight – super!	**sentimental**

FEB

3	Another **grey, cloudy day**.	**bored**
7	Yet another day of **drizzle** and **fog**.	**miserable**
12	**Heavy storms** and a few **sunny periods**.	**moody**
13	Everyone got a rise in salary except me!	**resentful**
21	Why, oh why can't I seem to do things right?	**frustrated**
27	Another series of repeats on telly – oh no!	**fed up**

MAR

4	**Showers and rainbow**s.	**confused**
9	Umbrella or parasol?	**uncertain**
14	Who am I? What am I?	**introspective**
17	Can I? Could I? Dare I?	**unsure of oneself**
24	Oh, sit still, will you!	**restless**
30	I think **the rain's going to ease off**.	**hopeful**

APR

2	**Sleet** and **biting winds**.	**edgy**
5	**Frosty mornings** and icy roads.	**touchy**
8	You won't have any fingernails left.	**nervous**
9	OK, OK, don't bite my head off!	**irritable**
16	I heard a cuckoo. Did you hear it?	**alert**
25	**The sun's coming out**.	**cheerful**

MAY

1	I think it's going to **clear up**.	**optimistic**
6	I've booked the holiday, so you can't say no.	**positive**
11	Just six more weeks and we'll be there.	**excited**
19	How about a ten-mile walk tomorrow?	**active**
22	Oh, I loved it! Adored it! Fantastic!	**enthusiastic**
26	You mean I've really won the Best Office Boy title?	**thrilled**

JUN

5	UK Best Office Boy Competition? No problem!	**confident**
13	Not a **breath of wind**.	**calm**
16	A **cool breeze**, a **cloudless sky**.	**refreshed**
19	I could lie here forever.	**relaxed**
24	It's too hot to move.	**idle / lazy**
28	Oh yes, this is the life!	**content**

JUL

1	She smiled at me! She actually smiled at me!	**exhilarated**
4	She said she'd come to dinner!	**elated**
7	Now I know how the winner must have felt.	**triumphant**
10	Jumping for joy!	**on top of the world**
18	Pinch me to let me know I'm not dreaming.	**up in the clouds**
28	Paradise must be like this.	**ecstatic**

AUG

2	I know I don't know you, but you can still marry me!	**wild / rash**
6	It's so **close** and heavy today, no air at all.	**weary**
9	**Sticky, thundery heat**.	**drained**
14	No energy, no emotion.	**exhausted**
19	She's gone. I've got nothing left.	**empty**
24	And it was going to be so good!	**disappointed**

SEP

1	And she was so, so nice.	**heart-broken**
4	That's the last holiday romance I'll ever have!	**disillusioned**
11	**The days are closing in**.	**gloomy**
18	It's going to be a **long hard winter**.	**depressed**
24	Why bother? Why care?	**disheartened**
29	I just don't understand.	**bewildered**

OCT

2	An **overcast sky**.	**dejected**
8	Why did you have to mention her name?	**easily upset**
12	**The rain's set in** for the day.	**distressed**
17	Why are there no new people to meet?	**lonely**
24	I don't want any new faces round here, thank you!	**hostile**
30	**Hailstorms** and **icy winds**.	**bitter**

NOV

1	Redundant, maybe? And thrown out of my flat? All alone.	**insecure**
2	To be or not to be?	**suicidal**
8	Nextdoor's music is really getting on my nerves!	**easily annoyed**
15	It's **brightening up**. I don't believe it.	**astonished / amazed**
16	It can't be true. I don't know what to say!	**overwhelmed**
17	Come on, let's fly to Paris for breakfast.	**light-headed**

DEC

6	Fancy dress parties and drinks round at our place.	**sociable**
9	Snowball fights.	**playful**
12	I must be the happiest man alive.	**over the moon**
18	Skating on frozen puddles and falling over laughing.	**frivolous**
24	Champagne bubbles and laughter.	**merry**
31	I haven't done so badly this year after all!	**self-satisfied**

You will notice that amongst the clues above you have the most common expressions relating to the weather – an important topic in England!

Practice

1. There are six people in the Bracewell family:
   grandfather, aged 86.
   Mr and Mrs Bracewell.
   Jenny, their 21-year-old daughter.
   Tommy, their 19-year-old son.
   Timmy, their 14-year-old son.

   Imagine how each member of the family felt on these six days of a week at the end of last year. Write one or two adjectives to describe each person's mood per day.

   On Monday, Grandfather felt sad but pleased for his grandson.
   Mr Bracewell was depressed and easily annoyed.

   Mon: Tommy announced he was going to Australia for a few years to find work.
   Tues: It was the second anniversary of Grandmother's death.
   Wed: Mrs Bracewell came back from a shopping spree during which she had bought half the local fashion store's stock.
   Thur: Mr Bracewell admitted that he'd lost his job.
   Fri: Timmy showed his (very bad) annual school report to the rest of the family.
   Sat: Jenny announced that she was getting married.

2. Discuss or write the answer to this question.
   How do the items below affect your moods?

   1 the weather and temperature
   2 your health
   3 work
   4 the world situation
   5 the time of day or week or year?

3. Describe to a partner or in writing, in as much detail as you can, how you have been feeling over the past few days. Think in terms of hours, minutes, even seconds, rather than 24-hour periods.

4. Describe a typical year's weather in your country for someone who has never been there. Comment on each season and particular months.

5. Write an article with the title: 'People with stable temperaments are boring'.

■ Below you might like to note:

   1 other adjectives or expressions you meet which describe our moods.
   2 further words or expressions about the weather.

   ....
   ....
   ....
   ....
   ....
   ....
   ....

Attitudes and relationships

Reading

Read through the text below to check on some of the language we use to describe our feelings for other people – from **adoring** them to **tolerating** them to **hating** them.

Tim and Lenny **can't stand** each other. They **loathe** each other, **hate the sight of** each other. Lenny seems to **envy** Tim his stripes and Tim **is envious of** Lenny's spots.

We all **have great respect for** Leo; **respect** mingled with **fear**.

Sammy **frightens** everyone. Even Tim and Lenny **keep out of his way**, and Leo admits to being **slightly afraid of** him. The chickens are **terrified** of him and the rabbits are **petrified**; they **nearly have a heart attack** if you just go up behind them and hiss.

Clarence always seems to have **a chip on his shoulder** - as if he has **a grudge against** the whole animal kingdom. The others **ignore** him.

Everyone **looks up to** George.

Zoe and Pat are **very close**. They seem to **enjoy each other's company** and **get on very well** together. I suppose they **have a lot in common,** same taste in clothes etc. Penny, who has a **love-hate relationship** with Pat, is getting **jealous**, though.

Percy makes everyone **feel a bit uneasy**; none of us can really **relax in his company**. We all remember past pricks and so are **wary of** him.

Nobody **trusts** Charlie; they say **you never know what he's thinking**.

Dear Henry is **amused** by everything and everybody.

Everyone **keeps their distance** from Ronny.

Everyone **admires** hardworking Sarah. She **impressed** us all last autumn particularly.

Oswald is very **badly treated**. Everyone **looks down on** him; even wise old Orville regards him **with contempt**. The poor chap, he's developed quite an **inferiority complex**, just because he can't fly.

There's **general sympathy** for Harry. I'm not sure whether we **pity** him for his ugliness or **feel sorry** for him having to carry all that weight around.

We're all **very fond** of Donna, but she seems quite **indifferent** to us. (I get the feeling that she's only **in love with** herself, just sitting around all day singing protest songs about Love and Peace and things.) It's difficult to **get through to** her.

Gordon is **fascinated** by the butterflies, absolutely **captivated**. They seem to find him pretty **intriguing**, too.

To a man, we're all **bored stiff by**, **fed up with** and **sick to death of** Polly, who goes on all day about nothing in particular.

We **detest** and **despise** Valerie for giving us all a bad name.

Everybody **despairs of** Lou and his friends, throwing themselves off cliffs like that.

We **resent** Bruin's and Bunny's popularity with children; their dressing up in people's clothes is definitely **frowned on**.

Secretly, I think we all still **miss** Dudley.

Practice

1   Use each of the expressions below to say or write a true statement about the way you relate (or have related in the past) to people you know or to particular groups of people. You will need to add a preposition with each expression.

    be in love   *I've been in love with Carlos since we were children.*

1 **feel sorry**	8 **hate the sight**
2 **be terrified**	9 **have great respect**
3 **can't get through**	10 **be wary**
4 **get on well**	11 **have a lot in common**
5 **be fascinated**	12 **feel indifferent**
6 **be fed up**	13 **be very fond**
7 **look up**	14 **look down**

2 Discuss or write the answers to these questions.

    1 How did you feel towards the members of staff (individually) in your last school?
    2 What are some of the problems that often occur between teenage children and their parents?
    3 What problems can occur between management and workers in a big company?
    4 'Most divorces are avoidable.' Do you agree?

3 Write part of a letter to a friend, describing how a close friend and you have **fallen out**. Explain what **went wrong** and why. Say how you felt about it.

4 You are a lawyer in a divorce case. Write part of your final speech, explaining why, in this case, a divorce should (or should not) be granted.

■ Add any other words about relating to other people as you meet them.

. . . .
. . . .
. . . .
. . . .
. . . .
. . . .
. . . .
. . . .
. . . .

Expressing oneself

Reading

Read this man's speech. See how soon you can tell what he is talking about. In it he includes over fifty variations on the words *say* and *speak*. See how many of them you can incorporate into your own use of English.

'Ladies and Gentlemen!
I hope you will excuse me for **butting into** your conversations in this way. I know nobody likes being **interrupted** at such a time, but I have been asked to **say a few words**, **make a speech** if you like, on this extra-special occasion. And **may I say** first what a pleasure and honour it is to have the opportunity to **address** you like this, this afternoon.
You know, ever since you first **hinted** to me that something of this sort might be on the cards, I have been **debating with myself** constantly as to how I could best **express** the **sentiments** I want to **convey** to you, here, this afternoon. And then when you actually **broke the news** and **announced** a date, I began to **consult** friends and acquaintances who have been in this position, **discussing** the subject with them **at length** and **in detail**.
I can **reveal** today, however, that the problems of **phrasing my message** have not been solved. I suppose if I were an actor, I could **recite** a relevant **speech** of Shakespeare's. Were I a priest, I might **preach** to you, but I fear it would be a poor **sermon**. As a politician, I could **read out** a prepared **statement** and then go on **repeating** 'No **comment**'. If you were a class of students, I might **give you a lecture**. Were you secretaries, I could **dictate** what I have to **say**. If we had more time, we could **chatter** and **gossip** together for hours. But you and I are none of these things, so I shall have to **put my message across** in more ordinary **terms**.
I suppose I could simply **declare** that this is one of the happiest days of my life and **claim** that I never thought I could be as happy as I am today. Or I could just **state** a few useless **facts and figures** and **leave it at that**. I could, on the other hand, **refer to** what great men – and women – have said or written on this theme, and just **quote** a few famous lines. I might also **mention** my own experience, **reminisce** a little, **recount** a few **anecdotes**, tell a few **stories** and make some significant **comment** on young people today.
Standing here, I can **assure** you, my main fear is not that I shall '**dry up**' – I have already **uttered** too many words on this **theme** to **be at a loss for words** now – but that I shall, in a rash moment, **blurt out** what I have to say, **gabble** away for a few seconds and **leave** too much **unsaid**, **unspoken**. Then again, while I stand here **thinking aloud**, **arguing** with myself, **contradicting** myself perhaps, you will no doubt be thinking, 'Why's the old man **rambling** on like this without **getting to the point**?' 'Why doesn't he just **come out with it**?' you'll be saying. '**Spit it out**!' I hear you cry.
Well, time marches on, and I can see that you have no need of **explanations** or **illustrations** from me; no **account** of my own life is required, no **descriptions** or **recommendations**. I shall not bother to **sum up** what I have said so far. All I should like to **add** on this – how shall I **put** it? – extra-special occasion is: I **hope** you'll both be very happy.'

Dialogue

The items in italics on the next pages are what people actually say. Below each of the items in italics is a statement about the way in which that person is expressing him or herself. The key words are left out and are in the Key at the back of the book. Try to complete each statement. Then check your answers.

PART ONE

1 *Hello. How are you doing? Nice to see you again. Haven't seen you for ages. How are you?*
He's simply ... an old friend; it's quite a warm, friendly ..... .

2 *This is Françoise. She's over here – er – staying with me for a few weeks. She's from Paris.*
Now he's ... a third party to his friend – a normal sort of ... .

3 *Look, would you like to join us? We're just going down the road to the Steakhouse for a bit of dinner.*
He's ... his friend to join them for dinner.
(For some reason, I don't get as many ... as I used to.)

4 *Well, er, that's very nice of you. Yes, I'd love to.*
She has ... the invitation; an informal ... , of course – nothing on paper.

5 *Oh no, I've just remembered. I have to meet Harold – you remember Harold? – at eight, so I'd better not come with you. Thanks all the same.*
Oh dear, now she finds she has to ... the invitation, because of a prior arrangement.

6 *Well, why don't we get together tomorrow, the three of us, and go for a picnic, something like that?*
He's ... a picnic tomorrow; a good ... in this weather.

7 *Look, I'll pick you up at your place, so you won't have to get a bus.*
He's ... to pick her up in his car; a gentlemanly ... .

8 *Well, er, I don't know, er, I mean, er, it's, er ...*
She's clearly very ..., ... over every word like that. I wonder what could be behind her ...

9 *Oh come on, you must come, really you must! We won't take no for an answer.*
He's ... that she comes with them tomorrow; he's very ... .

10 *Well, all right then. Fine, OK.*
Ah, good, she's finally ... to go. Thank goodness.

11 *Look, I'm sorry, but you won't pass this exam if you go on wasting time the way you have been these past few weeks.*
The teacher is ..., her student not to take things easy; a friendly ... this time – maybe next time it will be harsher.

12 *If I were you, I'd try and read twenty pages every day; write one or two compositions a week, and spend some time every evening just going through your notes.*
Now she's ... him as to how he can make progress; but will he listen to her ...?

13 *You're right. I'm sorry. I know I've let you down. I don't deserve to have a teacher like you. I really am dreadfully sorry.*
He's ... for not doing much work as he might
have done; it sounds like a sincere ..., but it's
easy to be ... when it suits you, isn't it?

14 *Oh come on now. It'll be all right. You'll do well. I'm sure you'll pass as long as you keep your head.*
She's ... him now that he will pass.

15 *James, things'll get better for you, I'm sure they will. Don't worry. Don't be upset. I do feel for you.*
Now she's .... with him, trying to ... him.
She's certainly a very ... teacher, but I'm
not so sure he deserves her ... . Male students of
thirty-five shouldn't need this sort of ... .

16 *Excuse me. Is this the customer service section here?*
She's ... as to whether she's in the right
place; she's probably at the .... desk.

17 *Well, look! I'm not satisfied with this jumper I got here last Saturday. I washed it once and you can see for yourself what's happened to it.*
She's ... about the garment she bought; the
girl probably hears hundreds of ... like this
every day.

18 *What do I want? I want my money back, of course. And I want it now!*
She's ... her money back; it sounds like a
pretty forceful ... .

19 *Look, if you don't give me that money this instant, I'll make life so uncomfortable for you that you'll wish you'd never set foot in this store.*
Now she's ... the poor girl; that's quite
a violent ... .

20 *You, you stupid little girl, you're a fat lot of use!*
That's unfair, madam, if you don't mind my
saying so. I just work here.
Now she's ... the girl, who sounds rather
offended. I'm not surprised. That was a nasty ... .

21 *Can I help to sort things out here? I'm the manager. We don't like to see our customers upset in any way – especially the young ladies and especially the beautiful ones – and especially the well-dressed, elegant ones.*
He's ... the woman on her appearance –
a big ..., as she's over seventy.

22 *So if you'd like to choose another jumper from our range, we'll happily exchange this one for it, even if the one you choose does cost more. All right?*
What he's ... sounds very fair – unless
someone can come up with a better ... .

23 *Congratulations, Marlon. Marvellous performance. Best Hamlet I've seen. I don't know how you do it.*
They're ... the actor on his performance; they're offering /
giving him hearty ... .

24 *Well, I'm very grateful. You're very kind. I appreciate that.*
He's ... them for their kind words; he's offering /
giving them heartfelt ... .

25 *Fantastic show. We were wondering – The way you expressed your – We thought*
perhaps you might get us – Incredible performance! Er, any chance of some free
tickets for our friends?
Ah, it was all ...; they were ...
him in order to get some free tickets.

PART TWO

26 *Comrade Stalin was the finest leader we have ever produced. He did more for*
our nation than any other. He deserves to be ... .
It's 1953, and Comrade Khrushchev is ...
Comrade Stalin; generous ... indeed.

27 *Comrade Stalin was a criminal. No-one in the history of our great country has*
done more to destroy ... .
It's 1956 and Khrushchev is ... Stalin as a
criminal.

28 *Right, now where were you? What were you doing? Who were you with? What*
was his name?
This is an ... ; the police are ...
the suspect, ... him about his activities at the
time of the crime.

29 *Look, come off it, Dad. I'm twenty-one. Stop treating me as if I was a baby!*
Oh no, it wasn't a policeman; it was a father. The
daughter is ... that she's not a baby any more;
youthful ... .

30 *Come on, tell me. You'll feel better once you've told me. Don't be shy.*
She's ... her husband to tell her the
latest bit of gossip. He seems to need ... .

31 *Do tell me. Really, you ought to. You've got to. Look, come on. Tell me, for*
goodness' sake.
She's ... him to tell her now – as if it
was terribly ... .

32 *No, no. And, for the last time, no!*
Oh dear, he has ... to tell her; a stubborn ... .

33 *Oh please, Winston, please. Don't keep things from me - please!*
Now she's ... with him, ... him to
tell her – on her knees perhaps.

34 *Look, I won't tell anyone, not a soul. I won't really.*
She's ... to be discreet; but will she keep her
... or break it?

35 *Well, all right then. The thing is – and you mustn't mention a word of this to*
anyone – the thing is, you know Tom's got this new secretary called Belinda?
Well, ...
Well, he's given in and is ... in her –
on this very ... matter; I suppose a husband
really should have ... in his wife, though,
shouldn't he?

36 *I propose ... (What about the unemployed?) (How would you like to live on £38 a week?) (Give us back our jobs!) I propose ...*
A few of the crowd are ... the politician.
Some ... are welcomed by politicians – it gives
them the chance to show how clever they are.

37 *As I was saying, I propose to increase basic income tax along the following lines.*
Ah, this politician has completely ...
the heckling.

38 *It was all your fault. If you hadn't opened your big mouth, neither of us would be in the mess we are in now.*
It seems one man is ... the other for the
trouble he's in – it's not clear whether he's to
.... or not.

39 *Yeah, OK. I realise that it wasn't so clever of me. I know I shouldn't have ...*
Ah, now he's ... that it wasn't the cleverest
thing to have done – an honest ... .

40 *And there's something else, I'm afraid. Er – when I told you I'd written to the tax people, well, I hadn't. I lied. The whole story was a lie.*
Now he's going further, actually ... that he
had lied – quite a serious ..., really.

41 *How could you? I mean, we agreed that the only way we were going to succeed was if we were both completely honest with each other. And now this!*
He's ... the other one now for what he did.
His eyes are ... and his voice full of ... .

42 *Oh, so you got ten per cent in the exam, did you? You genius! You must be so tired after all the work you did for it!*
He's ... his poor friend, ... of him,
... him as brothers do. Perhaps he's only joking,
though, simply ... the other boy's ... .

43 *I got 99% myself. Of course, I expected to do well. After all, I'm obviously the brightest student in the class.*
Now he's ... about how clever he is, the
little horror.

44 *You only got so many because you cheated. I saw you looking at Sarah Nicholls' paper, all the way through the exam.*
Ah, now his friend's ... him of cheating –
quite a vicious ... .

45 *What do you mean? I didn't. I didn't do anything of the sort.*
He's ... that he cheated – a fairly
forceful ... .

46 *Look, for Heaven's sake, you two; try and behave like sixteen-year olds, not six-year olds.*
Their mother's ... both of them, ...
them off quite firmly.

47 *Now get upstairs, both of you. And get that mess tidied up in your room. Go on, get upstairs.*
Now she's ... them upstairs to clean up
their rooms.

48 *It is my considered opinion that the defendant has not got one ounce of decent human feeling in his whole body ...*
The judge is ... the defendant as 'a pretty
nasty piece of work'. A strong ..., don't you think?

49 *Please excuse me, your Lordship, but could I possibly have a quick word with you?*
The clerk is ... a moment of the judge's time
– a very polite ... .

50 *It's just that, you won't forget, will you, that your wife asked you to pick up a few things from the supermarket on your way home, and it's very nearly quarter past five, so ...*
He's ... the judge about certain other
duties he has to perform – a timely ... .

Practice

1 Describe how you used to get on with members of your family when you were younger.

2 Write or relate two conversations you have heard in which people were being particularly kind, unkind or rude to each other.

3 Compare English and your language. Write or discuss the ways in which people seem to express their feelings towards each other in each language.

4 Write on one of the following topics.

1 A letter apologising to a friend following the big row you had last week and how rude you were to him or her.
2 'People don't really mean most of the things they say.' How far do you think this is true?

■ Add any other words about how we express ourselves as you meet them.

. . . .

Reacting to events

Reading

Read through the following texts, noting the rather strong idiomatic language we can use to describe our reactions to slightly unusual events.

Some moments from our family scrap-book, when we were all:

1 surprised.

... We all **got the shock of our lives** last Christmas. We were sitting round the fire, forcing third helpings of Christmas cake into our mouths, when the doorbell rang. It **made everybody jump**. Auntie Jane **nearly jumped out of her skin**. I was pretty **startled** myself, I must admit. Anyway, there at the door – **believe it or not** – was Uncle Mac, with an armful of presents. (It was the first time in living memory that he had ever given anything to anybody.) Everyone **caught their breath** when they saw him. **No-one could really believe their eyes**. Poor Aunt Flossie actually **fainted**, and Uncle Bill kept **blinking, as if he had seen a ghost**. And Granny, who had been talking non-stop since breakfast, was absolutely **speechless**. I thought **her eyes were going to pop out of her head**. I reckon **you could have knocked all of us over with a feather**.

2 emotional.

... I looked across and saw that **tears were already trickling down** Mum's cheeks. I must confess **a lump had come to my throat**, and I was having to **swallow** hard. When the priest started speaking, Julia **burst out crying**, and that was the signal for Mum to **break down**; she was completely **overcome**. By this time **tears were rolling down** several faces – including Dad's – and I had a horrible feeling that I was going to **burst into tears**. The priest's few words were very **touching**; I think he was almost **moved to tears** himself. I'm not surprised. They made such a lovely couple and Maggie looked great in white.

3 angry.

... I think it was Dad's side of the family that started it, when Uncle Mac started **calling** Uncle Bill **names**. Auntie Jane **took offence** immediately and then Granny joined in. She made Aunt Flossie **lose her temper** and soon after that Dad **blew his top**. That led to Mum **going berserk** – I've never seen her so **livid**. It wasn't long before Maggie, for some reason, started **insulting** Uncle Tom and then it was his turn to **see red**; he really **went mad** – 'furious' isn't the word for it. It was about then that Grandad, who had obviously been **seething** for some time, **hit the roof**. Things **quietened down** a bit after that and Granny dealt the next hand of cards.

4 afraid.

... Well, naturally most of us were **scared stiff**. Only Maggie **kept cool** throughout. Mum **went as white as a sheet** and even Dad **panicked** a bit. Auntie Jane's **hair stood on end** and Uncle Bill **ran a mile**. I must confess that **my heart missed a beat** or two. I mean, it's not every day that a tax inspector comes to your front door, is it? All the time he was with us, Uncle Mac was **twitching** as if he had an army of ants inside his shirt collar. Whenever the phrase 'failure to declare earned income' came up, Aunt Flossie **winced** and Mac's hand started **shaking** so much he couldn't light his pipe. It was obvious that Granny was **trembling** too when she tried to pick her cup of tea up – three times. Everyone **shuddered** visibly when the man said he would be back – everyone except Maggie, that is. She didn't **flinch** once, **didn't turn a hair**. She's either a very good actress or extremely honest.

5 embarrassed.

... I could see that Julia was **dying of embarrassment** – not surprisingly, in the circumstances. I bet the incident is still **on her conscience**. Anyway, I could feel that I was **blushing**, and the other chap was **as red as a beetroot**. Julia **had a terribly guilty look in her eye**, or rather, she **had guilt written all over her face**. She started **stammering** something about feeling tired and having come up for a rest. I **didn't know where to put myself**, I can tell you. I've never felt so small in all my life; **about two foot tall**, that's how I felt. I stood there for a few seconds **hoping a hole would open up in the floor and swallow me**. In the end I just **gulped** and backed out of the room.

6 amused.

... Well, everyone **burst out laughing**, of course. Uncle Bill **laughed his head off**, and Auntie Jane **nearly died laughing**. And you should have seen Granny; she was **in hysterics**. Even Uncle Mac **couldn't help laughing** when he realized what the cause of their laughter was. The vicar was the only one who didn't **see the funny side of things**; completely straight-faced, stony-faced he was. Granny was still **hysterical** long after Uncle Mac had turned round, **chuckling** to himself, and put the matter straight.

Practice

1 Choose the correct word to complete each sentence.

1 I couldn't ... my ears when they told me.
   a hear **b** believe **c** feel **d** accept
2 The Prime Minister was ... with rage.
   a wordless **b** silent **c** shivering **d** speechless
3 Poor girl, there were ... running down her face.
   a tears **b** lumps **c** shudders **d** cuts
4 I must admit, I nearly ... my sides laughing.
   a cut **b** broke **c** split **d** swallowed
5 I can tell you, my heart nearly skipped a ... .
   a beat **b** moment **c** break **d** turn
6 Everyone ... out laughing.
   a broke **b** burst **c** jumped **d** popped
7 They had joy ... all over their faces.
   a placed **b** arranged **c** poured **d** written
8 My ... stood on end when I saw him.
   a hair **b** head **c** heart **d** eyes

2 After a little thought, tell a partner or write about a memorably embarrassing, frightening or funny experience you have had.

3 Tell your partner or write the plot of a horror film you have enjoyed and still remember, or a comedy that amused you, or a thriller that kept you on the edge of your seat. Tell them about how you felt while you were watching it.

4 Write, for your college or company magazine, a review of a ghost story you have read.

■ Add any other words about our reactions to events as you meet them.

. . . .

. . . .

. . . .

. . . .

. . . .

. . . .

. . . .

. . . .

. . . .

. . . .

. . . .

. . . .

Sounds people make

Reading

In the following passages, you will meet about fifty of the noises we humans make, many of them without producing words. Read the passages and then do the exercises that follow.

1   Read the passage and decide whose thoughts are being described.

I'm awake, lying here **moaning**, and nothing's happening at all. Oh well, better start **crying** properly. Still no reaction. Right, they've asked for it. Here we go with a real **scream**. Ah, now I hear something next door. Must go on **sobbing**, so they realise it's serious. Here she comes, **muttering** to herself. Why is it always her? Never him? Ah, a bottle. Excuse me, but it's difficult to **suck** a bottle without making **sucking** noises, you know. Oh no, I've got **hiccups** again. Sometimes I seem to spend half my day **hiccupping**. Over the shoulder I go again. Oh dear, a **burp**. Pardon. Back to bed. Ah, I like it when she **hums** that song to me. Oh dear, we're both **yawning**. Time to sleep again. I can hear him **snoring** next door. 'Not a **murmur** now', she says to me, the same as always. There's no need to **sigh** like that, you know. You were a baby once.

2   It's been a hard day's night, as they used to say. My boss made my life hell today. Read the passage and find out what my job is.

I've never known a boss like him; you hardly ever hear him talking normally. He starts as soon as he comes into the office in the morning. If I'm two minutes late, he starts **shouting** at me. And you should hear him on the phone, **yelling** at some poor junior. When he asks you to do something, he just **barks** – like a fierce dog. And when he finds a mistake in your work, he **roars** like a lion. When someone asks him a question, he nearly always just **grunts**, like that. He'll sit for hours **grumbling** about the weather, the business, his colleagues, the market. And he will **mutter**! Half the time you can't understand a word he's saying. The worst thing is his dictation. He just **mumbles** all the way through the letter; I have to guess every other word. Then he **bites my head off** when I've written something he didn't want. I just start **stammering** and **stuttering**, and get out of the room as soon as possible.

3   The third group of noises come from a theatre. Read the text and find out what is happening on stage.

You can hear the audience **whispering** excitedly. Some of them are **clearing their throats**. Could they be nervous? Something's happening. The audience are **clapping**; polite **applause** at the moment. Two of the audience are being invited onto the stage. The rest of them are **cheering** and **calling out** things. Now something is happening on stage; you could hear a pin drop. The two members of the audience are doing exactly what they are told and the chairs they are sitting on are beginning to rise into the air. The audience are **gasping.** Oh dear, what's happened? They've suddenly fallen to the ground and look most upset. The audience are **booing** loudly. It hasn't worked. Now they're **whistling**. The whistling has changed to **hissing**, but there's nobody on stage except the two members of the audience. Now they're **chanting** that they want their money back. The manager's coming out on stage. Listen to them **groaning**.

| 4 | The fourth group of sounds comes from when I was ill last week. I really wasn't well at all. Find out what was wrong with me. |

It started on Monday. I really wasn't well at all. I was **sniffing** all day. On Tuesday I hardly stopped **blowing my nose** and **sneezing**. By Wednesday I had a pretty bad **cough**. I tried **gargling** with salt water but it didn't seem to do much good. If I had to go upstairs, I'd reach the top stair **panting** like a thirsty dog, and I'd still be **wheezing** five or ten minutes later. By Friday I'd **lost my voice** almost completely. I was **croaking** like a frog all day at the office.

| 5 | The fifth group of sound-words, shows how different people reacted to the same joke. |

Lady Thackeray-Smythe **laughed** politely. Her husband was **chuckling** minutes afterwards. A class of schoolgirls **giggled**. A class of schoolboys **sniggered**. An American TV audience **shrieked** and **howled with laughter**. Lady Thackeray-Smythe's maid **tittered**. Billy Bloggs **laughed like a drain**.

Practice

| 1 | To see how many of these words you have remembered, arrange the verbs in each of the columns below according to how loud they normally are: the loudest number 1, the softest number 6. Then write a sentence of your own for each verb to show what it means, or discuss your lists with a partner. |

mutter	hum	hiss
sigh	groan	pant
scream	boo	howl
yell	whisper	chuckle
whistle	roar	sob
gasp	mumble	sniff

| 2 | What noises made by other people annoy you most, and in what situations? If you think of other noises which have not been mentioned in this unit, try to find the words for them in a dictionary and write them in the space provided for your notes at the end of the unit. For example, I hate the sound of people making the bones in their fingers **click** and people **singing out of tune**. |

| 3 | List the sounds you would expect to hear in the situations below. |

  1 in a football stadium on a Saturday afternoon
  2 on a crowded beach in summer
  3 in the maternity ward of a hospital during the evening
  4 at the scene of a major disaster

| 4 | Write or act out your commentary for Radio South as you report on the tour of your town by members of the British royal family. |

| 5 | Write the middle paragraph of an article for the Daily Sensation. Describe the scene outside the tower block in which a terrorist bomb has just gone off. |

| ■ | Add any other words describing the noises we make. |

. . . .

. . . .

. . . .

Gesture, mannerism and body language

Picture story

Look at the picture story below and notice the way we describe the two cats' gestures. Then cover the words and see if you can recall them.

He's **licking his lips**.

She's **smiling**, **grinning**.

He's **staring** (**leering**) at her.

She's **frowning**, maybe **scowling**.

He's **winking** at her.

She's **pouting**.

He's **raising his eyebrows**, **pointing** at a glass.

She's **shrugging her shoulders**, **grimacing, making** (**pulling**) **a face.**

He's **nodding**.

She's **shaking her head**.

He's **blowing her a kiss**.

She's **sneering**.

He's **beckoning** to her.

She's **poking her tongue out at him**.

He's **scratching his head**.

She's **waving** (goodbye).

Practice 1

1 Check that you know the meaning of each of the verbs below. They all describe different ways of *looking*. Then choose the appropriate verb to complete each sentence. Finally, make sure you understand the other words and phrases in bold print in the sentences.

glanced   gazed   peeped   peered   stared

1 He... intently at the piece of paper in front of him, **wringing his hands** in despair.
2 He **stretched to his full height** and... over the wall to see what Lady Thackeray-Smythe's daughter was doing.
3 We... through the fog, **blinking**, trying to **catch a glimpse of** a moving light.
4 She stopped **fidgeting** and **fiddling** with her dress. She just sat, absolutely still, and ...out of the window, miles away, just occasionally **pursing her lips**, then **biting** them hard.
5 The referee... at his watch again, **made a sign** to the linesmen, then **blew the final whistle**.

2 Hungry? Thirsty? Feel like a cigarette? Before you do anything, just connect the two halves of these sentences correctly. To do this, decide which verbs go with which objects.

1 He **chewed**	**a**	smoke-rings.
2 She **licked**	**b**	his cigar.
3 He **puffed**	**c**	the sweets to make them last longer.
4 She **nibbled**	**d**	the tablets so as not to have to taste them.
5 He **sipped**	**e**	the tough meat before digesting it.
6 She **swallowed**	**f**	the chocolate biscuits to avoid eating too many.
7 He **blew**	**g**	the ice-cream and then her lips.
8 She **sucked**	**h**	the brandy.

3 Now match the two halves of this group of sentences.

1 My **stomach was rumbling**	**a**	so I **scratched** it.
2 We **breathed in deeply** (**took a deep breath**)	**b**	like a **dribbling** baby.
3 My **teeth were chattering**	**c**	and **tossing** and **turning** all night.
4 When the meal arrived, the dog started **drooling**	**d**	and my **mouth was watering**.
5 I was **sweating** (**perspiring**)	**e**	and then **exhaled** fully.
6 My **heart began to beat faster**	**f**	and I was **shivering**.
7 My **arm was itching**	**g**	and my **blood pressure went up**.

Reading

Here is a selection of verbs concerned with the physical contact people can have. Read through the two short texts and then do the exercise that follows.

1 When I was a boy, I couldn't stand:

being **tickled** on the soles of my feet.
being **patted** on the head by my parents' friends and told I'd grown.
being **smacked** by my father for something I hadn't done.
having my hair pulled and **my ear flicked** by a sadistic teacher of ours.
being **scratched** (on the cheek, arm, back, leg) by the girls in the class above.
being **pinched**.
being **kicked** and **stamped** on, **having my fingers trodden on** and **my face stepped on** in the annual Girls v Boys football match.
having my hair stroked by my grandma, as if I was a cat. They were terrible like that, our family, always **caressing** each other. I never understood the need they had to **touch** people – most embarrassing I found it.

2 An interview with a boxer:

Well, half the time he was just **slapping** me, with the open glove; that's illegal, you know – and he **poked** me in the eye several times with his thumb – it was awful – **pushing** and **shoving** me he was; he even tried to **wrestle** with me – **punches**? He can't **punch**. He **tapped** me, that's all he did – he hardly **touched** me with a proper **blow** – when he **knocked me out**? Let me tell you, he didn't really **hit** me even then, not properly – he **butted** me with his head, like the bull he is – next time I'll **knock him out** in the first round, believe me.

Now use the words in the text to describe what is going on in the playground of a very bad school.

Practice 2

1 The verbs on the right are in the wrong order. Decide which to use to complete each of sentences 1 – 6.

    1 The freed hostages ... their family and friends.   **shook hands with**
    2 The US President ... the Prime Minister.   **sat cuddling**
    3 I ... my mother-in-law on the cheek.   **squeezed**
    4 Charles ... her hand reassuringly as they stepped
       forward together to the altar.   **embraced**
    5 The Pope ... the President.   **hugged**
    6 Jack and Jill ... each other to keep warm.   **kissed**

2 If you are working alone, write a paragraph about the signs and gestures used in your country. If you can, compare them with the signs and gestures used for similar purposes in other countries.
If you are working in class, demonstrate and discuss the signs and gestures we make to express ourselves. In an international class, you may be surprised to discover how much body language varies from country to country.

3 Write or act out a conversation with a friend about one of the topics below.

    1 how lovely and peaceful the park was last Sunday afternoon
    2 how horrible the station was during the rush-hour on your way home this evening
    3 how unpleasant a bar was at closing time last Saturday night
    4 how moving it was to see some hostages reunited with their families

4 Write the page from your diary in which you describe the candidates' behaviour as you were all waiting to be called in for your oral exam. Begin: *There were five of us in the room...*

■ Add here any other words about body language, mannerisms and gestures that you may meet.

. . . .
. . . .
. . . .
. . . .
. . . .
. . . .
. . . .
. . . .
. . . .
. . . .
. . . .
. . . .
. . . .

Posture and movement

Reading

1 Look carefully at the picture and read the text below it. Note how we describe the different positions the people are in. Then identify the people in the picture from what they say.

When England won the World Cup Final, I was ...

A **sprawled** on the floor, **lying** half **on my stomach** and half **on my side, knees bent** and **with my feet in the air**, one hand propping up my chin.

B **standing on tiptoe, hands behind my back, chest out, chin up, shoulders back, stomach in**.

C **perched** on the arm of the settee, **my legs dangling** over the side, with the cat **curled up** on my lap.

D **crouching, leaning back** against the wall, **arms folded** and **swaying from side
   to side** as the play moved from end to end.
E **standing, feet apart, hands in pockets, stooping** a bit and **twisting my neck**
   to see the screen.
F **kneeling with my head bowed**, hands on hips, waiting for the stupid match to
   finish.
G **sitting forward with hunched shoulders** and **arched back**, my **elbows
   resting on my thighs** and my **hands clasped** in front of me.
H **sitting astride a chair, arms outstretched, rocking to and fro.**
I **reclining on the settee, legs crossed, head back, fast asleep.**

2 Read the text illustrating people's movements from one place to another. The verbs
  are in a column on the left, so afterwards you can test yourself by covering the left
  column.

I remember ... . Do you?

skipping	for hours in the back yard, with a worn-out rope,
hopping	races with one leg tied behind us,
rolling	down those slippery slopes, getting covered in mud.
racing	home after school as fast as we could,
stumbling	over the kerb,
falling headlong	on our knees, then
hobbling	home like wounded soldiers, pretending we had broken our legs, then
rushing	upstairs to be first in the bath.
skating	in the winter,
gliding	gracefully to the middle of the pond, then
crashing	into someone.
climbing	Farmer Staple's apple trees,
swinging	on the branches,
clambering	over hedges,
crawling	through bushes.
sliding	down the bannisters when our parents were out,
bouncing	up and down on their bed as if it was a trampoline,
tiptoeing	downstairs early Christmas morning to see the presents underneath the tree, then
creeping	back upstairs, so as not to be heard.

3 In this report of a football match, the verbs have been lifted out of the text and placed
  on the right. Read the text, guessing the meaning of the verbs that have been left
  out. Check that you can complete each sentence correctly and then test yourself by
  covering the right-hand column and trying to complete the text without its help.

Match Report

They looked superb as they ... on to the field,	**trotted**
battalions of green and orange. After only five minutes,	
however, the United number 9 ... to head the ball,	**dived,**
... with a goal-post and ... off the pitch with	**collided, staggered**
blood pouring from his forehead. A few minutes later,	
their number 8, who had done too much pre-match ...,	**jogging,**
was ... towards the goal-line when he ...	**galloping, collapsed**
with cramp. He had just managed to ... to the touch-	**limp**
line before the number 7 ... into a corner flag and	**bumped**
... flat on his back. The City number 10 went next,	**fell**
... over the United goalkeeper and doing a ... into	**tripping, somersault**
the net. The United number 9 ... back on, suffering	**wandered**
from concussion, just before half-time, but he was	

... off again.	**escorted**
At half-time, a streaker, ... on to the pitch. Five	**sprinted**
old ladies ..., a few were seen ... up and	**fainted, jumping**
down. Ten policemen ... after him and ...	**dashed, chased**
him for five minutes or so, until he ... over a	**leapt**
barrier and ... in the crowd.	**disappeared**
After 63 minutes, the 43-year-old City winger ...	**ambled**
towards the United goal. Up went the ball. The number 9	
... and thought he was going to ... like a	**stretched, soar**
bird towards it. Instead, he ... into the mud like	**plunged**
a champion freestyle swimmer starting a race, not	
noticing that the opposing number 5 had accidentally	
... on his right boot. The weary referee ...	**trodden, strolled**
towards the scene of the accident and gave a penalty.	
Immediately eight orange figures ... on top of him	**sprang**
and he ... to the ground.	**sank**
Five minutes later, the City number 8 ... forward	**stepped**
to take the penalty but while ... up to the ball he	**shuffling**
... on a patch of ice. About then, hundreds of	**slipped**
spectators ... on to the field. The United number 5 was	**surged**
... and ... to the ground. The referee finally	**pushed, shoved**
... his way out of the crowd and ... off like a	**elbowed, marched**
defeated general leaving the battlefield, never to	**return**
It was just another Saturday afternoon.	

Practice

1 Write about or discuss the topics below.

1 the moments in sport that excite you the most (as a spectator)
2 the series of instructions that you, as a keep-fit instructor, give your class as they do a particular exercise
3 the radio commentary you give as people of all ages, shapes and sizes cross the finishing line in a charity marathon race
4 the way people sit, move and react in an office on Monday morning at nine, compared with the way they sit, move and react on Friday afternoon at four.

2 Write a paragraph from your short story, describing a nightmare in which you were being chased.

3 Write a section of the film script for the most action-packed scene you can remember seeing in the cinema.

4 Write part of a letter to a newspaper complaining about some of the ridiculous things you or a relative of yours were forced to do on an organised sporting holiday.

■ Have you stood, sat or moved in any other way in your life? Can you think of any other ways in which people move without the aid of animals or vehicles? If so, write the appropriate words or expressions here.

. . . .

. . . .

. . . .

. . . .

. . . .

Actions and activities

Reading

In this section we look at a series of everyday, non-technical actions. Read the texts.

1 Dear Cinderella,
Your jobs for tonight:
sweep the **chimney**, **scrub** the floors,
beat the carpets, **hoover** the stairs,
dust the furniture, **polish** the silver,
make the beds, **change** the sheets,
tidy the house, **dig** the garden,
clean out the fireplace, **empty** the rubbish,
wash our underwear, **mend** the socks,
darn the shirts, **iron** the laundry,
cook the supper, **do the washing-up**,
dry the dishes, **put them away**.
Don't wait up for us. We might be late home.

The Ugly Sisters

2 Interior decorating

It was my first go at decorating. Everything started well enough. **Scraping** the old wall-paper off was great fun and didn't take us long because we were able to **peel off** quite big strips. What did take a long time was rubbing with sandpaper the walls to be **painted** and **papered**. Our walls were so smooth in the end that Dad went round **scratching** them to make sure the paint would go on all right. He was a great organizer, Dad. Throughout the day he gave us useful tips like: 'Just **dip** your brush in the paint' and 'Don't **squeeze** out the paint from the brush before you **apply** it,' and 'Just **dab** the paper with a wet sponge'. He also made us **wipe** each brush when we'd finished with it, then **soak** it in white spirit, **wash** it in soapy water and finally **rinse** it under a tap. A real perfectionist he was.

There was great excitement late in the morning when we started **unwrapping** the rolls of wallpaper and **unpacking** the tins of paint. I got the job of **shaking** all the tins, **levering** them open and **stirring** the paint. Meanwhile Uncle Mac and Grandad were **mixing** the paste, **unrolling** the paper and **spreading** the paste on the back. I watched admiringly as they **folded** the paper, **carried** it to the wall, **hung** it delicately (with the two ends **stuck** lightly together) from the top, then **pressed** down gently and **smoothed** out the lumps and bumps. I was terribly impressed.

It's difficult to say when exactly things started to go wrong. I think it was while I was **dragging** some of the rubbish downstairs that Uncle Jack started **flicking** his brush at Uncle Mac because he wouldn't let him have the stepladder. I got back in time to see Uncle Mac **drop** the ladder and **fling** a dirty cloth at Jack. Jack **picked it up** and **threw** it back. Then it got out of hand. Grandad **grabbed** a brush and **tossed** it straight at Uncle Bill, who went over and **tipped** a bucket of paste all over Grandad's back. Grandad then **seized** the empty bucket and **stuck** it on Bill's head. Uncle Mac came and **poured** a bucket of cold water over Dad's head. Dad **snatched** a brush from my hand and **scrawled** some rude words on the paper that Mac had

74

just **put up**. Not satisfied, he went over and **hurled** a half-full tin of paint at thesame wall. Still not satisfied, he **climbed** up the ladder, **knocking over** the other brushes and **spilling** another pot of paint as he went, **tugged** at the paper on the only remaining clean wall and **tore** it into shreds as it came away in his hands.

After that, things went from bad to worse.

3   A Golf Lesson

Right! Now, **place** the tee in the ground – that thing in your left hand – yes, **push it down** a bit more – no, **pull it out** a bit – no, **put it back in** – now, just **press** it into the ground – go on, just **slide it in** – stop! Good. Very good. Right now, **rest** the ball on the tee – try again – and again. Good. Well done. Fantastic. Now, here's your club – **take** it in your left hand – no, your left hand – **hold** it quite firmly – no, don't **grip** it like that – **let go of it** – just **grasp** it like this, not too firmly – relax. Wonderful. Right, now **wrap** the fingers of your right hand round here – can you **tuck** your scarf into your jacket? We don't really want that round the club, do we? – good, well done. Now **move** your hands backwards and forwards a little – **wiggle** your fingers a bit – relax. Right, stand here and **bring the club back** over your shoulder – no, the other shoulder – come on, **swing** it back, relax, **twirl** it round a bit – now, in a moment, **bring it down** fast and try to **hit** the ball right here in the middle. Try and **strike** it just – ouch! Yes, try and wait until I've **taken my hand away** next time – right, better insert the tee again – it's over there – good. **Pop** the ball on the tee. Good. Get hold of the club again. Good. Now, don't **lift** your head – **raise** your right elbow a fraction – **keep your eye on** the ball – right now, go! – O.K., well, you go and **fetch** the club from those bushes and I'll try and **replace** this piece of grass.'

Notes

1   You might like to add some more similar verbs here, but remember that many further action words appear in other sections.
2   Remember, too, that as soon as you have the name of a tool in English, *hammer, screw, measure* etc., you probably have a perfectly good verb as well: **to hammer, to screw**, **to measure**.

Practice

1   Write or give oral instructions to a partner on how to do the following things.

   1   put up wallpaper
   2   put an electrical plug on a lead
   3   serve in tennis
   4   ski
   5   bowl a ball in ten-pin bowling
   6   shave or make up

2   Write or tell your partner how easy it was for you to do the following things yesterday.

   1   plant those seeds in your garden
   2   clean out the fireplace
   3   get your car started
   4   make a desk for yourself
   5   paint the top floor windows
   6   clear the drains

3   Discuss or write about the jobs around the house that you really hate doing.

4 Write the part of a letter to a friend in which you describe how your try to lay some concrete, or build a little garden shed, or make yourself a new summer dress, but it all went disastrously wrong.

5 You have just produced a new tube of super-glue that you are about to market. Write the instructions for use that you will put on the packet.

■ Add any other words about other actions and activities as you meet them.

....

....

....

....

....

....

....

....

....

....

....

....

....

The universe

Quiz

True or false? Decide whether you agree with these statements or not. The answers are printed below the quiz.

1 Our **galaxy** is called the Milky Bar.
2 Our **solar system** has nine principal **planets**.
3 **Earth** is thought to have the highest density of all the **planets.**
4 A **constellation** is another word for **star**.
5 A **meteor** is sometimes known as a **shooting star.**
6 **Meteorites** can be bigger than meteors.
7 **Asteroids** are **orbiting rocks** found between **Mars** and **Jupiter.**
8 An **astrologer** would know more about the surface of **Venus** than an **astronomer**.
9 Halley's **Comet** was expected to appear in the 1990's.
10 UFO stands for **unidentified flying object**.
11 **Pluto** was first discovered during the twentieth century.
12 **Saturn** is further from **the Sun** than **Uranus**.
13 **Mercury** is the hottest **planet**.
14 **Neptune** is the nearest **planet** to **the Sun**.
15 A **light year** is nearly six thousand million miles.

Answers: **1** No, **The Milky Way**   **2** Yes   **3** Yes   **4** No, a group or cluster of **stars**   **5** Yes   **6** Yes   **7** Yes   **8** No, the other way round   **9** No. As expected, it arrived in the 1980s   **10** Yes   **11** Yes   **12** No   **13** Yes   **14** No, Mercury   **15** No, nearly six million million miles

Practice

1 Write or discuss the answers to these questions.

1 How much do you know about each of the planets in our system?
2 How far do you think man will get in space discovery in the next hundred years?
3 Do we really need to know what other planets and systems are like?

2 You are an astronaut reporting back to earth from outer space. Describe what you can see as you float through space.

3 Write part of a letter to a newspaper in which you argue space travel is (not) a waste of time and money.

■ Add any other words or expressions about the universe in the space provided.

. . . .

. . . .

. . . .

. . . .

. . . .

Physical geography

Game

There follows a selection of words describing a range of **geographical features**. Read each set of notes and see if you can guess which country is being described. The answers are given below.

1 – a **peninsula bounded by** a large **mountain range in the North** – **a wide plateau extending to** the ocean **in the South** – **unpredictable monsoon climate** – **population** (approximately 720,000,000) **concentrated in** the **northern plains** –

2 – enormous **forest areas** in the **interior** – **coastal mountains in the West** – numerous **islands off the north coast** – **lowlands in the North** – **continental climate, severe inland, more moderate by the sea** – **total area**: 3,851,809 square miles –

3 – a **wide variety of land and climate** – a huge **river basin in the North** – **thickly forested** – a vast **plateau in the South** – **densely populated in coastal belt to the East** – relatively **underdeveloped in central areas beyond the highlands** in the South-East – **lies on the Equator** –

4 – consists of four **main islands** – **mountainous** and **hilly** – many **active volcanoes** – **subject to earthquakes, typhoons** and **tidal waves** – **extends through** many **degrees of latitude** – the **climate**, therefore, is very **divers**e –

5 – **located** round the **mouth** of the Rhine and **opposite** the Thames **estuary** – a long **coastline** – most of the country **flat** and **low-lying** – large **areas in the West and North below sea level** – **subject to floods** – complex **network of canals** –

6 – **mountainous** with numerous **lakes** – **varied climate** according **to altitude**, ranging from **tropical** to **temperate** to **cold** – **highest point over 18,000 feet** (nearly 6,000 metres) – **desert in the West** – half of the country **lies inside the Tropic of Cancer** –

7 – **to the North** the **southern slopes** of a gigantic **mountain chain** – **tropical forests** and **jungle** – **highest peak** 8,845 metres – **fertile valleys** for **agriculture** in central **zone** –

8 – most **highly developed** country in its **continent** – **rich in mineral deposits** and other **natural resources** – **large industrialised urban areas** round **coasts** – rural in the **interior** – **rich vegetation**, good **irrigation** –

Answers: **1** India **2** Canada **3** Brazil **4** Japan **5** Holland **6** Mexico **7** Nepal **8** South Africa

Note the following rather tricky uses of the words *north, south, east, west* and the more general terms *northern, southern, eastern, western*.

The South of France	**southern France**
South Africa (a country)	**southern Africa** (a region)
The North Pole	**the southern hemisphere**
West Berlin	**western Europe**
East Germany	**eastern culture**
South-East Asia	**southern Europe**
South America	**the southern States of America**
South / North Korea	**Northern Ireland**
the south bank of the river	**Eastern block countries**

Practice

1 Make or find an outline map of your country or a country you know well and describe its **physical geography**, drawing in the key features.

2 Write or discuss the answers to the following questions.

1 Which country or countries might you choose to live in if you had to emigrate? Give the reasons for your choice.
2 What influence can a country's physical geography have on the lifestyle, standard of living and quality of life of the population?
3 Write out a page or two from the diary you kept during your solo flight around the world.

3 Write the opening of your speech at a conservationist 'Friends of the Earth' meeting, complaining about the ways in which man is interfering with and destroying his natural environment.

■ If your country couldn't be well described using the words and phrases given in this section, add any others you would need below.

. . . .

. . . .

. . . .

. . . .

. . . .

. . . .

. . . .

. . . .

. . . .

. . . .

. . . .

. . . .

. . . .

The plant world

Reading

Read through these two pieces of homework, noting some of nature's key words.

20.4.89   How Plants Grow (Biology Homework for Mr Chambers)

Of all the year's four seasons, it's Spring I like the best,
When Nature's clothes are not yet on, except its pants and vest.
The **twigs** are growing stronger, the **tree-trunks** stand up proud,
And on their **sprouting branches** the birds all sing aloud.
There's **blossom** on the **cherry trees** and **acorns** on the **oak**,
The **ash** and **elm** and **beech** look fresh, and everyone drinks coke.
The **hedgerow** is a lovely sight, it's getting on for June,
The **flowers** are in their tiny **buds**, they'll be **in bloom** soon.
And then we'll see their **petals** on top of healthy **stems**.
To me they are as precious as the most expensive gems.
There are **nettles** by the river, there are **rushes** by the lake,
There's masses of **moss** and thousands of **ferns**, the **thistles** and **thorns** are awake.
There are **needles** on the **pine trees** and beginnings of their **cones**,
And **fruits** growing on the **bushes**, the heavy **shrub**, it groans (under the weight, sir)
I know all the **plants** will **wither**, they'll **fade** and then they'll **die**,
The **clover** will be over, and I always wonder why.
And then in late September, oh dear, here comes the autumn.
The coloured **leaves** blow off the trees, last year I ran and caught them.

*No, this will not do. Our lessons are concerned with biology, not English verse. You
will do this again, and give it to me on Friday!*

24.4.89   How Plants Grow (Biology Homework for Mr Chambers)

Plants can be divided into ten categories, including **bacteria, fungi, algae** and less
common and much longer Latin names. One of these comprises all **flowering
plants, crops, trees** and most other **natural vegetation on land**.
Plants grow by a process called **photosynthesis**, which nobody really understands,
including me. The **leaves (or foliage)** absorb **carbon dioxide** from the air when the
pigment in them called **chlorophyll** is exposed to **sunlight**. Meanwhile, the **roots**
absorb water and **mineral salts** from the **soil** and somehow send them up the
shoot.
There is something poetic about the **reproductive process** in 'higher' plants. Every
cell contains two sets of **chromosomes**, each with a lot of **genes** arranged in pairs. I
think this is important. The **flower** is the reproductive part of the **organism**. It has
four main parts: **sepals** on the outside, then **petals**, then **stamens** which hold the
pollen grains or male cells, and inside the **style**, containing **ovules** in **ovaries** –
basically the female **seeds**. Then the bits of pollen are carried by the wind or insects
to the female part, two cells come together, **pollenation** has taken place, and the
thing is **fertilised**. This is a brief summary of how plants grow. Perhaps the picture
will help:

*Better work, but I think we could
probably do without the artistic
illustrations thank you. Our lessons are
concerned with biology.*

Practice

1 Only try to learn the following words if you are a real nature-lover. On the other hand, it might be worth being able to recognise them.
Try to find the answer to each question from the words printed below it.

1 Which one of these is not an **evergreen tree**?
a **cedar**   a **cypress**   a **holly tree**   a **laurel**   a **willow**   a **fir tree**   a **yew**
2 And which of these is not **deciduous**?
a **(silver) birch**   a **sycamore**   a **horse-chestnut**   a **poplar**   a **plane tree**
a **yew**
3 There are, of course, hundreds of different flowers: some wild, some cultivated, some both (like a **daffodil**). Which of these are normally garden flowers, and which wild? Mark them G or W respectively.

**iris   carnation   hyacinth   bluebell   daisy   marigold   orchid
lily   dandelion   pansy   rose   narcissus   crocus   snowdrop
primrose   poppy**

2 The following sentences are broken up into three sections, which have been mixed up. Try to rearrange them, so that they make more sense. They are describing where certain plants are usually found.

There was / were:

1 **waterlilies**	climbing up the walls	**in the jungle.**
2 **seaweed**	in a **clearing**	of the old house.
3 **a ring of toadstools**	in the **marshland**	and the **sea bed.**
4 **heather and gorse**	on the **pond**	**on the seashore.**
5 **reeds**	clinging to the **bark**	in the middle of the **meadow.**
6 **coral**	near an **oasis**	in the **forest.**
7 **long creepers**	on **pebbles** in **rock pools**	and **moorland.**
8 **moss**	all over the **reef**	**in the desert.**
9 **ivy**	on the **heath**	and **swamps.**
10 **cacti and palm trees**	among the **undergrowth**	of **the trees in the wood.**

3 Write or discuss the answers to these questions.

1 How do you feel schoolchildren can best be introduced to nature and the natural sciences?
2 How would you arrange, if you could, a garden of a hundred square metres?

4 Write part of an enthusiastic letter to a friend explaining why this present season is your favourite one.

5 Write an article for your local magazine entitled: 'City-dwellers don't know what they're missing'. Try to convince the reader of the joys of the countryside.

■ Add any other words about plants and flowers as you meet them.

. . . .
. . . .
. . . .
. . . .

The animal world

Quiz

Here's an animal quiz which will refresh your memory on some key words as well as the names of about 150 animals. There are a lot of words in bold print here. Don't despair! Your own language may help you a lot, and you only need to *remember* those words that you may need to use. You just need to *recognise* the other ones. Try to learn the most general terms, in particular.
Select the correct answer to each question.

PART ONE (not very difficult)

1 Which is the largest of the **ape** and **monkey families**, **full-grown**?
   a chimpanzee   b orang-outang   c gorilla
2 Which of these is not a **mammal**?
   a whale   b porpoise   c shark   d dolphin
3 Which of these is a **marsupial**?
   a kangaroo   b camel   c panda
4 Which of these hasn't got **a shell** on its back?
   a snail   b tortoise   c turtle   d crab   e octopus
5 Which of these hasn't got **tusks** but has got **whiskers**?
   a elephant   b walrus   c seal
6 Which of these hasn't got **horns**?
   a rhino(ceros)   b hippo(potamus)   c bull   d goat   e deer
   f antelope
7 Which of these has **spots** rather than **stripes**?
   a zebra   b leopard   c tiger
8 Whose **fur** might you expect to pay most for?
   a fox   b mink   c rabbit
9 Which member of the **snake family** is this?
   a viper   b boa constrictor   c cobra   d python   e rattlesnake
10 Which of these animals is not **carnivorous**?
   a hyena   b reindeer   c polar bear
11 Which of these **insects** doesn't **sting**?
   a ant   b wasp   c bee   d ladybird
12 Which won't **bite** you?
   a mosquito   b flea   c butterfly   d fly
13 Which of these **beasts** hasn't got a **hump**?
   a bison   b ox   c camel
14 Which of these **birds** can fly?
   a penguin   b ostrich   c goose   d emu   e kiwi
15 Which of these birds has the most impressive **tail**?
   a peacock   b pigeon   c sparrow   d budgerigar
16 Which of these animals does not normally **hibernate**?
   a bear   b squirrel   c dormouse   d rat
17 Which of these has most **legs**?
   a spider   b scorpion   c centipede   d beetle   e worm
   f piranha fish
18 Which of these birds' **feathers** aren't black?
   a blackbird   b crow   c raven   d blue tit
19 Which of these **creatures** is not **extinct**?
   a mammoth   b dinosaur   c pterodactyl   d buffalo
   e brontosaurus

20 Which birds are these?
    a the symbol of peace?
    b the announcer of spring?
    c supposed to be very wise?
    d with perhaps the most beautiful singing voice?

PART TWO (more difficult)

21 Which **member** of the **cat family** is this?
    a cheetah **b panther** **c lion**
22 Which of these is not **a fabulous creature**?
    a dragon **b unicorn** **c chameleon** **d mermaid**
23 Which of these **reptiles** is not an **amphibian**?
    a crocodile **b iguana** **c alligator** **d newt**
24 Which of these is not **related to the dog**?
    a wolf **b jackal** **c yak**
25 Which **breed of dog** is this?
    a Alsatian **b terrier** **c spaniel** **d Pekinese** **e poodle**
    f foxhound **g labrador** **h greyhound** **i bulldog**
26 Which of these is not **nocturnal**?
    a moth **b badger** **c bat** **d koala bear**
27 Which of these **creatures** has got **gills**?
    a lizard **b toad** **c lobster** **d dragonfly**
28 Which of these runners would win a 5000 metres race?
    a gazelle **b elk** **c wildebeest**
29 Which of these would win the high jump?
    a frog **b grasshopper** or **cricket** **c giraffe**
30 Which of these four is **a cross** between two of the others?
    a horse **b ass** **c donkey** **d mule**
31 Which of these animals has **hooves** as opposed to paws and claws?
    a stag **b hare** **c otter** **d racoon**
32 Which **rodent** is this?
    a beaver **b guinea-pig** **c hamster** **d mole**
33 Which of these is not **a bird of prey**?
    a hawk **b falcon** **c vulture** **d woodpecker** **e eagle**
34 Which of these is not **a wading bird**?
    a stork **b flamingo** **c swan**
35 Which of these does not normally **migrate**?
    a robin **b swallow** **c thrush**
36 Which is this **species of vermin**?
    a weasel **b skunk** **c stoat**
37 Which of these birds has the longest **wings**?
    a albatross **b seagull** **c humming-bird**
38 Which of these creatures is not **prickly**?
    a hedgehog **b porcupine** **c cockroach**
39 Which of these **cold-blooded sea creatures** has **tentacles** and no **fins**?
    a jellyfish **b swordfish** **c stingray** **d flying fish**
40 Which **bird**:
    a starts the day with its cry?
    b is a bit of a petty thief?
    c is found in the expression: to learn something **...-fashion**?
    d is found in the expression: **as dead as a** ...?

Answers: 1c 2c 3a 4e 5c 6b 7b 8b 9c 10b 11d 12c 13b 14c 15a 16d 17c
18d 19d 20 **dove cuckoo owl nightingale** 21c 22c 23b 24c 25h 26d 27c
28a 29b 30d 31a 32a 33d 34c 35a 36a 37a 38c 39a 40 **cock(erel)**
magpie parrot dodo

Practice

$\boxed{1}$ In the case of some **pets**, **farmyard animals**, and even some **wild** ones, we don't stop at giving them a basic name. The male and the female are given different names. Whereas we don't often have to ask, 'Is that a man or a woman?' when it comes to animals, 'Is it a he or a she?' is a fairly common question.
If you think these words may be useful to you in future, try to decide which of these pairs is **male** and which **female**.

mare	**fox**	**duck**	**goose**
stallion	**vixen**	**drake**	**gander**
buck	**dog**	**cow**	**lion**
doe	**bitch**	**bull**	**lioness**
ewe	**tiger**	**hen**	**cat**
ram	**tigress**	**cock**	**tom(cat)**

$\boxed{2}$ We also have a number of specific names for various animals' young. Match the grown animals, birds and insects (on the left) with their young (on the right).

dogs	**kids**
sheep	**lambs**
cows	**chicks**
pigs	**larvae**
horses	**puppies**
butterflies	**caterpillars**
cats	**cubs**
goats	**foals**
hens	**calves**
lions	**piglets**
insects	**kittens**

$\boxed{3}$ Then, of course, all animals have got to live somewhere. Work out which animals live where.

cows	dogs	lions	tame rabbits	canaries
pigs	bees	horses	wild rabbits	most birds
a **sty**	a **nest**	a **hutch**	a **den** (or **lair**)	a **hole** (or **burrow**)
a **hive**	a **cage**	a **kennel**	a **shed** (or **stall**)	a **stable** (or **stall**)

$\boxed{4}$ If you've learnt all those words, you must be a real **animal-lover**. Who knows when you might want to describe a hundred swans high above you, or two hundred buffalo **charging** or three hundred **cattle stampeding** towards you? If you do, you will need the words used to describe a group of animals. Match the group words below with the correct kind of wildlife.

1 a **herd** of	**a** fish
2 a **pack** of	**b** bees
3 a **flock** of	**c** wolves
4 a **swarm** of	**d** cattle, elephants
5 a **shoal** of	**e** sheep, birds

Note but do not try to learn (unless they are of particular interest to you) a **pride of lions**, a **school of whales** and other rarer group nouns.

$\boxed{5}$ There are words for the particular noises that animals make. Read the poem on the next page. It should help you to remember them. Then think of an animal and test yourself by trying to remember the word for the noise it makes.

In Praise of Fish

Cats **purr**
As they lick their fur;
Horses **neigh**,
Donkeys **bray**;
Hounds **bay**
At the bloody ground
Horrible sound,
Barking hounds,
Snapping and **yapping**,
Tails wagging.
Lions **roar**
If they hurt their paw.
Hawks **squawk**
If they hurt their claw.
But fish don't talk,
Thank the Lord.

Mice **squeak**,
Sheep **bleat** –
So do goats;
A frog **croaks**.
Most birds **cheep**,
Some **screech**,
But fish can't speak,
Thank Heavens.
Unlike fish,
Snakes **hiss**,
And like it or lump it,
Elephants **trumpet**.
Pigs **grunt**,
Flies **hum**,
But fish are dumb,
Thank God.

Wolves **howl**,
Dogs will **growl**
With a vicious **snarl**
If you steal their meal.
Piglets **squeal**
So you know they feel
While their mothers **snort**
As they're brought to the slaughterhouse.
Fish don't **buzz**,
As a queen bee does.
Ducklings **quack**,
And bulldogs **snap**
At the postman's boots.
Owls **hoot**,
But a fish is mute,
Thank Goodness.

6 Below you see a list of parts of animals' bodies. Take each word and find a creature in this unit which has it as part of their body.

a **tail**	**hooves**
hind legs	a **trunk**
stripes	**fins**
spots	a **hump**
udders	**fur**
horns	**scales**
tusks	**whiskers**
a **mane**	a **pouch**
wings	a **shell**
claws	**webbed feet**
paws	**feelers** or **antennae**
tentacles	a **beak**

7 Write or discuss the answers to questions 1 – 6.

1 Which animals make the best pets?
2 What, if anything, does keeping a pet teach a child?
3 Would you like your children to be brought up on a farm?
4 Why are we happy to eat certain animals and not others?
5 Which animals would you rather not touch? Can you say why?
6 Children get to know a lot of animals through books and toys. Think of about ten animals found in children's books. What image does each of them normally have?

8 Write part of a letter to a friend describing the afternoon you took a group of young children to a zoo or safari park.

9 Write the opening of your speech at an 'Animal Liberation' meeting, attacking the way animals are used and abused by human beings: in sport, circuses etc.

■ Add any other words about animals as you meet them.

. . . .
. . . .
. . . .
. . . .
. . . .
. . . .
. . . .
. . . .
. . . .
. . . .
. . . .
. . . .
. . . .

Food and drink

Study

1 Which of these **vegetables** can you find in the picture? Label each vegetable in the picture with the appropriate number.

1 onion	7 potato	12 cabbage	17 lettuce	22 celery
2 peas	8 beans	13 beetroot	18 tomato	23 cauliflower
3 asparagus	9 carrot	14 broccoli	19 chicory	24 artichoke
4 parsnip	10 turnip	15 swede	20 leek	25 marrow
5 courgette	11 mushroom	16 watercress	21 spinach	26 radish
6 brussel sprouts				

2 Now try and do the same with the different **fruit** below. Then mark your favourite fruit and vegetables by putting a ring round the number beside each of them.

1 apple	7 orange	12 cherry	17 pear	22 plum
2 apricot	8 peach	13 strawberry	18 raspberry	23 gooseberry
3 rhubarb	9 blackberry	14 grapefruit	19 banana	24 lemon
4 melon	10 grapes	15 pineapple	20 fig	25 date
5 nuts	11 coconut	16 currants	21 mango	26 lime
6 pawpaw				

Practice

Meat

This is a short section, in case you are a **vegetarian**! Most **cuts of meat** are spoken of in English which comes from 'polite' Norman French. The parts that *fall off* or out of the animal when it is cut up *(offal)* tend to come from Anglo-Saxon. Which of these meats are your favourites? Which wouldn't you eat for a million dollars?

a **joint of beef**   oxtail
beefsteak   ox tongue
stewing beef / steak

a **fillet of beef**
veal cutlets   **calf's liver**
veal escalopes   **calf's heart**
a **shoulder of veal**   **calf's foot**
lamb chops   **lamb's brains**
a **shoulder of mutton**   **sheep's head**
a **leg of pork**   **pig's kidney**
pork sausages   **pig's blood**

Note that the pig is also responsible for providing us with cured and smoked meat: **ham, gammon** and **bacon**.

Poultry

These are birds which can be eaten but are not hunted with a shotgun. Read the questions and select or write the appropriate answer for each of them.

1 Which of these five birds is white in the northern hemisphere but can be black in Australia?
   a chicken   b turkey   c swan   d goose   e duck
2 What is eaten with each of the above types of poultry in your country?

Game

Game is the group name for the wild animals and birds which are hunted and then eaten (**rabbits, hares** etc). Select or write an answer for each question.

1 One of these meats is not from a bird. Which is it?
   a pheasant   b venison   c partridge   d pigeon   e grouse
2 How popular is this type of food in your country?
3 Should shooting game as a sport be encouraged or discouraged?

Fish

Read the questions and select the appropriate answer(s) for each of them.

1 Which of these would you describe as white fish and which is oily?
   **a sole   b cod   c plaice   d trout   e haddock   f salmon   g eel
   h mackerel   i herring**
2 Some of the above fish are freshwater fish, that is to say they spend all or most of their life in a river. Some are sea fish. Underline the freshwater fish.
3 Ring your favourites in the list of fish in question 1. Then select how you like each of them cooked.
   **a grilled   b fried   c baked   d smoked   e in a sauce   f in a soup
   g in a stew**
4 One of these is not an example of shellfish (**seafood**). Which one?
   **a crab   b lobster   c shrimp   d prawn   e oyster   f cockle
   g mussel   h kipper**

Cereals and grasses

Match the list of cereals **1–6** with statements **a – f**.

1 wheat   2 maize   3 rye   4 barley   5 oats   6 rice

a Most **porridge** is made of it. It is also used to **feed** horses.
b It is the **staple diet** in the East.
c It provides **corn on the cob**, a lot of **cornflour**, and American whisky.
d It is used to make black bread, **cattle feed** and some kinds of American whisky.
e It is used a lot in **brewing** and soups and **malt** is made from it.
f It is used to make **white bread** and most **pasta**.

Pasta

Talking of pasta, below are a few of the approximately thirty types that are most commonly eaten. Ring those that you like most.

a spaghetti   b macaroni   c noodles   d ravioli   e lasagne

Herbs and spices

1 Which of these herbs do you like to use in your cooking? What sort of food do you use them with?

1 garlic	4 parsley	7 thyme
2 marjoram	5 rosemary	8 bay leaf
3 mint	6 sage	9 oregano

2 Which of these spices would you find it difficult to live without?

1 black or white pepper	5 nutmeg
2 cayenne pepper	6 cinnamon
3 vanilla	7 pimento (paprika)
4 ginger	8 chilli

3 Do you agree that if the **ingredients** of the meal have the proper taste you don't need all that **seasoning**?

What our food contains

Look at the advertisement on the next page, which lists for you some of the elements in the food we eat, for example protein, carbohydrates etc. Ask yourself how much you eat of each in a typical day's diet.

Food in general

1 Write or discuss the answers to these questions.

1 How careful are you about having a well-balanced or a calorie-controlled diet?
2 How healthy do you think healthfoods really are?
3 We should all 'eat, drink and be merry'. Do you agree?
4 What (in detail) are your favourite restaurant meals at about these prices:
   a £2.50? (cheap)
   b £5.00? (quite reasonable)
   c £10? (average)
   d £20 – 25? (expensive)

2 Write or act out a conversation with a waiter. You are ordering one of the meals you listed above. Remember the sort of restaurant you're in and be prepared to choose an alternative if what you ask for is unavailable.

3 Write a page from your diary. It is the fifteenth day that you have been on a really strict diet.

4 Write, in dialogue form, a conversation between a butcher and a regular customer who does not find any of the meat in the window particularly attractive or good value.

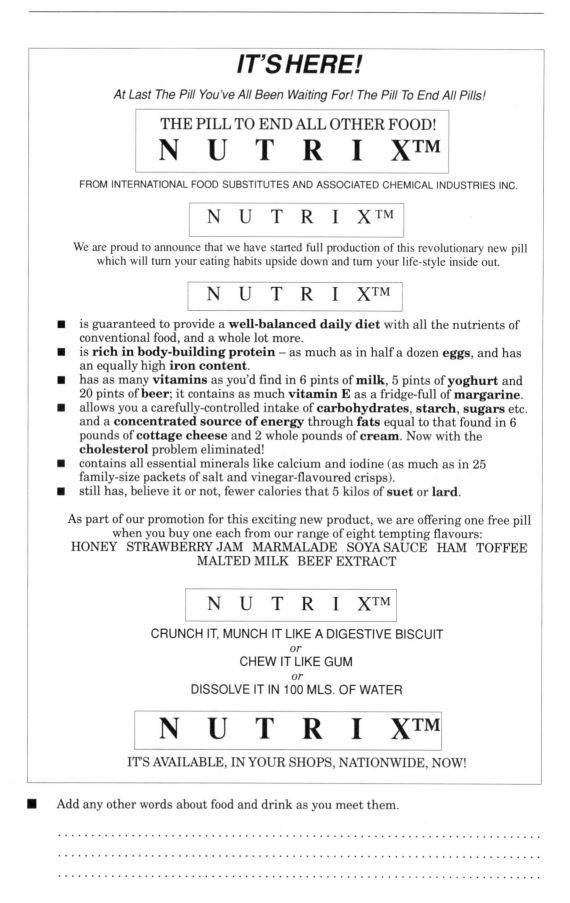

IT'S HERE!

At Last The Pill You've All Been Waiting For! The Pill To End All Pills!

THE PILL TO END ALL OTHER FOOD!
N U T R I X™

FROM INTERNATIONAL FOOD SUBSTITUTES AND ASSOCIATED CHEMICAL INDUSTRIES INC.

N U T R I X™

We are proud to announce that we have started full production of this revolutionary new pill which will turn your eating habits upside down and turn your life-style inside out.

N U T R I X™

- is guaranteed to provide a **well-balanced daily diet** with all the nutrients of conventional food, and a whole lot more.
- is **rich in body-building protein** – as much as in half a dozen **eggs**, and has an equally high **iron content**.
- has as many **vitamins** as you'd find in 6 pints of **milk**, 5 pints of **yoghurt** and 20 pints of **beer**; it contains as much **vitamin E** as a fridge-full of **margarine**.
- allows you a carefully-controlled intake of **carbohydrates**, **starch**, **sugars** etc. and a **concentrated source of energy** through **fats** equal to that found in 6 pounds of **cottage cheese** and 2 whole pounds of **cream**. Now with the **cholesterol** problem eliminated!
- contains all essential minerals like calcium and iodine (as much as in 25 family-size packets of salt and vinegar-flavoured crisps).
- still has, believe it or not, fewer calories that 5 kilos of **suet** or **lard**.

As part of our promotion for this exciting new product, we are offering one free pill when you buy one each from our range of eight tempting flavours:
HONEY STRAWBERRY JAM MARMALADE SOYA SAUCE HAM TOFFEE
MALTED MILK BEEF EXTRACT

N U T R I X™

CRUNCH IT, MUNCH IT LIKE A DIGESTIVE BISCUIT
or
CHEW IT LIKE GUM
or
DISSOLVE IT IN 100 MLS. OF WATER

N U T R I X™

IT'S AVAILABLE, IN YOUR SHOPS, NATIONWIDE, NOW!

■ Add any other words about food and drink as you meet them.

. . . .

. . . .

. . . .

Buildings and rooms

Games

1   Cover the right-hand column.
I have a room in a small **semi-detached house**. Two of my friends live in **mansions**. What sort of **accommodation** do (did) these people have, or what might they be living in at the moment?

1	a queen	a **palace** or **castle**
2	an eskimo	an **igloo**
3	a Red Indian a hundred years ago	a **wigwam** or **tepee**
4	a monk	a **monastery**
5	a nun	a **convent** (or **nunnery**)
6	an eighty-year-old with no living relatives	an **old people's home**
7	a soldier	**barracks** or **living quarters**
8	a cowboy	a **ranch(-house)**
9	a travelling sales representative away from home	a **motel**
10	a forester in Canada	a **(log-)cabin**
11	skiers in the mountains	a **chalet**
12	holiday-makers who find hotels too big or expensive – or both	a **guest house** (or **boarding house**)
13	a well-off couple holidaying in the South of France	a **villa**
14	a camper	a **tent** (or **caravan**)
15	a successful advertising executive	a **penthouse (suite)**
16	a tramp – if he's lucky	a **hovel**, **garden shed**, an **old hut**

2   Cover the right-hand column again.
I spend a lot of time in my **bed-sitting room** (**bedsitter**). In which room might it be a good idea to look for these people?

1	an artist	a **studio**
2	a dentist	a **surgery**
3	a novelist	a **study**
4	a carpenter	a **workshop**
5	some sailors	a **cabin**
6	a secretary	an **office**
7	some teachers	a **staffroom**
8	a prisoner	a **cell**
9	a dentist's patients before their appointments	a **waiting room**
10	a rugby player after a match	a **changing room**
11	some factory workers at lunchtime	a **canteen**
12	a gardener	a **shed** or **greenhouse**
13	some toddlers	a **playroom** or **nursery**
14	a photographer busy developing photos	a **darkroom**
15	some off-duty soldiers	a **mess(-room)**
16	a swimmer after her swim	a changing **cubicle**
17	a street-market trader	a **stall**
18	a secret wine-taster	a **(wine-)cellar**
19	a pilot, mid-flight	a **cockpit**
20	a corpse	a **mortuary** (**morgue**)

Practice

1 Note the areas, rooms and sections in the buildings shown below. Answer the following questions.
1 Which buildings are they?
2 What happens in the various parts of them?
3 Where would you expect to find the people listed below?

1 an usherette	7 a librarian
2 a surgeon	8 a sales assistant
3 a headmaster	9 a prompter
4 a guard	10 the defendant
5 the cast	11 a sister
6 a congregation	12 a local councillor

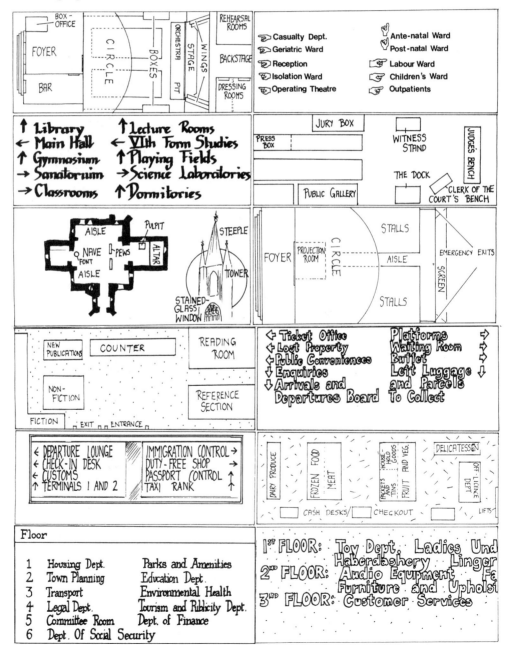

2 Two of the buildings on the previous page were, of course, shops. Shopping habits, like everything else, have changed a lot in the past twenty years. It was not long ago that names like **Hypermarket**, **Department Store**, **Boutique**, **Cash and Carry**, **Discount Store**, **Do-It-Yourself Supplies**, **Takeaway Food** had little or no place in our high streets.

My grandfather still refuses to shop in any of these places. Cover the right-hand column and say where you think he would go to buy the following things.

1 a nice piece of cod	a **fishmonger's**
2 a dozen blue envelopes	a **stationer's**
3 a box of soft-centred chocolates	a **confectioner's**
4 a copy of *Time* magazine	a **newsagent's**
5 a dozen pink carnations	a **florist's**
6 a bar of perfumed soap	a **chemist's**
7 a cauliflower or some broccoli	a **(green)grocer's**
8 a three-piece suit	a **tailor's**
9 half a dozen wholemeal rolls	a **baker's**
10 an ounce of pipe tobacco and a box of matches	a **tobacconist's**
11 a couple of pork chops	a **butcher's**
12 a packet of one-inch nails	an **ironmonger's**
13 a goldfish	a **pet shop**
14 a sack of coal	a **coal merchant's**
15 a seventeenth-century grandfather clock	an **antique dealer**
16 a pair of sheets and pillow cases	a **draper's**

3 Write or act out what you would say while showing the people mentioned around the buildings below.

1 new students around a boarding school
2 new guests around a hotel
3 new employees around a factory
4 new prisoners around a prison

4 You have an empty building about sixty metres by forty, and you have just made a fortune. Plan and draw the layout for using it for each of the following purposes.

1 a new supermarket
2 a sports centre
3 a library
4 a youth club

5 Write a paragraph for a travel brochure on a castle, church or cathedral which you particularly like.

6 Write an article for your school, college or workplace magazine entitled: 'The only sensible way to shop nowadays is in big stores'.

7 Write part of your letter to the sports centre, complaining about how confusing the signs are outside and just inside the building.

■ Add any other words about buildings and rooms as you meet them.

. . . .

. . . .

. . . .

. . . .

Furniture and household

Reading

Over the next day or two, read through this rather strange application form, noting how the couple describe the house in question and its furniture. As you read, answer the question below.

If the couple decided to sell the house next month, which of these features could they say that it had?

1 two **bathrooms**
2 **polished wooden floors**
3 a **slate roof**
4 **attractive wallpaper throughout**
5 **double glazed windows**
6 three **bedrooms**
7 a **spacious garden shed**
8 **excellent period fireplaces**
9 a **mature vegetable garden**
10 a **modern kitchen**

Application Form XYB / 43Z Sect. 51
To Join The Yuppies' (Young Upwardly-Mobile) Neighbourhood Scheme
Remarks:
(Please state briefly below any qualifications and/or
experience you have to support your application.)

When my wife and I **moved into** our present house, it was little better than a **slum**, completely **unfurnished** apart from a few bits and pieces which the former **occupant** had either forgotten to or – more likely – decided not to take with her. (These included an enormous **sideboard** that weighed a ton, a **chest of drawers** with its only remaining door hanging off, an ugly **bookcase** with all its **panes of glass** cracked, and a broken nineteenth-century **piano stool**.)

The **floors** then were just **bare boards** with one or two **mats** and **strips of lino.** We now have **fitted carpets** in every room except the bathroom (where we have special long-lasting **tiles** at over £20 per square foot,) and the kitchen (**polished parquet floor**), plus several sheepskin **rugs** in the reception rooms. On arrival, we found most of the **interior decorated** with faded, **flowery-patterned wallpaper,** peeling at the **picture rail.** We have **painted throughout** in magnolia (**windows** and **sills** wine-red or **stripped pine**) except in the lounge, where we have had **hessian** hung. A few tasteful reproductions and a number of old German **prints** (all expensively **framed**) are on the **walls**, along with some carefully selected **posters** in the children's rooms.

Numerous **structural alterations** have been **carried out**, notably the **conversion** of the old **garden shed** into a **second bathroom**, complete with **bath, basin, bidet** and **W.C.** (lambswool-covered **lavatory seat** and press-button **flush)** and the **extension** of the **conservatory** to make a **sun lounge** – with **window seats** all around it – **leading on to** the **newly-laid patio**. The **roof,** meanwhile, has been completely **renovated, slates** giving way to **tiles, double glazing** has been **fitted** on all windows, and the old **fireplaces** have been **blocked up**, except in the **lounge** which has retained its **grate** and **mantlepiece** for the old-world image it creates. In terms of **heating**, we have graduated from **electric fires** to **gas fires, convector heaters, storage heaters** and recently to full **gas-fired central heating** with extra-large **boiler** and double **radiators,** each with its own **thermostatic control**.

We have also **made** dramatic **improvements** in the kitchen. The old **installations** were **ripped out** last year and in their place came: a new **sink unit** with **mixer tap** and **double drainer**, a line of smart **cupboards** all along one wall and two **rows of shelves** along the other, a **split-level cooker, eye-level grill, double oven** – you name it, I think we've got it. Upstairs, the old iron **double bed** we inherited has been replaced by elegant **twin beds** with **interior-sprung mattresses** and **continental quilts** (**duvets**), of course. Our children, Alexandra and Charles, have recently moved out of their **bunk beds** and into **single beds** in **separate rooms**; these have been specially **equipped with** a **desk, blackboard** and **easel**, and **toy chest**. All bedrooms have **built-in wardrobes** now and my wife has her own personal **dressing table**.

Our more expensive purchases, apart from the above, include:
a **leather upholstered lounge suite** comprising a **four-seater sofa** – or should we say **settee**? – and two **armchairs**. (We remember with horror the year we had to make do with a **studio couch** plus a few **pouffes** and **cushions**.)
a **solid wood table** and set of **matching dining room chairs**, plus a **microwave oven**.
a new **shower unit** in the **master bathroom, plumbed in** of course, so that no unsightly **pipes** are visible.
new **stereo equipment, colour TV**, a **video recorder, home computer** and **cocktail cabinet**.

It may interest you to know, finally, that we have made a formal complaint about the ghastly **tallboy** and **divan** that our neighbours have had standing in their **back garden** for nearly six months. (Our garden, incidentally, has been recently **landscaped** and completely **transformed**: gone is the **vegetable patch**; in its place a neat **lawn** and **flower-beds**.) All our (new) friends say we have done a wonderful job on our **property**. One or two have invited us to join the amateur dramatic society and they are even giving us the names of private schools in the area.
I hope you will consider our application favourably.

Signature: ....
Date: ....

Practice 1

1   Write or discuss the answers to these questions.

   1 What do you like and what don't you like about the place where you live?
   2 What things would you like to have done to improve your room, flat or house?

2   Describe, in as much detail as possible, the most beautiful bedroom you can imagine.

3   Describe the poorest-looking house you remember being in.

4   Write or act out the conversation in a furniture shop between you and the sales assistant, as you try to decide what to buy for your new flat.

5   Write instructions to leave with the removal men who are helping you to move house. Tell them where everything is at the moment and where you would like it in your new home. Warn them about any particularly important or fragile articles.

6   Write the opening of the speech that you make as a tourist guide showing groups of visitors around the state room(s) of a palace, castle or large country house near your home.

7 Write the opening paragraph of your latest short story, in which you describe your feelings as you revisit the house in which you grew up, now much changed.

Game 1

Cover the right-hand column. On the left are listed the uses of some rectangular pieces of material that no household should be without. Guess what they are and then check your answers in the right-hand column.

1 things to sleep between	(a pair of) **sheets**
2 something to clean and polish table tops	a **duster**
3 something to wash your face with	a **flannel**
4 and to dry it with	a **towel**
5 something to wipe your mouth with after eating	a **serviette** or **napkin**
6 something to put round baby's bottom	a **nappy**
7 things to keep you warm in bed	**blankets** (**bedspread/duvet**)
8 something to blow your nose with	a **handkerchief** (**tissue, hankie**)
9 something to wash up with	a **dishcloth** or **scourer**
10 and dry the dishes with	a **tea-towel** or **teacloth**
11 something to cover the table before laying it	a **table cloth**
12 something to put hot dinner plates on	a **table mat**
13 something to clean the floor with	a **floor cloth**
14 things to stop people peeping through the windows at you	**net curtains** (or **blinds**)

Practice 2

Think for a moment about how important some of our **household gadgets** and **devices** are to us.

1 If you had to live without two of the following, which ones would you choose to leave behind?

a **fridge** (**refrigerator**)   a **dishwasher** (**washing-up machine**)
a **hoover** (**vacuum cleaner**)   a **washing machine**
a **dryer** (**spin** or **tumble dryer**)   a **freezer**

2 And which three of these?

an **iron**   a **sewing machine**
a **mixer**   an **electric kettle**
a **toaster**   a **coffee grinder**
a **liquidiser**   a **hairdryer**

3 Which of these do you prefer to be electric? All of them or not?

a **drill**   a **screwdriver**
a **saw**   a **sander**
a **razor**   a **lawnmower**
a **toothbrush**   a **whisk** (to beat eggs etc.)
a **typewriter**   **curling tongs** (or hair **curlers/rollers**)

Game 2

1 Look carefully at the pictures on the next page. In them there are **tools**, **appliances**, items of **crockery** and **cutlery**. Under each of them are four names. Only one of them labels the picture correctly. Decide which it is.
Then make sure you know the other words given in each group as well. Draw each of them and then try to give the English word for each drawing without looking at the book. Alternatively, write a sentence to show the meaning of each word.

a **garden fork**
a **spade**
a **rake**
a **hoe**

a **pair of shears**
a **shovel**
a **scythe**
a **sickle**

a **nail**
a **bolt**
a **screw**
a **nut**

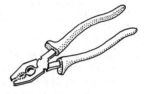

a **mop**
a **broom**
a **carpet sweeper**
a **brush**

a **hammer**
a **chisel**
a **spanner**
a **plane**

a pair of **scissors**
a pair of **nail clippers**
a pair of **tweezers**
a pair of **pliers (pincers)**

a **spatula**
a **corkscrew**
a **tin opener**
a **garlic crusher**

a **strainer**
a **grater**
a **peeler**
a **colander**

a **carving knife**
a **penknife**
a **cheese knife**
a **fish knife**

a **teaspoon**
a **ladle**
a **soup spoon**
a **dessert spoon**

a **mug**
a **teacup**
a **tumbler**
a **wine glass**

a **salt cellar**
a **sieve**
a **pepper mill**
an **eggcup**

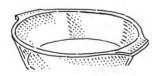
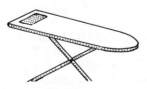

a **casserole dish**
a **baking tray**
a **mixing bowl**
a **thermos flask**

a **breadboard**
a **chopping board**
a **draining board**
an **ironing board**

2 Answer the questions. Then make sure that you know the meaning of all the words that are not the correct answer.

1 Which of these four instruments wouldn't be of much use to a carpenter?
a **vice**   a **stethoscope**   a **set square**   a **saw**
2 Which of these tools wouldn't interest a metal worker?
a **tuning fork**   a **file**   a **wrench**   a **lathe**
3 Here are four instruments we can look through:
a **telescope**   **binoculars**   **opera glasses**   a **microscope.**
Which would you use:
a to see more clearly what that ballerina looks like?
b to study the markings on the leopard over there?
c to have a good look at Venus this evening?
d to examine a drop of your blood?

3 Leaving aside mysterious inventions like **lie-detectors**, the **test tubes** and **bunsen burners** of the chemistry laboratory, the surgeon's **scalpel**, the dentist's **drill** and the fireman's **hose**, here is one more picture. What is this? Is it:
a a **pencil sharpener**?   b a **pair of compasses**?   c a **torch**?
d a **cigarette lighter**?   e a **bottle- opener**?   f a **rubber**?

Study and practice

1 Here are some more **instruments** and **gadgets** that **measure** things for us. Cover the right-hand column, and see if you can give their names. Then check your answers.
What is it that tells you:

1	how fast you're driving in your new sports car?	a **speedometer**
2	how much more air you need to pump into your tyres?	a **pressure gauge**
3	which way you're travelling in the desert?	a **compass**
4	what your temperature is?	a **thermometer**
5	how heavy you or the potatoes are?	a (pair of) **scales**
6	how many centimetres you are round the waist?	a **tape measure**
7	how much electricity or gas you've used this quarter?	a **meter**
8	how much you've spent at the supermarket?	a **cash register** (till)
9	how fast to play the piece of music?	a **metronome**
10	approximately how much oil you've got in the car?	a **dipstick**
11	how long a line is?	a **ruler** (**metal rule**)
12	how fast you've just run the hundred metres?	a **stopwatch**
13	when your line or surface is exactly level?	a **spirit level**
14	about the atmospheric pressure?	a **barometer**
15	how many degrees there are in an angle?	a **protractor**
16	how much alcohol there is in your blood according to the police?	a **breathalyser**

2   Finally, in this section, let's think about **containers** and **holders**. It's amazing how many there are in and around a house. On the left below you will see a list of them. On the right are examples of their different types. Some of them combine into one word, others remain as two words. Cover the words on the right and try to think of as many as you can for each container. Then check your answers.

BOX	**matchbox seedbox toolbox musical box**
BAG	**handbag carrier bag shoulder bag paper bag**
BOWL	**sugar bowl fruit bowl soup bowl goldfish bowl**
PAN	**saucepan frying pan dustpan**
BASKET	**laundry basket wastepaper basket shopping basket picnic basket**
CASE	**suitcase bookcase pencil case pillow case briefcase**
CAN	**oil can watering can petrol can**
TANK	**oil tank water tank fish tank**
POT	**flowerpot mustard pot coffee pot teapot**
RACK	**pipe rack cassette rack luggage rack**
RAIL	**towel rail handrail picture rail**
STAND	**umbrella stand hat stand microphone stand**
HOLDER	**pen-holder cigarette holder microphone-holder**
BIN	**dustbin rubbish bin litter bin pedal bin**
JUG	**milk jug measuring jug water jug**

Remember that we might put:

flowers in a **vase.**
candles in a **candlestick**.
water in a **bucket.**
money in a **purse, wallet, safe** or **piggybank**.

Practice 3

1   Write or give a partner detailed advice on each of the following situations.

1 His/Her garden looks a complete mess.
2 He/She has no idea what to take with him/her on his/her camping holiday.
3 None of his/her doors close properly because of the carpets.
4 He/She has always kept all his/her crockery, cutlery and kitchen utensils in one big cupboard. He/She has just bought some new kitchen units and has no idea where to put things so that they are easy to find.

2   Explain which odd jobs around the house you enjoy and which you hate. Give your reasons.

3   Describe how housework and people's attitudes to it have changed over the past thirty or forty years.

4   What bits and pieces are elderly peoples' houses full of in your country? Describe in some detail the objects in their sitting room, the spare room, the loft, the garden shed etc.

5   Write a letter of complaint to the shop where you bought a set of tools recently, almost none of which work properly.

6   Write, in dialogue form, a conversation in a furniture shop between an inquisitive customer and a knowledgeable assistant.

7 Write the list of wedding presents you want to circulate in advance to your guests. (This 'ordering' of gifts is customary in Britain. It avoids your being given six toasters and a hundred and ninety-two wine glasses.)

■ Add any other words about furniture and household appliances as you meet them.

. . . .

. . . .

. . . .

. . . .

. . . .

. . . .

. . . .

. . . .

. . . .

. . . .

. . . .

. . . .

. . . .

. . . .

Vehicles

Study and practice

1 Study the words for the parts of the car illustrated below. Then test yourself by covering the words and trying to recall them.

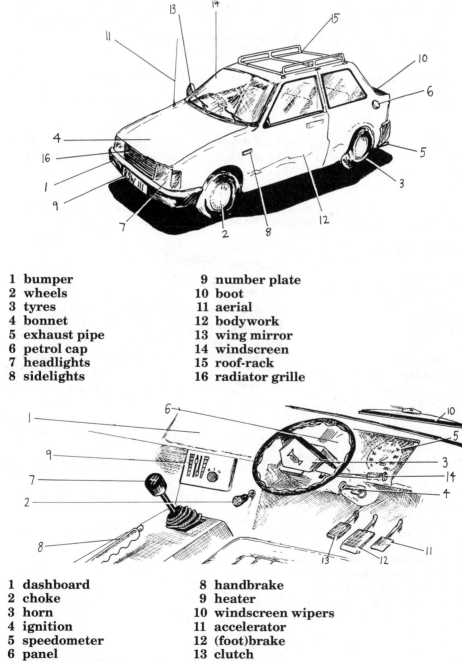

1	bumper	9	number plate
2	wheels	10	boot
3	tyres	11	aerial
4	bonnet	12	bodywork
5	exhaust pipe	13	wing mirror
6	petrol cap	14	windscreen
7	headlights	15	roof-rack
8	sidelights	16	radiator grille

1	dashboard	8	handbrake
2	choke	9	heater
3	horn	10	windscreen wipers
4	ignition	11	accelerator
5	speedometer	12	(foot)brake
6	panel	13	clutch
7	gear (stick / lever)	14	indicators

1 engine
2 fan belt
3 carburettor
4 battery
5 distributor
6 dipstick
7 radiator
8 (sparking) plugs

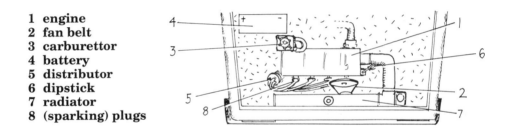

2 Fill each gap in the sentences below with one of the words you see illustrated above.

1 It won't start; either the ... is flat, or the ... are dirty.
2 It's got a nice spacious ... for your luggage, all-weather ... to reduce the risk of skidding in wet weather, and a ... showing you everything from the time you've been travelling to the ... you should be in at any given moment.
3 Fortunately the ... wasn't damaged when he drove into the back of me, but the ... is quite badly bent.
4 The first thing you do for an emergency stop is take your foot off the ... and press both feet down on the ... and the ... .
5 If you have the ... out for too long, the ... will be flooded with petrol.

3 Draw your own pictures with parts of the car missing or in the wrong place. Write under each picture what is wrong with it and how it should be drawn, or ask a partner to explain this to you.

4 Would you prefer to travel by bicycle? Take a look at the parts of the bike shown here; then test yourself by covering the words.

1 handlebars
2 bell
3 pedals
4 mudguard
5 tyre
6 valve
7 chain
8 saddle
9 crossbar
10 spokes
11 inner tube
12 pump

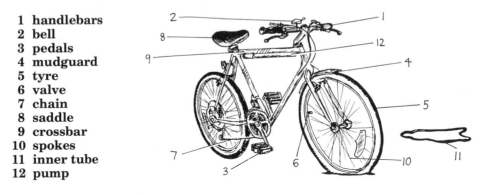

5 See if you can explain the difference between the following types of vehicle.

1 a **tandem**, a normal **bicycle**
2 a **wheelchair**, a **push-chair**
3 a **scooter**, a **moped**
4 a **trolley**, a **pram**
5 a **sleigh**, a **toboggan**
6 an **estate car**, a **hatchback**
7 a **tricycle**, a **three-wheeler**
8 a **lorry**, a **truck**, a **van**
9 a **bus**, a **tram**, a **coach**

Reading

Now read this advertisement.

PAN-ANGLO RAIL

We've come a long way since John and Mary were here!

TODAY WE OFFER YOU:

INTER-CITY SERVICES AT REGULAR INTERVALS
HIGH-SPEED LOCOMOTIVES
UP-TO-DATE **CARRIAGES**
LUXURIOUS **COMPARTMENTS**
BUFFET CARS   RESTAURANT CARS

PLUS:

EFFICIENT FREIGHT SERVICES IN PLACE OF THE OLD **GOODS TRAINS**
COMPUTERIZED CO-ORDINATION IN PLACE OF OLD **SIGNAL BOXES**
A VAST **NETWORK** OF **UNDERGROUND TRAINS**
REGULAR **CONNECTIONS** TO ALL **MAJOR STATIONS**

Oh yes, we've come a long way since John and Mary were here!

Practice 1

1. Write an angry letter to Pan-Anglo Rail. Compare what they say in their advertisement with what you personally experienced during an unbelievably unpleasant journey.

2. Do you agree that the vehicles on this and the next page are in the right order to show how dangerous they are? Write or say what you think.

racing car
motorcycle (motorbike)
juggernaut
motorbike and sidecar
sports car
(touring) **caravan**
car with **trailer**
police car
hearse

ambulance
saloon car
steamroller
taxi (cab)
tractor
milk float
horse and cart
invalid car

3 Note the parts of the strange-looking boat – or is it a ship? – below. Then draw three different kinds of boat and label each drawing.

1	oars
2	rudder
3	mast
4	sail
5	deck
6	hull
7	keel
8	funnel
9	porthole
10	cabin
11	port
12	starboard
13	stern
14	bow
15	propeller

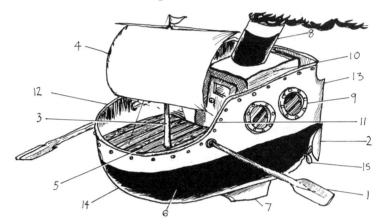

Quiz 1

Match each of the vessels below with a definition.

ark	**raft**	**punt**	**ferry**	**galleon**
tug	**rowing boat**	**launch**	**paddle steamer**	**barge**
lifeboat	**powerboat**	**lightship**	**yacht**	**canoe**
houseboat	**trawler**	**dinghy**	**submarine**	**liner**

1 Kon-tiki was a famous one.
2 Some people like to make their home in one.
3 One might be **transporting** coal up or down the Rhine.
4 Noah would have had problems without one.
5 A small boat, often made of rubber.
6 Full of brave men who go out to sea in all sorts of weather to help other people.
7 A **fishing boat** that drags a **net** along the **sea bed**.
8 A participant perhaps in a **sailing race** or **regatta**.
9 A boat to carry people and their things from one point to another – and back.
10 Didn't they used to travel down the Mississippi in one of these?
11 The Spanish Armada was composed of a number of these.
12 The QE2 is one.
13 An English form of **gondola** – propelled by a **pole**.
14 The river police might chase a suspect in one.
15 A Red Indian would have felt at home in one.
16 This one will take part in a very fast race.
17 You won't get far without oars in this one.

18 A stationary **vessel** that will guide and direct others.
19 You won't see it very often but it might see you through its **periscope**.
20 A little boat that will pull a much bigger one.

■ Serious **mariners** might make a note of any further **marine** vocabulary here:

. . . .

. . . .

. . . .

. . . .

. . . .

. . . .

. . . .

. . . .

Study

Try to learn any of the words below that you feel might be useful in a future flying career.

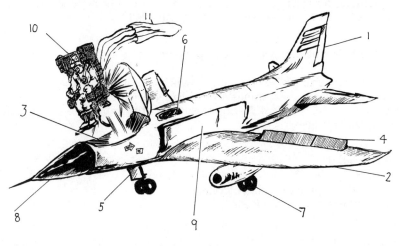

1 tail	7 wheels
2 wings	8 nose
3 cockpit	9 fuselage
4 flaps	10 ejector seat
5 undercarriage	11 parachute
6 window	

Quiz 2

Cover the right-hand column and try this little quiz. On your own or in teams, see if you can guess the year when these flying objects first appeared in the sky. (One point for the team nearest the actual date.)

a **hot-air balloon**	1783
a **helicopter**	1936
an **earth-orbiting satellite**	1957
a **manned spacecraft**	1961

an **aeroplane**	1903
a **jet plane**	1941
a **hovercraft**	1959
the first **supersonic manned flight**	1947
a **jet airliner**	1949

■ Add here any other words you meet concerning aeroplanes.

....

....

....

....

Practice 2

1 Talk in small groups about the following:

1 cars you (or your parents) have had and how good they were.
2 tips you know about how to run your car as economically as possible.
2 unpleasant journeys you have had by land, sea or air.
3 the problems for cyclists on the roads and what can be done about them.
4 airport and aeroplane security: can it be achieved?

2 Act out the following situations with a partner.

1 have a conversation in which one of you is a customer and the other a car salesman pointing out all the good things about his/her product(s).
2 give the other his/her first driving lesson, pointing out where everything is in the car and what it does.

3 Explain in detail:

1 how to mend a puncture on a bicycle.
2 how to change a wheel on a car.

4 Write a long list of things not working properly in your car for the mechanic to have a look at during its service.

5 Write a paragraph from a leaflet advertising your company's latest car, motorbike or bicycle.

6 Write the script for a commercial advertising your company's airline or cross-channel ferry service.

Clothes

Game

See if you can complete this crossword with the help of the clues that follow. The clues and the answers include most of the items of clothing you are likely to wear or see worn. The answers are on page 109.

Clues Across

2 The **sewing** round the bottom of a skirt, blouse, slacks etc. (3)

4 When you've **undressed**, you'll probably be this. (5)

6 A **military jacket**, but quite **fashionable**. (5)

9 A **fastener** that needs a **hole**. (6)

11 You may hear '**brassière**', but most people call it this. (3)

12 A **knitted woollen jacket**. (8)

15 An **anorak** is an example of one. (4)

17 Part of a **three-piece suit**. (9)

19 What a **dress** often used to be called and still occasionally is. (5)

21 You won't see it too often; it'll be under a **shirt** or **top**. (4)

23 If you haven't got 9 Across, this will help you to keep things together. (3)

27 Put in front of 15 Across to make one word that'll keep you warm. (4)

29 They used to be called '**knickers**', but this word is taking over. (7)

31 The **sole** is the front part of 51 Across; this is the back. (4)

32 You'll hear people call it a **sweater**, a **jersey** and a **jumper** as well. (8)

35 A **bathing costume** (**bikini** for ladies, **trunks** for men) is now often referred to as a **swim** ... . (4)

36 A cardinal's **robe** is often ... . (3)

37 A **corset** and a **girdle** are examples of ... **wear**. (5)

39 Apart from on the finger, you might find a **ring** on the ... . (3)

41 The part of the **jacket** to grab if you're angry with someone. (5)

42 Black **arm**-... are worn as a sign of respect for the dead. (5)

43 **Tight trousers** and **bootlace ties** were **in vogue** over thirty years ... .(3)

44 Hamlet was probably wearing **breeches** and a **chemise** when he said to himself: *'To ... or not to ... .'* (2)

107

45 An important part of gentlemen's **morning dress**. (3-3)

46 One of a pair that children often wear on their hands. (6)

48 The currency you'd probably use to buy a 64 Across. (3)

49 If you haven't got **buckles**, you may need these to keep your shoes on. (5).

51 A word for a **plimsol, clog** or **sandal**. (4)

52 To look like a he-man, you might need ... **shoulders** for your jacket. (6)

54 A top Roman wouldn't be seen in public without one. (4)

58 It stretches from the **cuff** to the **shoulder**. (6)

59 Wear it with a 22 Down **T-shirt** to look like a French onion-seller. (5)

61 Another way of saying '**a piece of clothing**'. (1-7)

64 An oriental **robe**, usually worn **barefoot**. (6)

65 Similar to a **petticoat**, it's another example of 37 Across. (4)

67 **Polish** and **varnish** are for furniture, but also for these. (5)

68 A lady who wears a **habit**. (3)

69 Something for Hindu ladies to wear, with or without a **veil**. (4)

70 The sergeant-major on parade might wear one over his **uniform**. (4)

72 Like a **slide** and a **ribbon**, something for ladies to put in their hair. (4)

73 In America they cover a man's legs; in England they don't. (5)

74 Something like a **shawl**. (5)

75 If the woman **wears the** ... at home, it means she's the boss. (8)

76 It will often be worn over a **pair of shorts**: a ...-**suit**. (5)

Clues Down

1 It often follows the words: cowboy, wellington, football. (4)

2 It might be a **boater**, a **bowler**, a **trilby**, a **fez**, or even a **turban**. (3)

3 A colloquial name for a **raincoat**. (3)

4 An artistic form of 4 Across. (4)

5 That rather smart **suit** could well be a ... **jacket**. (6)

7 A collar goes round this part of you. (4)

8 An **informal** but quite **elegant** variation on 9 Down and 18 Down. (6)

9 You can wear one with 53 Down. (3-3)

10 You can't get much more elegant than these, gentlemen. (5)

11 This will look good with 8 Down in the clubhouse after the game. (6)

13 Something to protect the hands of a boxer, housewife or skier. (5)

14 Something for the queen to wear when a **tiara** would be too informal. (5)

16 The number of red **shirts** in a full Manchester United **strip**, not counting substitutes' **kit**. (3)

18 You'll often hear a suit and ... . (3)

20 A **robe** worn by men of the church. (7)

22 Along with **check**, the most popular **pattern** on clothes. (7)

24 A **fold** on a **skirt, dress** or **gym slip**. (5)

25 What **dungarees** can do outside the kitchen, this will do inside. (5)

26 Something else you could put on instead of dungarees: an **over**... . (3)

28 A **silk fabric**, handsome jackets were made of it in 30 Down times. (6)

29 It's used on a **tie** or a baby's **nappy**. (3)

30 We describe **costumes** and **outfits** at the time of King Edward as ... . (9)

31 You might wear one in a game of cricket; you must wear one on a motor-bike; you would probably have worn one with a **suit of armour**. (6)

33 It helps you to know which way round to wear certain **articles of clothing** – stops you wearing them **back to front** or **inside out**. (5)

34 If you've got an ....-**neck shirt** on, you won't need an 18 Down. (4)

38 You might wear one in preference to **pyjamas**. (10)

40 Many soldiers' wives wore **chastity belts** during the Middle ... . (4)

47 To a large extent they have replaced **stockings** and **suspenders**. (6)

50 Worn on a horserider's heel to keep his horse going. (4)

53 An abbreviation for 5 Down. (2)

55 Often worn at the same time as a **dressing gown**. (8)

56 You don't see many people over sixty wearing blue ... . (5)

57 A form of 56 Down, named after a man called Strauss. (5)

59 It's part of a car, but a woman might wear it on her head. (6)

60 An engagement or a diamond one? (4)

62 The university professor may have to slip it on quite often. (4)

63 **Headwear** for the jockey and maybe the worker. (3)

64 What does a Scot wear under his ... ? (4)

66 If your **trousers** are this, use a belt. (5)

69 She was wearing a beautiful Japanese ... **scarf**. (4)

71 It'll cover the head; it is often part of a **duffel coat.** (4)

73 Take off your **dress**, put it on a **hanger**; take off your coat, put it on this. (3)

Answers
(Across) **2** **hem**   **4** **naked**   **6** **tunic**   **9** **button**   **11** **bra**   **12** **cardigan**
15 **coat**   **17** **waistcoat**   **19** **frock**   **21** **vest**   **23** **zip**   **27** **over(coat)**
29 **panties**   **31** **heel**   **32** **pullover**   **35** **suit**   **36** **red**
37 **under(wear)**   **39** **ear(ring)**   **41** **lapel**   **42** **bands**   **43** ago   **44** be
45 **top hat**   **46** **mitten**   **48** yen   **49** **laces**   **51** **shoe**   **52** **padded**
54 **toga**   **58** **sleeve**   **59** **beret**   **61** a **garment**   **64** **kimono**   **65** **slip**
67 **nails**   **68** nun   **69** **sari**   **70** **sash**   **72** **grip**   **73** **pants**   **74** **stole**
75 **trousers**   **76** **track(suit)**
(Down) **1** **boot**   **2** **hat**   **3** **mac**   **4** **nude**   **5** **dinner (jacket)**   **7** neck
8 **cravat**   **9** **bow tie**   **10** **tails**   **11** **blazer**   **13** **glove**   **14** **crown**
16 ten   **18** **tie**   **20** **cassock**   **22** **striped**   **24** **pleat**   **25** **apron**
26 **(over)all**   **28** **velvet**   **29** **pin**   **30** Edwardian   **31** **helmet**
33 **label**   **34** **open(-neck)**   **38** **slippers**   **40** Ages   **47** **tights**
50 **spur**   **53** **DJ**   **55** **slippers**   **56** **jeans**   **57** **Levis**   **59** **bonnet**
60 **ring**   **62** **gown**   **63** **cap**   **64** **kilt**   **66** **loose**   **69** **silk**
71 **hood**   **73** **peg**

Practice

1   Write or discuss the answers to the questions below.

1 What (exactly) did you wear to the last three parties you have been to?
2 What (again exactly) would you wear on each of the occasions listed below?
   a an open-air rock concert
   b a formal garden party
   c a new discotheque's first night
   d a summer afternoon on the river
   e a quiet evening at home
   f a barbecue on the beach
3 In which periods of history do you think men and/or women dressed especially
   attractively? Describe what you like about these clothes.
4 What clothes have you seen in the street or in shops recently that really appealed to
   you?
5 What clothes have you bought over the past year? How often have you worn them?
   Do you still like them? What condition are they in now?

2   Write, in dialogue form, a conversation between a teenager (claiming the freedom to
wear modern styles and colours) and his/her grandmother (complaining about a loss
of elegance).

3   Write out the shopping list of all the clothes you need for your new baby.

4   Write a (full) list of clothes to take with you on a four-week holiday touring the
United States.

■   Add here any other words or expressions that you meet to do with clothes.

. . . .
. . . .
. . . .
. . . .
. . . .
. . . .

Size, quantity, dimensions and measurements

Reading 1

There are **a lot of** quite common expressions in this text. Make a special effort to remember them and to use them regularly in your English.
As you read:

1 Write out the list of food and drink the writer's father-in-law made before the wedding celebrations. Don't panic! He was very rich!
2 Note down the phrases which are clearly exaggerated.

There was, quite simply, **masses of** the stuff – **enough to feed an army**, or **sufficient** to keep a **largish** family going for a year at least – and it wasn't only the **staggering quantity**. There was an **enormously wide range** of dishes, **ranging from huge** stuffed olives to **king-sized** prawns, from **giant-sized** crabs to **quite massive** crêpes.
The guests – and there were **millions** of them all over the place – had a choice of a **thousand and one** different cheeses, **no fewer than** fifty different salads, **dozens of** patés and **scores of little** savouries.
The meat – literally **tons of** it – had been cut into **exceedingly large** slices, an **inch thick**, and **broad enough to** overhang any **normal-sized** dinner plate. There was also **plenty of** fish, including a **monumental pile** of smoked salmon and an **immense dishful** of sea-food, plus an **abundance of** poultry and game.
There was an **excessive amount of** alcohol: two containers **of giant proportions brimful of** punch, (their **combined volumes** must have exceeded a **hundred cubic feet**), **countless magnums** of champagne and **innumerable** three-**litre** bottles of sparkling wine. There were **gallons of** the stuff.
The fruit salad was served in a **colossal** dish, **several feet in diameter**. Into it had gone **enormous** cherries almost **the size of** oranges and **gigantic** oranges **as big as** footballs, bananas nearly a **foot in length** and **mammoth** melons **like** footballs. A **substantial quantity of** liqueur brandy had also found its way in.
The cake was **a mountain**, **consisting of** a **large number of** sections, each providing **ample portions** for **a couple of** rugby teams. **Altogether** it was **over three metres in height** and **getting on for a metre in width**. The layers of cream on each block were **some three centimetres thick**.
Despite **numerous** predictions that **far too much** food had been prepared, **very little** was left at the end. True, a **fair amount of** cheese remained – a **reasonable proportion of** which was fortunately still usable – but **apart from** that, **hardly anything**: **a few crumbs of** cake, **one tiny piece of** fish, a **minute portion of** ham, a **negligible amount of** jelly, a **teeny-weeny drop of** punch, but **not a trace of** the fruit salad in the bottom of the bowl.
There was a **great deal of lengthy** speculation as to the **astronomical sum total** of the cost; it was never disclosed. A spokesman for my new father-in-law said, 'It **wasn't small**', and my mother-in-law still reminds me occasionally that it was '**quite a few pounds' worth**'.

Game

The size, strength or capacity of things can be measured in many different ways. Cover the column on the right and complete the following sentences with an appropriate word or phrase of measurement or size.

1	It's just a normal family car: a five-... .	**seater**
2	He's bought himself a new 750 ... Kawazaki.	**c.c.**
3	My old van has a **maximum** ... of just over 50 ...	**speed** **m.p.h. (miles per hour)**
4	We really need another 100- ... bulb.	**watt**
5	We could also do with an extra 13-... plug.	**amp. (ampère)**
6	This 25-year-old whisky is 85%	**proof**
7	Her wedding ring is 24-... gold.	**carat**
8	It's over 85 ... Fahrenheit **in the shade** today.	**degrees**
9	We sailed across the Atlantic in a 20,000- ... liner.	**ton**
10	The ship was travelling at an **average speed** of 28	**knots**
11	Winds of gale ... 9 were reported.	**force**
12	The Krakatoa explosion (1883) happened too long ago for the **intensity of its sound** to be measured in	**decibels**
13	The recent earthquake gave a **reading of** point 7 on the Richter	**scale**
14	The Empire State is a 102- ... building.	**storey**
15	My parents live in a two-... flat.	**bedroomed**
16	The Government has a 24-... **overall majority** in Parliament.	**seat**
17	The town has a ... of 24,000.	**population**
18	We have our own 60-... orchestra.	**piece**
19	The article in the newspaper ran to four	**columns**
20	Hong Kong has the highest ... of population of any country in the world.	**density**
21	My girlfriend's ... ... are 38 25 38.	**vital statistics**
22	She passed her final exams with a ... 3.	**grade**
23	The Tower of Pisa leans at an ... of several ... to the vertical.	**angle** **degrees**
24	Rank in the services is usually indicated by the number of ... on one's sleeve.	**stripes**
25	Parts of the Pacific Ocean are known to be well over 30,000 feet in	**depth**
26	Britain has a two-... system of central government consisting of the House of Commons and the House of Lords.	**tier**
27	The people voted to remain in the Common Market by a ... of two to one.	**ratio**
28	Redundancies are being announced now at a ... of a thousand a day.	**rate**
29	Most symphonies have four	**movements**
30	Songs that have more than four ... are often too long to be recorded commercially.	**verses**
31	A number of rock-groups now own their own 16 or 24-... recording equipment.	**track**
32	The man thought to have been the **heaviest** ever is reported to have been over 70 **stone** in	**weight**
33	The final of the tennis championship – men's singles – was **the best of** five	**sets**
34	The 800 metres is normally a two-... race.	**lap**
35	The duke and duchess' farm extends over an ... of 640 **acres**.	**area**
36	After doing that exercise I feel in need of a ... whisky rather than a	**double, single**

Reading 2

Many quantities are set for us by the way various products are prepared or packaged for sale. Read through the shopping list, then test yourself on the words by covering first the right-hand column then the left-hand one.

Who said you don't get much for your money nowadays? For less than £300 you could buy a whole **case of** best-quality champagne. Or you could buy all of the following and still have some change.

a **string of**	imitation pearls
a **bar of**	soap
a **family-size tube of**	toothpaste
a **sample sachet of**	shampoo
a **loaf of**	wholemeal bread
a **carton of**	low-calorie yoghurt
a **500g tin of**	baked beans
a **packet of**	salt and vinegar flavoured crisps
a **bunch of**	grapes
a **pack of**	eight different breakfast cereals
a **few sheets of**	greaseproof paper
a **pair of**	sheets
a **pad of**	writing paper
a **roll of**	toilet paper
a **box of**	matches
a **bundle of**	firewood
a **sack of**	coal
a **bottle of**	cognac
a **barrel of**	English beer
a **can of**	Australian lager
a **crate of**	brown ale (24 bottles)
a **few sticks of**	celery
a **jar of**	pickled onions
a **5lb bag of**	potatoes
a **50p book of**	stamps
a **giant-sized block of**	ice-cream
a **set of**	spanners

Practice

1. The words **sort**, **kind** and **type** could be used to complete many of the questions below. Naturally enough, though, we have a number of other words which might be used. Use one of the eight words listed below to complete the sentences.

brand	**family**	**model**	**race**
branch	**species**	**style**	**group**

1. What ... of astro-physics is Aunt Sally studying?
2. Which ... of reptile would you least like to have in your bedroom?
3. Which Fiat ... is supposed to be the most economical to run?
4. What ... of music was popular before The Beatles?
5. Which ... of soap-powder do you usually use?
6. What age-... are most of the unemployed in?
7. What ... of people did the English descend from?
8. What ... of animals does the cheetah belong to?

2 Here are eight more words and eight more sentences for you to complete.

form	category	part	grade
make	breed	department	bracket

1 What ... of speech is the word 'down'?
2 What ... of dog is least trouble to look after?
3 Which ... of petrol do you use, two star or four star?
4 What salary-... do most teachers fall into?
5 Which ... of your branch are you working in at the moment?
6 What ... of car would you say is the most reliable?
7 What ... of corporal punishment do you personally hate most?
8 What ... of book would you list *War and Peace* under: fact or fiction?

3 Think of a big city that you know or have seen photographs of in books. Describe the impression it made on you when you first arrived there.

4 Discuss why English is in some ways so easy and in others so difficult.

5 Imagine you had a dream last night which involved a horrible creature of gigantic proportions. Describe the monster.

6 Imagine you are taking part in a meeting to discuss the siting of a new airport near your home. Consider the possible effects of the noise and the traffic on the local population and the countryside. Write a statement which clearly expresses your feelings and views.

7 You have just visited a Third World country with appalling problems. Write a one-minute speech for a radio news programme on the country's limited resources and enormous needs.

8 Write down, after discussion with a partner if possible, a list of all the things (including food) that you will need to put in the nuclear fallout shelter you have just built.

9 Write the first minute of your Olympic Games Opening Ceremony commentary in which you describe the scene in front of you.

■ Add here any other words or expressions you may meet.

. . . .

. . . .

. . . .

. . . .

. . . .

. . . .

. . . .

. . . .

. . . .

. . . .

. . . .

Shapes

Game

Decide which of these shapes describes each chocolate. Then look at the picture and try to describe the shape of each chocolate without the help of phrases **1 – 14**.

1 **pyramid-shaped**
2 **spherical**
3 a perfect **cube**
4 **crescent-shaped**
5 a **spiral**
6 **pear-shaped**
7 **conical**, a **cone**

8 **oblong**, with a **convex** top
9 **rectangular**, with a **concave** top
10 **round**, with a **serrated edge**
11 **semi-circular, half-moon shaped**
12 **square**, with an **uneven surface**
13 **cylindrical, log-shaped**
14 **triangular, three-sided**

Practice

1 And now some sophisticated work on the English alphabet. Which word (in capital letters) is being described below? Describe other words in the same way. When you can do this, you are doing very well with the vocabulary of this unit.

First letter
One **full-length perpendicular** line **is joined at the top** and **at its centre point** by two **parallel** lines, the former slightly longer that the latter, **extending to the right horizontally**.

Second letter
A **symmetrical, wedge-shaped figure**: two **straight but oblique** lines **slanting down** to the **base** from **a common point** at the top; these are **bisected** by **a single horizontal line.**

Third letter
A **long vertical line is connected at two points** – at the top and **halfway down** – to a **curved, semi-circular line running to the right**. From **the centre intersection a sloping line** drops to the **baseline at an angle of 45 degrees to the perpendicular**, again to the right.

2 Match the adjectives on the left with a suitable noun on the right.

1	**hollow**	skin
2	**rough**	roadsign
3	**pointed**	swimming pool
4	**oval**	shoes
5	**triangular**	roof
6	**sloping**	cheeks
7	**sharp**	staircase
8	**spiral**	blade

3 Discuss or write the answers to these two questions.

1 Do you like modern art? Can you describe any modern works of art that you either really liked or strongly disliked when you saw them?
2 Where have all the curves gone – from cars, cups, watches, buildings, phones, bottles and clothes? How true is it that circles and curves are disappearing and giving way to more angular shapes? Give examples of this trend and any exceptions that you can think of to support your argument.

Game

Finally, a drawing game. Try to draw each of the items below, spending a maximum of three seconds on each.

1	a **dotted** line	7	a **rough** sea	13	**rolling** hills
2	a **crooked** line	8	a **steep** hill	14	**wavy** hair
3	an **octagon**	9	a **bumpy** road	15	a **meandering** river
4	a **pointed** chin	10	a **sharp** bend	16	**undulating** countryside
5	a **jagged** edge	11	a **gentle** curve	17	a **calm** sea
6	a **hollow** tree	12	a **smooth** surface	18	an **oval** face

■ Add here any more words about shapes as you meet them.

. . . .

. . . .

. . . .

. . . .

. . . .

. . . .

. . . .

. . . .

. . . .

. . . .

. . . .

. . . .

Substances, materials and textures

Quiz

1   Even if chemistry lessons are a thing of the (distant) past for you, try this exercise on elements, metals and gases. Cover the column on the right and see if you can say which elements, metals and gases these symbols stand for. Each one has a simple clue beside it to help you.

Ag	a twenty-fifth wedding anniversary	**silver**
Zn	a bluish-white metal	**zinc**
Al	light to carry and silvery to look at	**aluminium**
U	named after a planet	**uranium**
Au	an olympic winner	**gold**
Sn	a can is made of it	**tin**
Ca	think of your teeth	**calcium**
S	think of matches	**sulphur**
CO	breathe out	**carbon dioxide**
Pu	nuclear power can come from this	**plutonium**
Fe	the most widely used metal of all	**iron**
Pt	describes a particular type of blonde hair	**platinum**
H	think of the bomb	**hydrogen**
P	gives out light in the dark	**phosphorus**
Hg	used in thermometers	**mercury**
Ni	and an American coin	**nickel**
O	life-supporting	**oxygen**
N	80% of the air	**nitrogen**
Cu	maybe the first metal used by man	**copper**
NaC1	commonly known as salt	**sodium chloride**

2   Does that bring back memories of acids, alkalis and smelly experiments? If you're in good form, try these. What alloys or other substances will you get if you mix the following? (Keep the right-hand column covered.)

copper and **tin**	3rd place medal	**bronze**
copper and **zinc**	a band	**brass**
iron and **carbon**	knives	**steel**
lime, clay, sand and **water**	brick walls	**cement**
the above plus **gravel**	for a path	**concrete**

Practice

1   In a recent nightmare, my grandson was saying to his girlfriend: 'Your hands are like **vinyl**, the skin on your face is like purest **acrylic** and your hair is like real **polystyrene**'.
How do you feel about recent changes in the materials that things are made of? Read the text on the next page. Decide which of the items in the right-hand column have their advantages and which items in the left-hand column you really prefer. Give your reasons.

The old / *The new*

The old	*The new*
lace handkerchiefs	**paper** tissues
satin bed-**linen**	**nylon** sheets
cotton pyjamas	**polyester** shirts
tweed jackets	**denim** tops
woollen cardigans	**acrylic** sweaters
flannel trousers	**cord(uroy)** slacks
leather shoes	**suede** uppers, **man-made** soles
feather (preferably **down**) beds	**polyurethane-foam** pillows
velvet curtains	**vinyl** upholstery
marble floors	**formica** worktop, **polystyrene** tiles
solid wood funiture	**chipboard** units
(of **teak, pine, mahogany, oak**)	**hardboard** shelves
cast iron pots and pans	**stainless steel** saucepans
china tea-service	**smoked-glass** cups
porcelain dinner plates	**enamel** mugs
steel cutlery	**plastic** spoons
brown paper	**polythene** bags
wooden boats	**fibreglass** yachts

2 Most materials are happy to act as adjectives as well as nouns.

> Sheffield produces a lot of **steel**. It has quite a large **steel** industry. I need a **steel** bar to put across this cage-door.
> Most materials, however, can also add a letter or two to make another adjective with a different, more figurative meaning.
> He gave me a **steely** look. (a bit like steel)

Cover the second and fourth columns below. Choose nouns to go with the two lists of adjectives, then see how many of yours are the same as the ones the book suggests.

1	a **leather**	jacket	a **leathery**	steak
2	**rubber**	gloves	**rubbery**	lips
3	a **glass**	eye	a **glassy**	look
4	a **silk**	scarf	**silky**	hair
5	a **grass**	skirt	a **grassy**	slope
6	a **mud**	hut	**muddy**	boots
7	a **stone**	wall	a **stony**	silence
8	a **skin**	disease	a **skinny**	person
9	a **tin**	drum	a **tinny**	sound from a cheap radio
10	an **ice**	cube	an **icy**	stare
11	a **wire**	coat-hanger	a **wiry**	marathon runner
12	an **oil**	well	an **oily**	rag
13	a **silver**	chain	**silvery**	hair
14	a **meat**	pie	a **meaty**	discussion
15	a **gold**	tooth	a **golden**	opportunity
16	a **metal**	container	a **metallic**	voice
17	a **milk**	bottle	a **milky**	complexion
18	a **smoke**	signal	a **smoky**	room
19	a **wooden**	leg	a **wooden**	actor
20	a **grease**	gun	a **greasy**	rag
21	a **soap**	bubble	**soapy**	water
22	a **woollen**	jumper	a **woolly**	argument

Note the two exceptions: a **wooden** leg, a **wooden** actor (unnatural); a **woollen** jumper, a **woolly** argument (vague, confused).

Practice

1 Discuss or write the answers to these questions.

1 Are **precious metals** and **stones – diamonds, emeralds, rubies, sapphires**, etc. – as beautiful as their prices suggest?
2 How have materials for clothes, household goods, furniture etc. changed during your lifetime? In what ways are these changes for the better and in what ways are they changes for the worse?
3 What is being done in your country to counter the dangers of certain materials in use today: **asbestos, lead, DDT, nuclear waste, nicotine?**
2 Write a paragraph from your latest short story in which the hero, blindfolded, stumbles through a **cardboard** box factory in an attempt to escape from his pursuers. Describe his feelings as he comes into contact with various substances and surfaces during the chase.

■ Add here any more words about substances as you meet them.

. . . .

. . . .

. . . .

. . . .

. . . .

. . . .

. . . .

. . . .

. . . .

. . . .

. . . .

Colours

There are an enormous number of words and expressions describing colours in English. A lot are mentioned in this unit. Try to remember and begin to use those of particular use to you.

Game

1. You and your partner have been invited to attend a dinner in aid of charity. It is not an occasion for a suit and an evening dress, but you can't go in jeans and a T-shirt. Below, for each garment you are going to wear, you are given a choice of four colours. Choose an outfit for both of you which you think will look attractive.

For him

jacket:	**navy blue**	**white**	**dark brown**	**crimson**
trousers:	**royal blue**	**khaki**	**fawn**	**sea green**
tie:	**multi-coloured**	**yellow**	**bright orange**	**emerald green**
shoes:	**reddish**	**buff**	**peach**	**black**

For her

skirt:	**deep blue**	**russet**	**lavender**	**pale blue**
blouse:	**salmon pink**	**tangerine**	**lilac**	**pearl**
jacket:	**olive green**	**mauve**	**rose**	**yellowish**
tights:	**flesh-coloured**	**tan**	**bright pink**	**turquoise**
shoes:	**rust-coloured**	**violet**	**greeny-blue**	**jet black**

2. You and your partner are going to decorate two of the rooms in a flat. From the alternatives below, choose a colour scheme for each room.

The kitchen

ceiling:	**pure white**	**greyish**	**light green**	**amber**
walls:	**brick red**	**sandy-coloured**	**steel blue**	**lemon**
tiles:	**whitish**	**pitch black**	**shocking pink**	**brownish**
woodwork:	**reddish-brown**	**coffee-coloured**	**smokey-grey**	**scarlet**

The bedroom

ceiling:	**brilliant white**	**off-white**	**lime green**	**sky blue**
walls:	**copper**	**dazzling white**	**beige**	**chocolate**
woodwork:	**purple**	**cream-coloured**	**bronze**	**straw-coloured**
carpet:	**mottled blue and green**	**golden**	**maroon**	**charcoal grey**
curtains:	**bottle green**	**silvery grey**	**indigo**	**gingery red**

Practice

1. Colours love to be used idiomatically. Cover the column on the right and complete each sentence with the appropriate colour.

1. He was ... **with envy** as he watched his friend riding his new bike.   **green**
2. When his father told him later he couldn't have a new bike, he went ... **with rage**.   **purple / white**
3. I'm all ... **and** ... after being in that crowded underground train for half an hour.   **black, blue**

4 The student went as ... as a beetroot when the lecturer gave her one of his famous ... **looks**.	red
	black
5 You can be sure to find quite a few ... **movies** in that ... **light district**.	blue
	red
6 I can't really believe that Nero was as ... **as he is painted**.	black
7 I felt sorry for those ... recruits, getting Sergeant 'Squash 'em' Sanders on their first day.	green
8 You're ...! You're just afraid of what your wife will do to you if you do.	yellow
9 I feel so ... when I see you, hand-in-hand with another man.	blue
10 My fingers were ... **with cold** and I imagine my face was as ... **as a sheet**.	blue
	white
11 I'll need your resignation **in** ... **and** ... of course.	black, white
12 She came out of that ... **comedy** about making pies from murder victims with her face a ghastly shade of	black
	green
13 You've got to stop looking at the world through ... **tinted spectacles,** stop considering these matters in terms of ... and ..., and start realising there's a huge ... area in between.	rose
	black, white
	grey
14 My father-in-law was hundreds of pounds **in the** ... after paying for our splendid ... **wedding**.	red
	white

2 Each of the concepts on the left can be expressed with a word or phrase that includes the colour given. Cover the right-hand column and see if you think of each idiom.

Black

1	a person who refuses his union's instructions to strike	a **blackleg**
2	a member of the family who fails to live up to the others' standards	a **black sheep**
3	illegitimate trading, perhaps of goods in short supply	the **black market**
4	a number of people under suspicion, or in danger of unfavourable treatment	a **blacklist**

Red

5	caught in the act, in the middle of a crime	**caught red-handed**
6	a special, very important occasion	a **red-letter day**
7	an excessive amount of bureaucracy	**red-tape**
8	a very special welcome for a very special guest	the **red carpet**

Blue

9	very, very rarely	**once in a blue moon**
10	suddenly and unexpectedly	**out of the blue**
11	those doing manual, not clerical or administrative work	**blue-collar workers**
12	someone of noble birth, an aristocrat	someone with **blue blood**

3 Write or discuss the answers to these questions.

1 Which of the following do you prefer? Why?
   a sunrise or sunset?
   b April or October?
   c black and white photos or colour ones?
   d pastel colours in rooms or strong, bright colours?
   e paintings by six-, eleven- or sixteen-year-olds?

4 What is your favourite colour – and be as precise as you can – for each of the items below?

a	cars	**g**	sheets
b	team sports kit	**h**	handbags
c	soap	**i**	swimming costumes
d	personal writing paper	**j**	dinner plates
e	front doors	**k**	toothbrushes
f	armchairs	**l**	ink in a felt-tip pen

5 Write, in dialogue form, a conversation in a shop. A customer is trying to get the assistant to mix exactly the shade of paint that he or she wants to decorate the sitting room walls.

■ Add here any other words or expressions about colours as you meet them.

. . . .

. . . .

. . . .

. . . .

. . . .

. . . .

. . . .

. . . .

. . . .

. . . .

. . . .

. . . .

. . . .

The condition things are in

Reading

Most of the things around us are not **in perfect condition**. They're in some way **defective**, **flawed** or **damaged**. Here is an undiscovered masterpiece by singer-songwriter Dod Billion to help you with the vocabulary on this subject:

Without-you-it's-just-impossible Blues
Music and lyrics by Dod Billion

Our toothpaste tube is **leaking**,
My razor blades are **blunt**.
The hot tap keeps on **squeaking**
And the cold one's **back to front**.
The bathroom door **won't lock**
And the windows are all **stuck**.
The water-pipes are **blocked**
And the basin's full of **muck.**

(Chorus)
I don't know what to do
Without you.
I don't know how to do it.
Without you it's
Just impossible Blues.

All our food's **gone stale**
And the fruit's all **squashed**.
The dishwasher's **failed**
So the plates are **unwashed**.
The kitchen table's **split**
And the saucers are all **chipped**,
And the curtains are **twisted**
And the table-cloth is **ripped**.

I don't know what to do
Without you.
I don't know how to do it.
Without you it's
Just impossible Blues.

All our records are **scratched**,
One or two have been **smashed**,
All our glasses are **cracked**,
And my homemade beer's **flat**.
The cutlery is **tarnished**
The liquidiser's **faulty**,
The shelves are still **unvarnished**,
They're beginning to **warp**, you see.

I don't know what to do
Without you.
I don't know how to do it.
Without you it's
Just impossible Blues.

All the woodwork is **rotten**,
And the metalwork's **rusty**.
Believe me, I've forgotten
What it's like under the **dust**.
The car **doesn't go**,
It just **splutters** and **jerks**,
And the battery's very **low**
So the lights **don't work**.

The windscreen is **shattered**
And the bodywork is **dented**.
The seats are in **tatters**
And the steering-wheel's **bent**.

I don't know what to do
Without you.
I don't know how to do it.
Without you it's
Just impossible Blues.

My favourite white shirt
Is **marked** and **stained**.
You can't see it for **dirt**
And the dirt's **ingrained**.
My socks **have got holes in them**,
And most of them are **torn**.
My shoes **have got no soles on them**,
The heels are **badly worn**.
My trousers are **creased**
And my jacket is **faded**.
It's covered in **grease**;
And I feel so **jaded**.

I don't know what to do
Without you.
I don't know how to do it.
Without you it's
Just impossible Blues.

(Extra verse)
My life's **in a mess**
It's all **twisted** and **tangled**.
I feel so **depressed**
As if I'd been **mangled**.
I'm absolutely **shattered**.
I feel so **beaten** and **battered**.
My dreams are in **tatters**;
The only thing that matters –

Is that I'm not with you,
And I don't know what to do.
I don't know how to do it.
Without you it's
Just impossible Blues.

Practice

1 Apart from the things that Dod sings about in the song, what other things could be described with the following adjectives? Try and think of four items for each.

   leaking *a pen, a bottle, a tap, a roof*

1 blunt	5 chipped	9 twisted	13 blocked
2 split	6 tarnished	10 faulty	14 warped
3 rotten	7 dented	11 bent	15 stained
4 torn	8 creased	12 faded	16 tangled

2 Many of the words in this unit do not only describe physical states and conditions. Decide what they mean in each of the sentences below. Then write a similar sentence of your own to illustrate the meaning of each word.

   1 This defeat has **dented** United's hopes of the championship.
   2 You've **shattered** all my illusions about him.
   3 There seem to be **leaks** of official information nearly every day.
   4 Hopes of finding any survivors have **faded**.
   5 Her reputation has been **tarnished** for ever.
   6 He's got a rather **warped** and **twisted** sense of humour.
   7 My German's a bit **rusty**, I must confess.
   8 I got a bit **stuck** on number 3 in this exercise.

3 Write or talk about topics 1 and 2.

    1 the state of three possessions of yours which are not in perfect condition
    2 the untidiest person you know

4 Write or act out a conversation in which you, as a guest at a hotel, complain to the manager about the **appalling state** of your room.

5 Write a letter to your landlord. Complain that everything in the flat you rent from him is still **in** the same **poor condition** as it was the last time you asked for some improvements to be made.

■ Add here any other words or expressions about conditions of things as you meet them.

. . . .

. . . .

. . . .

. . . .

. . . .

. . . .

. . . .

. . . .

. . . .

. . . .

. . . .

. . . .

. . . .

Parts and components

This unit has two functions. It is both a quick revision of numerous items already mentioned in this book and an introduction to some more **bits and pieces** that go to make up a number of everyday objects.

Quiz

1 Below you see groups of four words. In each case, the words are all parts of an everyday object. Decide what each object is.

1	dial	receiver	mouthpiece	hook
2	handlebars	pedals	chain	valve
3	tap	plug	overflow	pipes
4	bowl	cistern	flush	seat
5	lens	shutter	flash	meter
6	knob	aerial	screen	switch
7	plug	socket	lead	wires
8	hands	winder	face	strap
9	buckle	laces	tongue	stitching
10	lining	hem	seam	pleat
11	petal	stem	seed	leaf
12	flap	slot	drawer	tray
13	keys	ribbon	golf ball	cover
14	roots	trunk	twig	branch
15	neck	top	cork	label
16	handle	latch	hinges	frame
17	wing	tail	nose	fuselage
18	boot	clutch	gears	brake
19	lid	handle	spout	brim (or rim)
20	cuff	sleeve	button	collar

2 Guess what is being described in each of the paragraphs below.

1 It **is composed of** two thin **metal arms welded at one end** to a short **rod**. The rod allows the two **metal strips** to move together and away from each other. One arm is some twelve centimetres in length and ends in a **pin** with a **sharp point.** The other is shorter and is joined at the end to a thick **metal ring** which has a **hole** through it and a **thread** around the inside. A small **disc** or **wheel** can be **screwed** over it.

2 Well, for one thing, there should be a **plastic cover** clipped on to the **base** here, and more important, this **spring**, the **coil** here, is broken. So when you press this **plate** here, the two **bars** go down into the **holes**, but they don't come back up again.

3 Right, I've got all the **poles**, the **pegs** are in that bag plus the extra **brackets** and the **clips** for the **flaps**, you've got the **ropes** there, haven't you? I think we're about ready to go.

Practice

1. Decribe three everyday objects so accurately that somebody listening to you or reading your paragraphs could guess what you are talking about. Use item 1 in the exercise above to get some ideas.

2. List all the things you can think of that are missing or need repairing around your house. Work out how much it would cost you to replace or repair them all.

3. Write a list of contents to put in a do-it-yourself plumber's **kit**.

4. Write instructions on how to put together a self-assembly piece of furniture.

5. Write, in dialogue form, a conversation between an angry customer who is taking back a three-month-old dress or suit. It is in a terrible state. The assistant has to try and make excuses for the state of the hem, the seams, the lining, the cuffs, the button-holes and so on.

■ If you come across any more words about parts of everyday objects, make a note of them here:

. . . .

. . . .

. . . .

. . . .

. . . .

. . . .

. . . .

. . . .

. . . .

. . . .

. . . .

. . . .

What things do

There are over a hundred verbs – mainly intransitive – in this unit. You may need to work on the unit in small chunks or else come back and do it again several times in order to remember most of the new vocabulary well enough to use it in conversation or in writing.

Reading 1

1 Read this dramatic text on **destruction**, **bombs**, **smoke** and **fire**.

The first bomb **went off** at 2.36. The **explosion wrecked** three stores just off the main square, **destroying** several vehicles and **rocking** even the tallest building in the city. The pedestrian precinct **caught fire** at once, **bursting into flames**, as if someone had **set fire to** it with a giant torch, and sending clouds of smoke shooting up into the sky. We could hear, rather than see, a number of other houses **crumbling**.

The fire began to **spread**. Smoke was soon **pouring** out of the buildings in the next block, **hovering** over the skyscrapers and then **drifting** away towards the sea. We saw one huge office block **collapse** at the base and then quite simply **fall apart**.

The smoke was just beginning to **clear** and the flames **die down** when the second bomb **exploded**. Immediately the air **thickened** again as clouds of even blacker smoke **billowed** out of a hotel nearby.

When the smoke finally **disappeared**, half the city had **vanished**. Hours later the fire was still **smouldering** and tiny **wisps of smoke** were **rising from the ashes**. The city **lay in ruins**. Then Robert Redford and Jane Fonda appeared, and you knew that everything was going to be all right.

2 Now have a look at this 'light-filled' letter.

Dear Roland,
What do you think of this?

Shot One (5 secs.)
The sun is **shining** – the mountainside is **bathed in sunshine**.
The freshly-fallen snow is **glistening**.
A couple are standing in ski-clothes, cheeks **glowing**.
The woman is smiling, teeth **gleaming**.
Narrator: **A ray of sunshine**.

Shot Two (7 secs.)
Moonlight. The stars are **twinkling**.
The **rippling** water of the lake is **shimmering**.
The same couple are in fur coats, standing by the lake, **reflected** in water.
The woman is still smiling – a **dazzling** smile, teeth **gleaming.**
Narrator: **A radiant smile**.

Shot Three (8 secs.)
Picadilly Circus with the **flashing** neon lights of the advertisements.
Camera moves through the **glare** of car headlights into the interior of a Rolls Royce.
The same couple are sitting in back, their **eyes dancing**.

The woman is wearing a **sparkling** diamond necklace, her teeth still **gleaming**.
Narrator: **A ray of hope**.

Shot Four (10 secs.)
The couple are at a table in a high-class restaurant, **illuminated** by **glittering** chandeliers and **flickering** candles.
The woman has a **beaming** smile on her face, her teeth still **gleaming**.
Narrator: Now ... New! Improved! Whoosh! For you! Yes, for you! Now! New! Whoosh! The toothpaste of the stars! n

See you for the filming on Saturday. Don't forget to ask Robert and Jane.
Regards, Harvey

3 Read this extract from a diary. As you read, guess where the writer was at the time.

Monday
It's been **pouring with rain** all day.

Tuesday
It's been **bucketing down** again from morning to night.

Wednesday
Another rainy day. It hasn't stopped once. I got **drenched** when I ran across the road to the corner shop. My clothes were absolutely **soaked**; **soaked to the skin** I was.

Thursday
This is quite a storm! The water has **come up** so far, it's beginning to **lap** around people's doorsteps. It's already **covering** all the pavements and **swirling** round the blocked-up drains.

Friday
It's like a river outside. Water is **streaming** through the streets, **cascading** over buses and cars, **sweeping** everything along its path. Earlier I noticed a kitchen sink **floating** past; it **sank** within a few seconds, though.

Saturday
Water is **gushing** into the ground floor of people's homes and **spraying** the upstairs windows. Aaron phoned to say that his roof was **leaking**, that enormous raindrops were **splashing** onto his window-sills and **dripping** on the carpet, and that water was **trickling** down all his walls. I would have liked to help, but ...

Sunday
It's still **drizzling**, even now. When I think of the trouble waiting for those people – horrible brown mud **oozing** under their doors and **submerging** all their furniture – I'm glad I saw that advertisement for this ark.

Practice 1

Which of the words below do you associate with items **a** – **d**?
a destruction   **b** water   **c** light   **d** fire

1 **trickle**	9 **ripple**
2 **drenched**	10 **glow**
3 **crumble**	11 **glisten**
4 **shimmer**	12 **cascade**
5 **drizzle**	13 **splash**
6 **smoulder**	14 **float**
7 **wrecked**	15 **collapse**
8 **soaked**	

Study and practice

The fourth and last text is on what cars do, or at least, what my car does. Read the text and try to guess the meaning of the verb that should be in each of the gaps. Then look at the list of verbs below the text and choose one to fill each gap.

I don't really mind my car ... two or three times every morning when it's cold, ... after a few miles so that I have to stop and let the engine cool down, ... every month or two around town, only ... fifteen **miles to the gallon**, ... to the right every time I brake, ... whenever the roads are wet, ... oil and ... the rain **in**, but I do object to it ... of petrol on the motorway, in the middle of nowhere. I'm seriously thinking of getting rid of it and getting another one.

**letting   overheating   losing   stalling   breaking down   doing
skidding   veering   running out**

Practice 2

1 Tell a partner or write about a road accident that you have been involved in or a witness to.

2 Write or act out a conversation in which you and a friend both insist that your car is worse and more unreliable than the other's. (How many times has it broken down this year? How many new parts have you had put in? How much has it cost? What faults has it still got?)

Game

Have a look at the way this verb-game works. Read down the columns. (Notice how flexible in meaning a lot of English verbs are.) Then try to play the game yourself, starting with one of the verbs in this unit.

Things **move**	Buildings wobble	Roads **bend**
The earth moves	Buildings **fall down**	Rubber bends
The earth **rotates**	Leaves fall	Rubber **burns**
Wheels rotate	Leaves **turn** red	Flames burn
Wheels **spin**	The tide turns	Flames **dance**
The earth spins	The tide **comes in**	Dancers dance
The earth **revolves**	Fashions come in	Dancers **rock and roll**
Some doors revolve	Fashions **change**	Ships rock and roll
Some doors **slide**	The wind changes	Ships **sink**
Land slides sometimes	The wind **gets up**	Metal sinks in water
Land **subsides**	A storm gets up	Metal **expands**
Noise subsides	A storm **breaks**	Our lungs expand
Noise **grows**	Waves break	Our lungs **contract**
Flowers grow	Waves **erode** land	Metal contracts
Flowers **fade**	Rust erodes metal	Metal **cools**
Colours fade	Rust **spreads**	Coffee cools
Colours **run**	Butter spreads	Coffee **spills**
Buses run	Butter **congeals**	Liquids spill
Buses **stop** – sometimes	Blood congeals	Liquids **solidify**
Clocks stop	Blood **flows**	Some gases solidify
Alarm clocks **go off**	Water flows	Gas can **escape**
Cakes go off – ugh!	Water **evaporates**	Heat can escape
Cakes **rise** – or should	Liquids evaporate	Heat **melts** snow
The sun rises	Liquids **freeze**	Snow melts
The sun **sets**	Rivers freeze	Snow **thaws**
Jellies set	Rivers **meander**	Ice thaws
Jellies **wobble**	Roads meander	Ice **cracks**

Ceilings crack
Celings **leak**
Pens leak
Pens **write**
People write
People **move**
Things move

Practice 3

1. What do these items do? Match each thing with an appropriate verb from the right-hand column. Be careful! The verbs are not in the right order.

1	a clock	**rings**
2	a volcano	**flows**
3	a kettle	**bounces**
4	a bell	**flushes**
5	a ball	**erupts**
6	a violin string	**swings**
7	a toilet	**stretches**
8	a pendulum	**boils**
9	a river	**strikes**
10	elastic	**vibrates**

2. How do the items on the left start – as far as we are concerned? As above, match left with right, one verb per noun.

1	a bird	**sets sail**
2	an aeroplane	**comes out**
3	a flower	**arises**
4	a plant	**takes root**
5	a ship	**falls**
6	day	**breaks**
7	a problem	**takes off**
8	night	**breaks out**
9	a war	**comes up**
10	the moon	**hatches**

Practice 4

1. Describe the sights and sounds you experienced as you witnessed the following natural disasters. Keep your English simple and clear.

1. an **avalanche**
2. an **earthquake**
3. a **hurricane**
4. a **tidal wave**

2. Explain the processes below as if you were talking to a six-year-old. Remember to keep your English clear and simple.
   1. how electricity works
   2. how the earth moves round the sun
   3. how blood moves around our bodies
   4. gravity

3. Describe the plot of a disaster movie you remember seeing, mentioning some particularly memorable scenes in greater detail.

4   Discuss or describe in writing the rather special qualities required by reporters and correspondents who are sent here, there and everywhere to cover the world's trouble spots.

5   Write an entry for your diary as you crossed the Atlantic in a small boat and the weather turned nasty.

6   Write a paragraph from your first romantic novel, in which you describe sunrise in the mountains.

7   In your new capacity as reporter on the local newspaper, write an article on the warehouse fire you were sent out to cover last night.

8   Write part of the letter you write to a newspaper to complain about the sensational and undignified way in which tragedies and disasters are presented on TV news programmes.

■   Add here any other verbs you meet which describe what things do.

. . . .

. . . .

. . . .

. . . .

. . . .

. . . .

. . . .

. . . .

. . . .

. . . .

. . . .

. . . .

. . . .

. . . .

. . . .

Noises things make

Game

We frequently find it difficult to describe a sound precisely. Notice how often English speakers say: *There was **a sort of bang*** or *I heard **a kind of crack***. However, there is clearly a difference between a **thud** and a **squeak**, a **rattle** and a **roar**. One thing which will also help you is that most of the words of this kind can act as both a noun and a verb.

Try, in each section of ten items below, to find a sound on the right that can be caused by each item in the left-hand column. (Most of these words can be used as nouns and verbs, which is something!)

1	sack of potatoes falling from a great height	creak
2	bacon frying in the pan	rustle
3	a loose floorboard or door that needs oiling	bang
4	leaves in the breeze	screech
5	a clock	thud
6	keys in a pocket	tick
7	a bomb	sizzle
8	wind through the trees	purr
9	a well-tuned Rolls Royce engine	jingle
10	tyres when one brakes suddenly	whistle

11	kettle boiling	plop
12	wine glasses or little bells	grate
13	knives being scraped together	hum
14	a sugar lump dropped into the tea	splash
15	something heavy dropping into the sea	pop
16	something's loose under the car bonnet	jangle
17	the quiet, background sound of a fridge	click
18	the old jailer's keys	tinkle
19	champagne corks coming out	rattle
20	a light being switched on	hiss

21	the high-pitched sound of a factory machine	crackle
22	rain on the roof	squeak
23	wood burning on the fire	swish
24	a tap that can't be turned right off	squeal
25	a whip or a bone breaking	crash
26	curtains in a draught	whine
27	little pigs or again tyres after sudden braking	roar
28	lions or a powerful engine	crack
29	mice or the chair leg moving on the floor	drip
30	a car going into a wall	patter

Practice

1 List other things or events which might cause each of the noises and sounds listed above.

2 Explain what causes noise pollution in our society and suggest some remedies if you can.

3 Describe the sounds and noises around us that you hate most and that you find attractive.

4 If you are working in a group, act out a meeting at which two of you are factory managers and the other two are representatives of the workforce who are unhappy about their working conditions in the factory.
If you are working alone, write what you would say at this meeting. Choose whether you wish to be a manager or an employee.
The main grievances are the number of hours worked without a break, the volume of noise in the factory and the lack of anywhere relaxing to spend one's time off.

5 Write a paragraph from your new novel, *A Ghost Story*, in which the heroine is woken up at three in the morning by *(the ghost of your choice)*.

6 Branching out into screenplay work, write a scene (without any dialogue) for your new horror movie. It's set in an old country house at midnight, during a thunder storm.

7 Write an article on one of the following topics.
1 the experiences of a soldier (in the trenches) during the First World War
2 what you could hear when you stood still and listened at a funfair

■ More noises exist. If you hear any, note down the words for them here.

. . . .

. . . .

. . . .

. . . .

. . . .

. . . .

. . . .

. . . .

. . . .

. . . .

Births, marriages and deaths

Reading 1

Read the text several times over the next day or so, doing the exercise following it each time. This will help you to remember and use the key words in the text.

Having a baby

The day I got the results of the **pregnancy test – positive, 'pregnancy confirmed'** – I was over the moon. I sat down and made out a shopping list straightaway.

List for Baby

cot (or crib)	for baby to sleep in
pram and pushchair (and a carry-cot)	to transport him or her
2 dozen nappies	for him or her to wear (underneath)
safety-pins	for his or her nappy
high-chair	for him or her to sit in at meal-times
bib	round his / her neck when he's / she's eating
dummy	for him or her to suck
rattle	for him or her to shake
toys and dolls (and a teddy-bear)	for him or her to play with
potty	for him or her to sit on to avoid nappies as soon as possible
masses of cotton wool	for general cleaning and wiping

I couldn't believe it: me a **mother-to-be**! Actually **pregnant**! **Expecting**! '**An expectant mother**' – that was my favourite description of me. My friends all joked about me being on some kind of **fertility drug**, **conceiving** as I did so soon after our wedding.

I had the customary **morning sickness** for a while, but after that, no trouble. I went along to the **ante-natal clinic** every fortnight and started doing all the proper **breathing exercises** like an excited child.

And I read! Book after book on the subject of **childbirth**: how big the **foetus** is in the **womb** at the various stages, the pros and cons of **confinement** at home, how 15% of **pregnancies** end in **miscarriage**, the dangers of this and that. Some of it wasn't very pleasant reading, I can tell you.

The feeling of relief was indescribable when, at the beginning of the fifth month, the doctor said he could hear the baby's **heartbeat**. He was a fully-trained **gynaecologist**, by the way – or was he an **obstetrician**? – I can't remember. A few days later I felt the first **kick**, and that was a pretty exciting moment, too.

It was in the twenty-eighth week that things began to go wrong. I had had several **blood tests** before, but after this one I was told my **blood pressure** was far too high – there was a risk of **blood poisoning** – and I would have to go into hospital. There followed a period of **heartburn**, **cramp**, **vomiting** and **insomnia**. I kept overhearing bits of conversations: 'may have to **induce labour**', 'if the baby is

premature, we'll ...' etc. My mind was filled with visions of **incubators, induction, Caesarian operations** and appalling **complications**. And the baby wasn't **due** for another six weeks!

When the time came, I was **in labour** for twenty-three hours. I remember shouting through a haze as they took me into the **labour ward**: 'No **drip**! No **drugs**! No **stitches**! Please!' I came out having had them all, and in the end it was a **forceps delivery** – or so I'm told.

After all that, I just looked forward to the simple joys of **motherhood**. When they told me I couldn't **breast-feed** and she would have to be **bottle-fed**, my **post-natal depression** really started. Some nights I would lie awake mumbling 'Never again'.

It's been pretty well the same story each time, but after the fifth I gave up saying 'Never again'. I really do think that the stork system of having babies has a lot of advantages.*

Practice 1

Find all these figures and places in the text. Then show how they are relevant, as in the examples.

15%	*That's how many pregnancies end in miscarriage.*
masses	*That's how much cotton wool she bought.*

1 28th
2 23 hours
3 at least 5
4 2 dozen
5 the **ante-natal clinic**
6 every 2 weeks
7 the labour ward

■ Add any further vocabulary that you feel is relevant to babies here.

....

....

....

....

....

....

Reading 2

There are two stories below, one about marriage, and one about divorce. Start in the middle column, which both stories have in common. Then read each story. When you have finished, cover the left-hand and right-hand columns in turn and try to remember the marital expressions.

	For the six months of our	
engagement, we		**trial separation**, I
	seemed blissfully happy, so	
we		I
	decided to go ahead and	
get married.		**get a divorce**.
	There were lots of decisions to make: whether to	

have a **civil marriage**
in a **registry office**
or **marry in church** and
have a **white wedding**. We

finally decided on the latter.
After that, it was mainly
a question (I thought) of

sue on the grounds of
incompatibility or his
cruelty or his
adultery. I

where to have the
reception and where
to go on our
honeymoon.

how much **alimony** he
should pay and how much
maintenance for the
children.

The night before,

he had a **stag party**
organized by his **best man**
while I had a **hen party**
with some girlfriends.

I spent hours recalling
all our **anniversaries** and
going through
correspondence with my
solicitor.

When we arrived at the

church,

we made a strange trio,
I must say: me as

divorce court,

the **bride**,

Richard as

the **plaintiff**,

the **(bride-) groom**

and my little sister as

the **respondent**,

my **bridesmaid**.
The **vicar** (**priest**)

had a lot to say and

the **co-respondent**.
The **judge** (**magistrate**)

the **service**

took ages.

the **case**

'Gwendoline Mary, do
you take this man,
Richard Percy, in **holy
matrimony**, to ...?

'I hereby **dissolve**' – or
did he say '**annul**'? –
this marriage ... and
award a decree nisi to ...'

My father

gave me away,

was in court with me,

and cried.
It seemed very strange
for a few days to say,

'I'm a **married woman**.'

'I'm not a **divorcée**, but
I will be in six weeks' time
when I get a **decree
absolute**.

But I never regretted it
Well, ...

◾ Add here any other words about marriage that you meet.

. . . .

. . . .

. . . .

. . . .

. . . .

Reading 3

Look through these thoughts on death over the next few days, noting some of the many words and expressions that may be required on this delicate subject.

1 Most of our relatives are **dead**. It's a big subject. We all **die**.
The priest says we have **gone to meet our Maker – gone to a better place**.
Close relatives say we have **passed away**. Schoolboys say someone has **kicked the bucket**. Legally speaking, we are referred to as **deceased**.
There are a hundred and one ways to die. Most people would like to die from **natural causes – of old age**. Many don't, as you can see below.

2 **Causes of Death** among US males aged 25 to 44

1	**Accidents**	19,744
2	**Heart Diseases**	10,628
3	**Cancer**	7,690
4	**Homicide**	7,369
5	**Suicide**	6,868

Notes

1 **Accidental death** covers many things, of course. A fair proportion of those above will have been **knocked down** in a road accident, many will have **died at the wheel of their car**. A few will have died in **plane crashes**, some will have **drowned** at sea. Some will have been **burnt to death** in a fire, a number **gassed**, rather more **electrocuted**. A lot no doubt **suffocated** or were **asphyxiated** in an airless room or fire, one or two will have **choked to death** on a fish-bone.

4 There are a hundred and one ways of being **killed**. If you are an important celebrity, you can be **assassinated**. Remember the **assassination** of JFK and the subsequent **murder** of his suspected **assassin**? You can be **stabbed to death** with a sword or knife. You can be **shot** with a gun like Bonnie and Clyde. You can be **poisoned** with something you didn't order in your dinner. You can be **strangled** with a piece of string or scarf. The Boston **Strangler** might ring a bell?

3 War brings with it a language of its own: **missing, presumed dead; fatally wounded**; he **laid down his life for** his country; she **sacrificed herself** for the sake of her comrades. In wartime, and even sometimes in peacetime, one hears of **massacres** and **slaughter**, with hundreds of **victims** and often no **survivors**.

4 There are other ways of being killed, apart from being **murdered** or being **killed in action**. **Capital punishment** is one of them. Many countries still retain the **death penalty** for **serious offenders**. If you are **sentenced to death** and are not **pardoned** or **reprieved** at a later date, then you will be **executed**; perhaps **hanged** – with a rope, or **electrocuted** – in the electric chair, or **guillotined** – remember the French Revolution, or **shot** – by a **firing squad**, or **garotted** or **beheaded** or … But enough is enough, I hear you cry. Agreed. If I could just remind you, though, that a couple of thousand years ago you might have been **crucified** – on **a cross**, or **stoned to death**, like some Christian **martyrs**.

5 There are a hundred and one ways of **committing suicide**. Many of the horrors above you can do to yourself, but the most popular method is to take an **overdose** of drugs like Marilyn Monroe and too many others.

Is **euthanasia** murder? Is **voluntary euthanasia** the same as suicide? Are they all crimes or do you believe that **mercy-killing** can bring welcome **release**?

The statistics deal only with men aged twenty-five to forty-four. Twenty-five is very young, but death can come earlier. The **infant mortality** rate in some countries is as high as one in three. Despite the advances in medical science, many babies are **stillborn**, and the number of inexplicable **cot deaths** continues to give cause for alarm.

For many people, all these figures are somewhat overshadowed by the fact that millions are **dying of hunger**, **starving to death**. Some are **dying of thirst,** many more of **malnutrition**. Is there a **bloodbath** waiting round the corner, do you think? A **holocaust** waiting for the spark?

6 A lot of things have to be done after death. An **inquest** may have to be held to determine how we died. This might involve a **post-mortem** or **autopsy**. Then, most of the arangements are made by a firm of **funeral directors** – or **undertakers**. Much depends on whether we have chosen to be **buried** or **cremated**. For **burial**, we will be concerned with a **coffin,** in which to place the **body**, a **hearse**, in which to transport it, a **grave**, in which the coffin will finally be placed, and a **cemetery** (or **graveyard**), in which the grave will be dug. For **cremation**, more simply, an **urn** to hold our **ashes,** and a **crematorium** to hold the service. In either case, one might expect **wreaths** to be brought to the **funeral service** and an **epitaph** to be **engraved** on our **headstone**. Then it will be time for the **will** to be read; **death duties** may have to be paid; our **heir** will **inherit** our **estate**; our **widow** or **widower** will no doubt be **in mourning** for a long time to come.

We are unlikely to have a **tomb**. Napoleon has a tomb in Paris, but that honour is reserved for people like him. Nor will our **corpses** be laid to rest in a **mausoleum**. It is extremely unlikely that someone will compose a **requiem in our honour** or build a **statue to our memory**, and almost certain that we shall not **lie in state** for even a day. An **obituary** in *The Times* would be asking a lot. No, I think the most we can hope for is that someone might recognize our talents **posthumously** and **dedicate** something to us then. **RIP**, as we say, or rest in peace.

Practice 2

1 Below you will find definitions of some of the important words in the text. Try to give the word for each of them. If you cannot remember it, read the text again to find it.

1 a person who murders someone important
2 a large decorative grave with a space inside
3 be unable to breathe air; dying or killing in this way
4 to kill by pressing on the throat with the hands
5 someone put to death for their beliefs
6 poor condition of health resulting from lack of (good) food
7 to burn the body of a dead person at a funeral ceremony
8 an arrangement of flowers such as those given at a funeral
9 a statement of how you want your things to be be shared after your death
10 a piece of music written for a dead person

2 Write or discuss the answers to these questions.
1 What poems, plays and films have you read and seen which deal with the subject of death? What was your reaction to them?
2 How would you summarise modern thinking about the way babies should be born? Do you agree with these theories?
3 What needs to be done to make a wedding ceremony successful?

3 Write or act out a conversation in which you ask someone how her recent pregnancy went and how the baby is doing.

4   Debate or write an article on the following subject: *If the institution of marriage breaks down, so will our society.* Take five minutes to think of your ideas, arrange your arguments, consider your strategy. Then argue!

5   Write, in dialogue form, a conversation between a parent and his or her child of five who has just asked what happens to us when we die.

6   Write an article for your local paper describing the funeral of a national hero or heroine in your country.

7   Write a part of your letter to a friend describing how everything went wrong at another friend's recent wedding.

■   Add here any words to do with death that you meet.

. . . .

. . . .

. . . .

. . . .

. . . .

. . . .

. . . .

. . . .

. . . .

. . . .

. . . .

. . . .

. . . .

. . . .

Work

Game

First, a game to test you on the words for some jobs and professions. Cover the column on the right. Who would you contact or call on in the situations below? Then look at the column on the right. Try to find the appropriate person for each situation. Be careful! They are not in the right order.

1 a filling has come out of one of your back teeth
2 you think your eyes need testing
3 you find you have an ingrowing toe-nail
4 your back hurts and your doctor can't help
   (Find four people.)

5 your fringe is getting a bit too long
6 you want a portrait photograph of yourself
7 you have decided to sue somebody
   (who might refer you to another lawyer)
8 you fancy a holiday in the sun
9 you want advice on investment or insurance
10 your grand piano isn't sounding quite right
11 you want to find a 400-year-old grandfather clock
12 you are planning a church wedding
13 your car won't start
14 you want to place a bet on the 3.45 race at Ascot
15 someone in the family has just died

16 you want to learn to drive
17 you want to buy a pedigree alsatian
18 you have decided to sell your house

19 you want plans drawn up for a new house
20 you want to go ahead and have the new house built
21 you are moving house and have a furniture problem
22 you have lots of old iron you want to get rid of
23 you want new windows put into the house
24 your new fridge is leaking
25 you like the idea of new wallpaper throughout the house
26 water is gushing from your kitchen taps even when turned off
27 all the lights in your house have fused
28 you think your neighbours just might be neglecting their little child
29 your house is on fire
30 you think you are going crazy

a **chiropodist**
a **broker**
a **dentist (dental surgeon)**
a **vicar (priest)**
a **hairdresser (hair stylist)**
a **bookmaker**
an **architect**
an **osteopath**
a **driving instructor**
a **solicitor**
a **barrister**
a **(dog) breeder**
a **(garage) mechanic**
a **photographer**
a **piano tuner**
a **chiropractor**
an **optician**
a **masseur (masseuse)**
a **building contractor (builder)**
an **antique dealer**
a **travel agent**
a **scrap metal dealer (merchant)**
a **physiotherapist**
an **undertaker (funeral director)**

an **electrician**
an **estate agent**
a **maintenance engineer**
a **glazier** (and a **carpenter**)

the **fire brigade (firemen)**

a **psychiatrist**
a **social worker**

a **removal firm**
a **plumber**
an **interior decorator**

Practice 1

1 The jobs below are grouped according to the results of a survey on average weekly earnings in Britain. Group A earn the most, Group J the least.

1 Look through the groups to find the following:
employers, employees
white-collar (office) workers, blue-collar (factory and manual) workers,
manufacturing industries (factories), service industries (other), **professions,**
skilled workers, semi-skilled workers.
2 Note any jobs that you think are in the wrong group. Which group would you put them in?
3 Decide how fair you think earnings are in Britain.

Group A
medical practitioners (doctors, etc.) pilots specialists in finance, insurance / tax inspectors university lecturers
Group B
police inspectors fire-service officers prison officers sales managers marketing executives company secretaries personnel / industrial relations officers
Group C
ship's officers advertising executives public relations officers journalists (reporters) electrical / electronic engineers local government administrators
Group D
mechanical engineers civil engineers computer programmers systems analysts accountants teachers in further education **metallurgists public health inspectors production engineers policemen**
Group E
industrial designers surveyors draughtsmen ambulancemen technical sales representatives welfare workers primary / secondary school teachers
Group F
toolmakers and **fitters furnacemen welders (skilled) security officers, guards** and **detectives laboratory technicians sales supervisors bus / coach drivers sheet metal workers**
Group G
lathe operators train drivers and **signalmen motor mechanics (skilled) bricklayers postmen mail sorters catering supervisors joiners shipping** and **travel clerks telephonists**
Group H
packers, bottlers, canners, fillers chefs and **cooks plasterers hotel / pub / club managers midwives** and **registered nurses painters** and **decorators refuse collectors (dustmen) bakers** and **confectioners hospital porters storekeepers**
Group I
shop assistants, salesmen, shelf-fillers caretakers bus conductors bleachers and **dyers gardeners butchers barmen**
Group J
road sweepers general farm workers kitchen hands nursing auxiliaries waitresses

2 Work is obviously more than just having a job. Here is some union business for you to consider. You will probably meet quite a lot of this language again some time in your career.

1 If you are working alone, go straight to task 2. If you are working in a group, roleplay a part of the meeting with the following agenda. (Choose the points that look most interesting.) Before you start, allocate roles. You'll need at least two **employers**, possibly a **full board**, then three or four **representatives of the workforce**, each preferably with some special responsibility. Have a few minutes in your two camps now before you begin the meeting, to discuss strategy.

2 Write the **Directors**' reply to some written requests from the **union**. You will make some concessions, of course, but will want to reject some of the proposals.

Agenda for **Works Council** Meeting with **Employers** 19.03.89 14.30

1 **Minutes of Meeting** of 18.03.89
2 Plans for more **job stability: supplementary pensions**
                                                sickness benefit schemes
   Disputes Procedure
   Renegotiation of '**Hiring and Firing**' Procedures
                             (motion for the **reinstatement** of **Shop Steward**
                             Jack Hartley, **dismissed** 18.03.89)
   Redundancy Agreement
3 **Recruitment**, **Promotion** and **Transfer of Personnel**
   Training Requirements
   Hygiene, **Comfort** and **Amenities** at **Workplace**
4 **Classification of Jobs, Responsiblity Allowances**
5 **Negotiations for Annual Wage Increase**
   Provision to relate all **Pay** to Government's **Retail Price Index**.

Please add below any other points that you would like to be raised.
6 **Time and a half** and **time off in lieu** of Bank Holiday working
7 Special **rates for overtime** and **unsocial hours**
8 **Double time** after lunchtime Friday
9 Review of **Working Conditions + canteen, rest room facilities**
10 End of **time and motion** studies
11 Increase in **uniform allowance**
12 **Flexi-time** proposals
13 **Workers' representation** on the **Board**
14 Reduction in **Hours of Work**, Increase in **Holiday Entitlement**
15 Minimum **Compensation** for **Industrial Injury**
16 **Incentive Bonus Schemes**
17 **Productivity Deals**!!!
18 **Danger Money**!
19 Proposals for **Profit-Sharing** Systems
20 Plans for Setting up of **Workers' Co-operative** – w.e.f. next Monday!

Study

An important aspect of work is our position, our status.
Here are some of the ranks in the three British armed services.

Navy	*Army*	*Air Force*
admiral of the fleet	**commanding officer** (C.O.)	**air marshal**
lieutenant	**colonel**	**wing commander**
able seaman	**warrant officer**	**pilot officer**
petty officer	**brigadier**	**flight lieutenant**
cadet	**sergeant**	**squadron leader**

commander	lance corporal	marshal of the air force
captain	private	flight sergeant
commodore	commander-in-chief	air commodore
First Sea Lord	major	group captain
leading seaman	captain	
	general	

Practice 2

Now look at various **ranks** and **positions** you can have in the following places. There are eight gaps. Read items **1 – 8** and write the appropriate number in each.

1 Sergeant	5 Countess
2 Shop steward	6 Earl
3 Staff nurse	7 Housemaster
4 Vicar	8 Secretary of State

Police
Commissioner
(Chief) Superintendent
(Chief) Inspector
...
Constable

Politics
Prime Minister
...
Junior Minister
Back-bencher
Parliamentary Private
 Secretary
Mayor
Councillor

Company
Chairman
Director
Shareholder

Union
Union Leader
Member of the Executive
...
Branch Secretary
Conference Delegate

Priory
Abbot
Prior
Friar
Canon
Monk

Hospital
Matron
Sister
...
Orderly

School
Headmaster/ -mistress
Principal
Director of Studies
Deputy Head
Head of Department
... / -mistress
Senior Teacher
Supervisor of Studies

Aristocracy
King
Prince
Duke
Marquis
... / Count
Viscount

Convent
Mother Superior
Abbess
Sister
Novice

Catholic church
Pope
Cardinal
Bishop
Deacon
Priest

Protestant church
Archbishop
Dean
Canon
...
Parson
Curate

Aristocracy
Queen
Princess
Duchess
Marchioness
...
Viscountess

Reading

Not everybody has a **regular**, **steady job** with a **fixed income**. Some are **self-employed** and work for themselves, some work **part-time**, some work **irregular shifts**, some are **unemployed**. Some have a job, but it isn't what it should be. Some are apprentices, earning very little while they are being trained.

Read the words of the song below, noting how many people there are who are not Number One. The key-words have been printed on the right so that you can test yourself later.

I know you've always got to have a kind of ...	**substitute**
who will throw all the balls back into play.	
And you couldn't really do without a ...	**deputy manager**
longing for the manager's holiday.	
And the company will always need a ...	**vice-chairperson**
praying for the chairperson's death.	
It's clear that somebody has got to be the ...	**second string**
and someone has to make do with	**second best**

Someone must accept that he's the ...	**twelfth man**
waiting impatiently to play in the team.	
Someone's got to act as the ...	**trainee secretary**
typing out ream after ream.	
Someone's got to be the magician's ...	**assistant**
holding the maestro's gloves.	
And someone's got to work as the ...	**auxiliary junior**
wishing she was one step above.	

I suppose there'll always be a place for the ...	**failed musician**
turning the pianist's pages.	
And you're always going to find a ...	**would-be trainer**
who'll clean out the animals' cages.	
And can the cast do without the poor ...	**understudy**
fidgeting in the wings?	
Can the golfer get around without his faithful ...	**caddy**
carrying his clubs and things?	

I know that someone's got to be the ...	**student dentist**
getting on everybody's nerves.	
And there'll always be a need for a ...	**stand-in speaker**
aware that she was ...	**first reserve**
And it's no disgrace to be a plumber's ...	**mate**
carrying the boss's tools,	
Or the **temporary relief**, a ...,	**supply teacher**
A stranger in a hundred schools.	

I guess there'll always be a job for the ...	**commis waiter**
Peeping through the restaurant door.	
You can't have a fight without a heavy-weight ...	**challenger**
Landing in a heap on the floor.	
And you'll often hear the stories of the ...	**stand-by sailor**
Who never quite made it to sea.	
I know all that, but I can't help wondering	
why it's always got to be me.	

Practice 3

1. Describe the **structure** of a **company** that you know or of a typical company in your town. Mention the number of **employees**, the **working conditions**, the chances for **promotion**, the **directors**, etc.

2. Describe how you think work will have changed in 15, 30 and 45 years' time. What new jobs will there be? What jobs will have disappeared? What will most people's working conditions be like?

3 Write or act out an interview between a **candidate** and his or her **prospective employers** from the point where the **interviewee** is invited to ask questions.

4 Write an enthusiastic letter to a friend or your parents after the first week in your first job.

5 Write the first two paragraphs of a magazine article that has the headline: *Is any job better than no job at all?*

■ Add here any other words about employment you may meet.

. . . .

. . . .

. . . .

. . . .

. . . .

. . . .

. . . .

. . . .

. . . .

. . . .

. . . .

. . . .

Earning and spending money

Reading

Look, everyone, I think we ought to try and economise a bit this month – go carefully on our spending money, cut out a few luxuries, just generally cut down a bit. OK?

Below is an English family's budget in pounds sterling for next month. Look at it to see where their money is coming from and how much is going out. Note down how you think they could save money and any differences between this budget and a family budget in your country.

Income

Basic salary (gross 380, after tax):	335.00
Overtime payment:	56.50
Productivity bonus:	10.00
Royalties on 'Son of Jaws':	35.50
Son's **wages** (4 x 45 net):	180.00
His **tips** and **commission**:	25.00
Basic Earnings:	642.00
plus **extras**:	
Jim's **college grant** (240 – 3, **tax-free**):	80.00
Freda's **scholarship** (120 – 3):	40.00
Child Benefit (7.50 x 2 x 4):	60.00
Dad's **pension**:	136.00
Ted's **dole money** – **unemployment benefit**:	146.00
Dad's dividend on his BP **shares**:	13.00
Interest on Mum's **savings** (bank **deposit account**):	3.50
Tax Rebate (Tax year 1980 – 81):	4.50
Winnings on the Derby:	2.50
Total extras:	485.50
Total Income (all sources):	1127.50

Outgoings

National Insurance Contributions:	46.00
Mortgage payment:	175.00
Rates (**Direct Debit**)	39.50
Gas and Electricity – **Quarterly Bill**s:	164.00
Alimony – **maintenance money** to ex-wife:	173.50
HP instalment on car:	88.00
Road Tax:	80.00
Speeding **fine**:	35.00
Life Insurance premium:	48.00
Deposit on new washing-machine:	45.00
Accountant's **fees** (3 months **overdue**):	25.00
Repayment on **Credit Company loan** (**Standing Order**):	60.00
Interest on **overdraft** on **current account**:	45.00
Other **bank charges**:	10.00
Subscription to magazines	10.00
Donation to 'Help the Aged':	5.00
Contribution to Labour Party **funds**:	7.50
Jenny and Jim's **pocket money**:	60.00
Stake money for football pools and horse-racing:	18.50
Church **Collection**:	1.00
Total Expenditure:	1136.00

Balance: –£8.50

Practice

1. Act out or write a conversation between various members of this family, discussing how perhaps they could **cut down** and **save a little money.**

2. Below are a number of ways of **saving** or **making money**. Note down which you think are sensible and which you would not recommend. If you are working in a group, discuss your notes. If you are working on your own, write a brief summary of them.

    1 **buying in bulk** to **beat inflation**
    2 looking out for genuine **reductions** and real **bargains** in the sales
    3 buying supermarket **brands** rather than **brand-name products**
    4 buying **economy-size** packets and tins of things
    5 collecting packet tops that offer **discounts** on the next **purchase,** have '5p off' labels on them or contain forms for **special offers**
    6 looking out for special **HP** (**hire-purchase**) **deals** at **good rates of interest**
    7 delaying **payment of bills** until the **final demand**
    8 taking your holidays **out of season** at **cheap rates**
    9 buying **second-hand** clothes in **jumble sales** or **charity shops**
    10 buying products that offer **trading stamps** or **gift vouchers** or **competitions** with once-in-a-lifetime **prizes**
    11 using the telephone at **off-peak, cheap-rate** times
    12 **shopping** only at places where money can be **refunded** rather than goods **exchanged**
    13 changing your **foreign currency** when the **rates of exchange** are favourable
    14 checking your **bank statement** and **cheque counterfoils** to make sure there are no errors
    15 looking after **receipts** and **guarantees**

3. Which expression from the list of comments below would you use about yourself at the moment? Notice how many expressions we have for rich and poor, reflecting our obsession with money, and how we often refer to *pence* as *p* in everyday conversation.

    He's a **multi-millionaire**.
    She **inherited** millions (an oil-**heiress**).
    They **won a fortune**.
    She's got **more money than sense**.
    They're **made of money**.
    He's a very **wealthy** businessman.
    She's **extremely well-off**.
    You're looking very **prosperous**.
    They say we're living in an **affluent society**.
    He's **comfortably off**.
    Money doesn't buy happiness, but it helps.
    I'm a bit **hard up** at the moment, actually.
    I'm **down to my last ten p**.
    He's **broke**.
    They're **on the breadline**.
    I **haven't got a penny** to my name.
    I'm afraid we're **bankrupt**, gentlemen.
    Now I know what it's like to be **poverty-stricken**.
    I'm **running into debt**.
    I **owe** money everywhere.
    I'm **heavily in debt**.
    I'm a few thousand **in the red**.
    I'm **up to my ears in debt**.
    I wonder if it's true that **crime doesn't pay**!

4   Note down the various ways in which shops and firms in your country encourage you to buy their products.

5   Act out or write a conversation between a friendly **bank manager** and a newly-married couple. They are asking for advice on **financial matters**: how to manage their **salaries**, **savings**, **monthly outgoings**, etc.

6   Act out or write an interview between an employer and an employee who is trying to explain how difficult it is to '**make ends meet**' on his or her **salary** and is therefore asking for **a rise**.

7   Write a reply to your bank manager's letter enquiring about your £200 **overdraft**. Explain why you have one and what you're going to do about it.

8   Write the opening of your speech to a meeting of your town's Young Socialists on the inequality in present-day society and the unfair **distribution of wealth**.

9   Write the first paragraph or two of a brochure announcing that you have set up as a **financial adviser**. Outline the services you will be offering, the **benefits** that clients will receive etc.

■   If you meet any other words to describe your finances, add them here.

....

....

....

....

....

....

....

....

....

....

....

....

....

....

....

....

Health and illness

Reading 1

[1] Study the 'case history' below. Then write ten headlines for the President's ten-day illness, from *President taken ill* to *The nation holds its breath*.

'You're **in perfect health** ... **as fit as a fiddle** ... there's **nothing wrong with you.**'

'I feel a **bit off-colour** ... rather **under the weather** ... I do **feel funny** ... I really **don't feel well** ... I think I'm **sickening for** something ... I **feel feverish** ... like **death warmed up.**'

'He's been **taken ill** ... he's **in a coma** ... **fighting for his life** ... still **critically ill** ... **in a very critical condition** ... **no change** ... still **seriously ill** ... still **hasn't regained consciousness** ... is **responding to treatment** ... **off the danger list** ... showing **signs of coming round** ... **making progress** ... his **condition is satisfactory** ... he's **come out of the coma** ... he's **as well as can be expected** ... **comfortable** ... **no change** ... he's **turned the corner** ... he's **on the mend.**'

'We all wish you **a speedy recovery** ... **get well soon** ... we're glad you're **over it.**'

'**The worst is over** ... he's **almost completely recovered** ... he's **practically cured** ... he's **convalescing** ... **coming along nicely** ... he'll **be on his feet again soon** ... he'll **be out and about again** in a few days.'

'He's **had a relapse** ... he's **no better** ... he's **getting worse** ... his **condition is deteriorating** ... he's **getting weaker** ... he's **slipping away** ... **fading fast** ... his **life is hanging by a thread** ... it's **just a matter of time** ... he **could go at any second!**'

'He's **made a miraculous recovery** ... he's **as good as new** ... **as right as rain** ... he'll **live till he's a hundred.**'

[2] After all that, do you feel well enough to read on? Note the ways that illnesses can be spoken of and reported in the text below.

Examination Fever

For most of the year, most of us had been **allergic to** work; apparently there had been a **history** of such **allergies** in the school.

Throughout the spring there had been quite a few **cases** of 'Exams are stupid', which proved **highly contagious** among friends.

Then in late May, one or two of us **suffered a mild attack of** 'Gosh, is it really next month?' and we seemed to **give** that to the others rather rapidly. You could tell how it was **spreading** from improved attendance at lessons.

An even more **serious outbreak** was that of the very **infectious** 'I don't know a thing' two weeks before. At about the same time everyone seemed to **catch** 'You're no good!' from the teachers. Then there was **a bout of** 'I don't really care' followed by a few **chronic cases of** 'My parents will kill me'. This again proved very **catching**; half the class **was down with it** in the week leading up to the exam itself, and it had **reached epidemic proportions** by the Friday before.

By this time, those who had been **suffering from** 'It'll be easy for me' had **made a total recovery**.

That Friday there was a 'What if I'm suffering from **amnesia?**' **scare**, and this had developed by Monday into a **touch of** 'I can't even remember my own name'.

There were also, of course, the normal **isolated cases of** 'My pen doesn't work' and several pupils had a **sudden fit** of 'Where's the toilet?'

Afterwards there were a couple of **complaints of** 'I know I've failed', but generally the worst seemed to be over. Such **diseases** are rarely **terminal**. And after all, we had a **convalescence** and **recuperation** period of six and a half weeks to follow.

Practice 1

1 Without looking back at the previous two texts, try to supply the missing word that completes these expressions:

1 under the ...	7 as ... as a fiddle
2 it's just a ... of time	8 a bit ...- colour
3 ... the mend	9 fighting ... his life
4 suffer ... **hayfever**	10 allergic ... dust
5 to go ... with **'flu**	11 as right as ...
6 turn the ...	12 just a ... attack of nerves

2 Here, on this rather unpleasant page, are some of the best-known and least-wanted diseases and conditions, arranged according to where they strike or what causes them. However, in each group there is one that should not be there. Can you identify it?

*The **heart** and **blood vessels***
poor circulation
high blood pressure
a **stroke**
heart attack
jaundice
cardiac arrest
heart failure

*The **stomach** and **intestines***
appendicitis
stomach ulcer
polio
a **hernia**
constipation

Infectious fevers
measles
chickenpox
German measles (rubella)
smallpox
pleurisy
glandular fever
yellow fever
scarlet fever
whooping cough
influenza
leprosy
malaria

*The **lungs** and **respiratory system***
diphtheria
catarrh
sinusitis
tonsilitis
laryngitis
asthma
angina
cholera
bronchitis
tuberculosis (TB)
lung cancer

The liver
gallstones
cirrhosis of the liver
hepatitis
cancer of the liver
coronary thrombosis

The blood
anaemia
pneumonia
leukaemia
a **haemorrhage**
a **blood clot**

Food poisoning
typhoid
dysentery
diarrhoea and **vomiting**
salmonella
mumps

The joints
rheumatism
enteritis
arthritis
fibrositis

The nervous system
migraine
epilepsy (epileptic fits)
Parkinson's disease
multiple sclerosis
muscular dystrophy

Mental disorders
schizophrenia
manic depression
neurosis
paranoia

3 This is a section on **symptoms**, possible **diagnosis** and **remedies**. These six exchanges between **doctor** and **patient** have been mixed up. Decide which response should follow which question.

1 I've been **suffering from insomnia** lately. Do you think I might be **heading for a nervous breakdown?**

2 I seem to have some sort of **stye** or **infection** in my right eye. Do you think I might have **conjunctivitis?**

3 I can't stop scratching this **place** on my foot. Do you think it's **athlete's foot?**

4 I've got a rather **sore throat**, and I keep feeling a bit **flushed**. Do you think it could be **'flu?**

5 I've got a **big bump** on the back of my head. Do you think it might be more than a **bruise?**

6 I keep getting **shooting pains** down my shin and ankle. Is it possible that I've **broken** or **sprained** something?

a Possible. Try this **lotion** for a few days to **stop the itching**, then start putting on this **powder** at night.

b Unlikely, but I'll let you have some **cough mixture** to **relieve** the **symptoms**. You can get yourself some **lozenges**, if you like.

c I would doubt it. Here, rub this **cream** in for the next few nights to help **reduce the swelling**.

d No, of course not. But I'll **prescribe some barbiturates** – sleeping pills – to help you get a good night's rest. OK?

e I wouldn't have thought so. But I'll give you a **prescription** for some **drops** to try and **clear it up**.

f Well, the **X-ray** didn't show anything. If it's so **painful**, you'd better have some **crutches** to walk with and some **painkillers** to **ease the pain.**

4 Rearrange these six paragraphs in the same way.

1 I've got a **dull ache** in my arm and occasionally I get a **spasm**. Could it be a minor **fracture**, a **chipped bone** or something?

2 I've got these tiny little **bumps** all over the back of my **neck**. Do you think it might be **gland** trouble?

3 I've **come out in a rash** on my chest. Do you think it could be a **skin disease** like **impetigo** or **dermatitis?**

4 I keep getting **short of breath**. Is there any way I could be **suffering from asthma?**

5 I think I've got an **ulcer** in my mouth. Do you think it could be a **sign** that I'm **run down?**

6 I feel so **feverish**, and I'm sure I've **got a temperature**. I'm so afraid that there's **something wrong with my heart**.

a Mm, sounds a bit like it. I'll make you out a **prescription** for some **penicillin**, and some menthol **inhalations** might speed up the **recovery**.

b It's just possible. I'll **strap** it **up** anyway and put it in a **sling**. That should reduce your **discomfort** quite a lot.

c Oh, I shouldn't think so, but I think perhaps you ought to start **taking** these **tranquillisers**, to at least **get your blood pressure down**.

d Oh no, no, no. You'd know if it was. I'll give you some **ointment to rub in** to **get rid of** the **inflammation**.

e Probably not. I'll put you on a **course of tablets** to **prevent them from spreading**. They should go soon.

f It might well be. I'll **put you on antibiotics** for a while anyway, to **lessen the risk of serious infection**.

Reading 2

Observations of a Hospital Porter

Ambulance siren,
Brakes squealing,
Screeching. **Bleeding.**
Stretchers wheeling.
Anaesthetic.
Operations.
Amputation.
Blood transfusion.
Every hour
A siren blares
Another night
At St Mary's.

Practice 2

A Nurse's Lament

Complete the text below by filling each gap with one of the following verbs:

***dressing setting giving taking saving fitting sterilising taking out
transplanting taking off performing.***

Well, don't you think it's unfair? There they are upstairs, ... **bones,** ... **skin grafts,**
... **pacemakers,** ... **organs,** ... **lives** and exciting things like that. And here I am
spending the whole of my day ... **people's pulse,** ... **injections,** ... **bandages,**
... **stitches,** ... **wounds** and ... **bottles.** And to think they earn four times as much
money for all the fun they have!

Reading 3

Prevention is better than cure.

HIS LIFE IS IN YOUR HANDS

Beautiful, isn't he? The sort of child any parents would be proud of.
Hard to imagine that until a few months ago this little boy was **in mortal danger** and
nearly **lost his life.**
Without proper **vaccination** he was at the mercy of every **germ, virus, bacterial
disease** around.
Don't take the risk!
Make sure your child is fully **inoculated.** Today!

GIVE YOUR CHILD A FAIR CHANCE – TO LIVE!

Practice 3

1. Write or act out conversations in a doctor's surgery – rather longer than the ones you read earlier – in which a doctor, a patient and the patient's mother, wife or husband discuss how the patient should recover from the operation he or she is about to have.

2. List and give reasons for five golden rules for keeping healthy.

3. Debate or write about the topic: *Nobody wants to live till they're a hundred and ten.* Organise your thoughts carefully before you begin.

4. Describe the remedies or treatments you have heard of for the complaints and accidents listed below.

   1 a bad **burn**
   2 **nosebleed**
   3 **frostbite**
   4 **hiccups**
   5 a **hangover**

   6 a fish-hook in the finger
   7 a **cold**
   8 a person who's **fainted**
   9 a person who's **nearly drowned**

5. Write a letter to a friend from your hospital bed, describing your way of life for the past few weeks, before and since your operation.

6. Write, in dialogue form, a conversation between a **GP** (General Practitioner or family doctor), a parent and a very **spotty** child.

■ Add any more words you need to describe any further illnesses you may catch or hear of.

. . . .
. . . .
. . . .
. . . .
. . . .
. . . .
. . . .
. . . .
. . . .
. . . .
. . . .
. . . .
. . . .

Sport and games

Jigsaw reading

These extracts from sporting commentaries were in pairs, but they have been mixed up. Decide which extract goes with which. Then guess which sport is being referred to in each extract. The answers are given at the end of this unit to help you.

1 ... and now, just when it looked as if Wallburger was going to **win the bout on points**, ...

2 ... at this stage, with the recent loss of Scherzo's **bishop, knight** and both **rooks**, we can only be a couple of **moves** away from **mate** ...

3 ... and in **pole position** on the **grid**, on his favourite **circuit**, with its short **straights** and tight **bends**, is Marconi Libido – three times **winner** here and currently **leading** the **championship table** ...

4 ... then her legs shooting out in front of her, **landing** feet apart in the **pit** – a beautiful **leap** ...

5 ... Frankfurter has produced a left **hook** from nowhere, midway through the thirteenth **round**, to put him on the canvas. And it doesn't look as if he's going to **beat the count** ...

6 ... so it looks as if it's going to be the fast finishers who can sprint to the line who are in with the best chance. Down the back straight, ...

7 ... a **forehand drive return of service** – fine **shot** – Lumbago can't get it. It's in!

8 ... you can see it again now in **slow motion**; her foot hits the **board**, perfect **take-off** – the cycling movement she performs in **mid-air** ...

9 ... his **king** is now virtually **defenceless**. And in fact it's all over. Scherzo has **resigned**, his ...

10 ... and also crossing into the inside lane from lane number two ...

11 ... so, a free kick just outside the United **penalty area**! Kipov dummies over the ball. Hansov takes it – across the goal. Pizov goes up for it but he's **fouled** by Robson. It's a penalty in injury time.

12 ... That's it! **Game, set and match** to Andante ...

13 ... And they're off! Down goes the flag and they're away on the first of eighty laps.

14 ... so, the first lap in 53.4 seconds. There's the bell and at the moment, the Kenyan is out at the front, leading by a couple of metres, and it's a slow time ...

15 ... and this is her third attempt with the bar at 1 metre 81 ...

16 ... a red flag, his third no-throw in a row, so he's out of the competition ...

17 ... Two-one, and now a dramatic chance for an equalizer. Remember, if the match ends in a draw at full-time, it will be decided on penalties ...

18 ... and the Russian team are disqualified for handing on the baton too late ...

19 ... steps into the circle, composes himself, spins rounds – oh dear! ...

20 ... slow **approach**, **up** and she's **over**, and at a **new record height** ...

Game 1

1. Look at the groups of four words below. Try to decide in which sport all four words would be used. Then try to add a word of your own to each group. In one or two cases, more than one sport may be associated with the four items. These answers are also given at the end of the unit.

1 table	5 course	9 mat	13 ring
net	hole	horse	ropes
bat	flag	bars	corner
backhand	clubs	beam	bell

2 court	6 reins	10 table	14 board
baseline	fence	pocket	square
serve	whip	cue	pawns
volley	winning post	red	queen

3 pool	7 bow	11 track	15 racket
butterfly	arrow	pedals	shuttlecock
breaststroke	target	handlebars	smash
turn	bull	lap	lob

4 foil	8 boat	12 corner	16 rink
epée	rope	goal-kick	puck
sabre	ramp	striker	stick
hit	tricks	goalkeeper	goal

2 Below are three other short games for you. Don't worry if you don't win; they are only games to help you remember the words.

1 Here are some of the men's **world records** that existed in 1987 in certain **athletics events** (**outdoor** as opposed to **indoor**). Cover the column on the right and see if you can guess which **event** goes with which **record**.

1 2.42m.	2 9.93secs.	**high jump, 100 metres**
3 2.13m.	4 12.93 secs.	**pole vault, 100m. hurdles**
5 8.90m.	6 37.83secs.	**long jump, 4 by 100m. relay**
7 17.97m.	8 43.86 secs.	**triple jump, 400 metres**
9 22.64m	10 8 mins. 5.4 secs.	**shot, 3000m. steeplechase**
11 74.08m.	12 2 hrs. 7 mins. 13 secs.	**discus, marathon**
13 84.74m.	14 8847 **points**	**hammer, decathlon**
15 104.80m.		**javelin**

2 Now look at the column on the right and select the appropriate instrument used by each of the officials on the left. The name of the official's sport is given to help you.

football
the **referee**'s
the **linesman**'s
the **trainer**'s

boxing   gun
the **judge**'s   scorecard
the **second**'s   watch
                                  whistle
athletics   chair
the **starter**'s   sponge
the **timekeeper**'s   towel
                                  flag
tennis
the **umpire**'s

3 And now, who wears what? Cover the column on the right. Which **sportsmen / women** would you expect to find wearing these **clothes and accessories**?

1 **helmet**, thigh and shoulder **pads**, **boots**	**speedway rider** or **American footballer**
2 **cap, goggles, trunks**	**swimmer**
3 **shorts, vest, spikes**	**sprinter**
4 **shorts, gloves, gumshield**	**boxer**
5 **mask, breastplate, gym shoes**	**fencer**

Reading

For many people, sport is a question of **winning** or **losing**. Note the numerous expressions concerning sporting **success** and **failure** in the text that follows.

The Village Sports

The **sports** were held as usual on the **recreation field**, next to the glove factory. **Officials** outnumbered **spectators**, but there were more **competitors** than ever before.

Maggie was the star, as always. Apart from **winning** the women's **sprints** and **tying for first place** in the **long jump**, she was **champion** again in the (approximately) **50 metres freestyle**, **retaining her title** for the fifth time. She **led from start to finish** in the running – the others **didn't stand a chance** – and she was **in a class of her own** in the swimming; it was a **walk-over**, completely **one-sided**. She was across that pond and back before some had reached the other side.

Dad did well too. There was a **field of fifteen** for the 400 metres – to the bicycle shed and back – and Dad was an **outsider** before the **race** because he's unfit; but he **excelled himself** and **came second**. Was he proud of his **runner's-up** medal? You should have seen him!

Our family were **reigning champions** in the **Five-a-side football competition** and **hot favourites** to **win the cup** again. We did, but only just. The **final** – against our old **rivals**, the Lavenders – finished in a **draw**, despite two **own-goals** by Uncle Mac, and we **kept the trophy** on **goal difference** from earlier **rounds**.

After that, things began to go wrong and we suffered a number of **defeats**. Uncle Mac and little Donald were in a **photo finish** for **last place** in the father-and-son race – or would have been if someone had had a camera. They were just about **overtaken on the line** by old Mr Grey with his fifty-year-old son on his back; it was probably a **dead-heat** actually.

Then we were **outclassed** in the boxing. Uncle Bill was a **beaten finalist** at **middleweight**, but Uncle Mac was **knocked out** in the second round at **heavyweight** and at **lightweight** I **was stopped** in the first round. (I swear that Bobby Lavender is over 50 kilos.)

Because of my disappointing performance in that **event**, I was **relegated** to the **substitutes' bench** for the tug-of-war and Aunt Flossie **was promoted** to our **first team**. I felt so ashamed. Our **opponents** in the first **heat** were the butcher's family from Number 15 and they **slaughtered** us.

Then things went from bad to worse. Granny was **well beaten** in the over 70s' 200-metres **handicap**. She was **towards the back of the field** for most of the race and **failed to finish the course** in the end. Then Auntie Jane had all kinds of problems in the sack-race and was just an **also-ran**. She did get a **consolation prize** for **finishing** – two minutes after the others – but we had been hoping for a **victory** in that event. And then, worst of all, Grandad was **disqualified** in the egg-and-spoon race for having stuck the egg to the spoon. What's more, he's **been banned** from **entering the competition** for five years.

I've noticed over the past few years how the village sports have been getting more and more serious. It's a pity, really. I blame television ... for everything.

Practice 1

As further practice of some of the vocabulary in that text, answer the questions below.

1 Who is the reigning Wimbledon women's singles champion?
2 How many spectators does your country's largest football stadium hold?
3 Why might you bet money on an outsider?
4 Who were the beaten finalists in the last football World Cup?
5 Whose athletes are usually hot favourites to win most gold medals in an Olympic Games?
6 Who was the runner-up in last season's Formula One Drivers' Championship?
7 Are there heats for a marathon?
8 When might you be disqualified in a 100 metres sprint?
9 Who gets the gold medal when there's a dead heat?
10 Why might someone be banned from taking part in a sport for a period of time?

Riddle

Answer this question. If you need help, the answer is printed at the end of the unit.

Question: In sport, what one thing can you **hold**, **set**, **break**, **smash** or **equal**?

Game 2

And finally here's a little game – to add a few more words to your vocabulary and test your knowledge of sport. In each of the items below, something is wrong. See if you can spot each mistake.

1 So Miss Cupido finally wins **six – love**, seven-six (after the **tie-break) seven – five.**
2 Stravinski gets **the white flag** at the end of this year's Monte Carlo **Grand Prix**.
3 The Russian **gymnast**, Nelli Navelikova, now on **the rings** ...
4 And now they're coming to the last **fence** of this year's Derby ...
5 Another **basket** for Hooper; that puts Canada **into the lead** for the first time in the match: 38 to 35.
6 So with this 6 – 2, 6 – 3 victory, Abdul Kabul becomes the new squash **singles champion**, taking over from his **doubles partner**, Sadiq Khan.
7 Two more **gates**, two more **poles**, he's through them, round them. Nothing can stop him now becoming the new **downhill ski champion of the world**.
8 Such a **talented athlete**, **strong swimmer**, **powerful cyclist**, a **first-class shot**, he would be almost sure to win the **Modern Pentathlon** if he was a better **rider**.
9 Uwakana, in the slightly darker **shorts**, Japanese **judo champion** for the past four years, facing his **team-mate**, Onawawa ...
10 After three **rounds** of golf, we have **a three-way tie** between the three Americans all on a total of 148, with Juan Carlos one shot behind.
11 In this 4 by 100 **individual medley**, at the end of the third **leg**, as they change from **backstroke** to **freestyle**, Allegro **is leading by a metre from** ...
12 And that's very **good marks** for the **Olympic ice-dance champions**; two 9.7s, one 9.8, two 9.9s and a 9.6.

Practice 2

1 Explain the rules of at least two of the following sports. Then give any tips you can think of about how to do each sport well.

1 **polo**	6 **weightlifting**
2 **baseball**	7 **netball**
3 **croquet**	8 **squash**
4 **rugby**	9 **volleyball**
5 **cricket**	10 **bull-fighting**

2 Describe your sporting heroes, both now and when you were a child. Explain why you admire(d) them.

3 Describe, in as much detail as possible, a match, competition or race that you will never forget.

4 Discuss what you think are the main problems facing international sport today.

5 Discuss your attitude – angry, enthusiastic or indifferent – towards sports that:

a use animals.
b use machines.
c involve physical violence between contestants.

6 Write a paragraph from your novel in which the hero, after months of hard training, goes out on the track for the 1500 metres final.

7 *Sport divides more than it brings together.* Write part of a magazine article that you submit on this theme.

■ Add here any other words about sport that you may come across.

. . . .
. . . .
. . . .
. . . .
. . . .
. . . .

Answers
Jigsaw reading: **1, 5** boxing   **2, 9** chess   **3, 13** motor racing   **4, 8** long jump
6, 14 800 metres race (running)   **7, 12** tennis   **10, 18** relay race   **11, 17**
football   **15, 20** high jump   **16, 19** throwing the discus (field event)

Game 1: **1 table tennis   2 tennis   3 swimming   4 fencing   5 golf
6 horse-racing   7 archery   8 water-skiing   9 gymnastics
10 snooker** (or **billiards**)   **11 cycling   12 football   13 boxing** (or
wrestling)   **14 chess   15 badminton   16 ice hockey**

Riddle: a **record**

Entertainment

Reading 1

Spend some time trying to absorb the language of the theatre and stage contained in this text.

Confessions of a would-be actor

After playing Joseph in a **nativity play** at the age of five and a half, – I can still remember the three **lines** I had – my **theatrical career** really took off. I was chosen to be the back end of the **pantomime** horse in our school end-of-term Chrismas **show**. Success there, or rather lack of it – the horse's seams came apart soon after our first **entrance** – led to my being given the job of **stagehand** for all future **productions**. Even **scenery** falling over in the middle of an Italian **light opera** and last-minute panic over the missing **set** for an **ancient Greek tragedy** failed to persuade our **drama teacher** that I would be less of a risk **on stage** than off. (That, in fact, is not strictly true. I did have a **walk-on part** once in a French bedroom **farce** – as an apparently dumb police constable – but to everyone's horror I tried to **exit** with the wrong **character** at the end of the wrong **scene**, **stage left** instead of **stage right**.)

On leaving school, I joined an **amateur dramatic society**, full of enthusiasm but rather short on **experience**, **technique** and **timing**. For some years, I was restricted to **bit parts** in **sketches**, **satirical revues** and one or two **slapstick comedies**. My finest hour came when I had to **stand in** for a member of the **cast** who had been taken ill – I was the general male **understudy** – and take the part of the **villain** in a Victorian **melodrama**; lots of **overacting** and **asides** to the **audience**. I had only a very short **rehearsal** beforehand and I thought my **performance** was reasonably competent. The **producer**, however, suggested that I took up some less public hobby, like pottery or rug-making.

Not deterred, I joined a **repertory company** as **stage and costumes manager**, also responsible for **props** and **make-up**. And I was their **prompter** as well. During my time with them I wrote a number of **scripts**, most of which were rejected, but one of which was accepted and performed. It turned out to be the most terrible **flop**. I didn't do much acting there – just one part, if I remember rightly, in the **chorus** of a **musical**, a **revival** of *West Side Story*. Nobody '**discovered**' me. What I had always wanted was to **play** the **hero** in something like *Romeo and Juliet* or to have a **leading part** in an Oscar Wilde **comedy of manners**. When I turned fifty, however, I began to accept that it was probably not going to happen.

You can imagine my surprise and delight, then, when some nights ago I learned that I had landed the **title role** in Shakespeare's **classic play** *Macbeth* with the Royal Shakespeare Company. I couldn't believe my luck. *Macbeth*: that superb **monologue** before Duncan's murder, the **passages** with the witches on the heath, that fantastic *Tomorrow and tomorrow and tomorrow* **speech** in **Act** Five, **Scene** 5. The **dress rehearsal**, with **co-stars** Olivier and Glenda Jackson, was a dream. And with **the first night** to follow – ten **curtain calls** – bouquets – **reviews** the next day: '**Smash hit!**' 'Don't miss it!' 'A **box office** winner!' 'Triumph for new Macbeth!' 'A **Star** is ... '.

And then that horrible ringing sound in my ears ...

Practice 1

1   On the right are some of the ways we classify films. On the left are some film **titles**. Match each title with the most appropriate kind of film from the column on the right.

    1 Last Days of the Black Rock Gang   a **cartoon**
    2 Bridge over the Seine   a **western**
    3 John loves Mary loves Tom loves Judy   a **science fiction movie**
    4 Born to be a Star   a **disaster movie**
    5 Light Years from Yesterday   a **travelogue**
    6 The Blood of the Innocents in White   a **documentary**
    7 The London to Glasgow Express   a **war film**
    8 Avalanche   a **(Hollywood) musical**
    9 Goldilocks at the Teddy Bears' Picnic   a **horror film**
  10 Wildlife and the West   a **blue movie**
  11 Bonaparte and Alexander   a **thriller**
  12 Casablanca to Cape Town in 20 days   a **historical film**
  13 Life begins at Midnight in Amsterdam   a **romantic comedy**

2   In what situation might you say the following? Match each question with one of the situations on the right.

    1 **What's on?**   You want to know whether the actors are any good.
    2 **Who's in it?**   You can't see a free seat anywhere.
    3 **What's it about?**   You need to know what time to get to the cinema.
    4 **Where's it on?**   You're thirsty.
    5 **What time does it start?**   You're leaving the cinema with a friend.
    6 **Where shall we sit?**   There are three cinemas in town and you don't know which is showing the film you want to see.
    7 **Where's the bar?**   You haven't a clue what to go and see.
    8 **What did you think of it?**   It might be a horror film and you wouldn't enjoy that.

3   Here are some of the categories for the annual **Academy Award Winners**. Each winner gets an **Oscar**. Look back over the past few years – not just this year – and note down who you would give your awards to for as many as you can of the categories below. If you don't know the name of the person involved, then just give the name of the film. If you are working in a group, compare and discuss your notes with a partner.

Best film
Best **Actor**
Best **Actress**
Best **Supporting Actor**
Best **Supporting Actress**
Best **Director**
Best Original **Screenplay** (**script**)
Best **Screen Adaptation**
Best Cinematic **Photography**
Best **Editing**
Best **Special Effects**
Best Original **Score** (music)
Best **Costumes / Wardrobe**
Best **Title Sequences / Credits**
Best **Short** (film)
Special Award for Services to the **Cinema Industry**, the **motion picture business**, the **dream factory**, the **movie world**

Game

There are, of course, more aspects to **film-making** than those listed above. Match each person (**1 – 5**) with what they would say (**a – e**).

1 **Director**
2 **Producer**
3 **Continuity** Girl
4 **Clapperboard** Man
5 **Cameraman**

a Can't you get on with the **shooting**? This is costing me money.
b **Scene** 24. **Take** 25!
c Your **make-up**'s thicker and you're wearing a different dress.
d Clear the **set**! This is supposed to be a **film studio**! Get those damned **extras** out of here! **Action**! **Cut**!
e Rolling!

Reading 2

Finally in this unit – leaving aside **nightclubs** and **floor shows**, **variety shows** and **puppet shows**, **music-hall** and **carnivals**, **fairgrounds** and **fashion parades**, a song about the **circus**:

The whole thing's fake. The **sawdust**'s like cake.
The **tent** itself's unsafe, and it tilts.
The **singer**'s songs don't rhyme. The **band** can't keep in time.
And the chap can never climb on to his **stilts**.

But the one saving grace in this fifth-rate place –
The only **act** that's guaranteed to please –
The only reason that I go to this rotten awful **show**
Is that tiny little girl on the **trapeze**.

The juggler drops the **balls**. The **tightrope walker** falls.
And **performing fleas** are always such a pain.
The **fire-eater**'s bald. And the **audience** are appalled
As the **lion-tamer**'s mauled yet again.

The **clowns** aren't funny. It's a total waste of money.
I don't know why they have shows like these.
The only thing worth seeing in the whole **performance** being
That young twenty-year-old girl on the trapeze.

The **ventriloquist** moves his lips. The **acrobat** always trips.
And the **conjuror**'s got no **tricks** left up his sleeve.
The **high-diver**'s head is like a square loaf of bread.
I wouldn't be seen dead in there, believe me.

If it wasn't for the fact that there's this super little act
That gets me going weak at the knees,
I think you know the reason why I come back every **season**:
It's that middle-aged girl on the trapeze.

The **ringmaster** stutters. The **comedian** mutters.
And the **strong-man** splutters in despair.
The **midget**'s five foot five; I'm surprised he's still alive
Because the **knife-thrower**'s knives go everywhere!

The Russian **sword-swallowers** have lost all their **followers**;
So many knives they've borrowed stay below.
And the **disappearing rabbits** with their rather special habits,
Keep appearing just as rapidly as they go.

So even now, I must confess, the thing I like the best –
I don't know if there's anyone who agrees –
I've really just come back for that one three-minute act –
It's that elderly artist on the trapeze.

Practice 2

1 Write or discuss the answers to these questions.

1 Which **clip** from a particular film would you never tire of seeing?
2 What **trailers** have you seen recently that really made you want to go and see the film?
3 Can you think of any **scenes** from films you think should have been cut? Or can you think of any entire film you think should have been banned?
4 Which of these features do you, in general, like a film to have:

a a happy **ending**?
b a complicated **plot** or a simple **storyline**?
c lots of action?
d a political or social **message**?
e totally naturalistic **dialogue**?
f **larger than life** or **true-to-life characters**?
g (in the case of foreign films) **subtitles** or **dubbed dialogue**?
h lots of **close-up shots** of people's faces?
i long **sequences** of desert, jungle, etc?
j a fair number of **stars** or a cast of '**unknowns**'?

5 What can the cinema offer that the theatre can't – and vice versa?
6 Which plays have you seen which you have also seen the **film** of? How did the two versions compare?
7 Would you let your ten-year-old son go off to Hollywood to be in a film, with or without you there?

2 Write a favourable **review** for a play you have seen.

3 Write an unfavourable review for a film you didn't like.

4 Write part of a **fan letter** from a young teenager to an actor or film star.

■ Add here any other words that you meet about the theatre, cinema or circus.

. . . .
. . . .
. . . .
. . . .
. . . .
. . . .
. . . .
. . . .
. . . .
. . . .

Games and hobbies

Reading

Have a look through the following extracts from a scrapbook. In it, the writer gives us an impression of the various **pastimes** and **hobbies** that he enjoyed at different times in his life.

As you read, ask yourself how his **interests** and **activities** compare with yours at each stage of your life. Decide what you and the writer have in common and how you differ. Also identify the words for the things in the illustrations.

0 to 5
Nursery Rhymes
with Mummy and Daddy
Jack and Jill
went up the hill
and **Fairy Tales**
with Uncle Bill
Once upon a time
there was a handsome prince.

Dummies and **rattles**
and big **soft toys**
teddy bears, **dolls**
that walked and talked
abacus, **bricks**
and **jigsaw puzzles**
crayons, **plasticine**,
paints and **chalk**.

Swings and **roundabouts**
climbing frame
see-saw, **slide**
and **playground games**
castles in the **sandpit**
bucket and spade.
'Jennifer pushed me.'
'He called me names.'

6 to 10
Feet stuck
on the **rocking horse**
toes squashed
on the **tricycle**
knees grazed
coming off the **scooter**
bottom sore
from the **bicycle**.

163

Model aeroplanes
sticky fingers
missing bits
and breaking things
train sets
and making **pastry**
cut-out shapes
and **rolling-pins**.

Keeping pets
like mice and hamsters
rabbits in their hutch
and snakes in jars
puppies and kittens
in kennels and baskets
canaries in cages
with budgerigars.

On Sundays, we went to **Sunday School**. 'Well, you're going, whether you like it or not. Whatever would Jesus say?' Before that, we usually managed half an hour of **skipping** in the garden. I still think giving my little sister my treasured three-year-old **skipping rope** was my most generous juvenile act. Afterwards, there was **hopscotch** on the pavement – were we really as blind to traffic as children are today? – or, if it was raining, '**doctors and nurses**' indoors.

And then, every now and then, horror of horrors, a party with **party games** like **pass the parcel** and **musical chairs**. I am convinced that my present unease in the company of ladies can be traced back to the afternoon when, as a seven-year-old and as a **forfeit** – or was it a **prize**? – I was required to leave the party room with a gigantic ten-year-old girl and plant a kiss on one of her cheeks.

Boy Scouts
and **Girl Guides**
uniforms, badges
passwords, camps.
Collecting coins,
the future **numismatist.**
The would-be **philatelist,**
collecting stamps.

Birds' eggs
and garden insects,
wild flowers
carefully placed on
scrapbook pages
or under mattresses.
No-one had heard of
conservation.

Reading **comics**,
first *Mickey Mouse*
then *Roy of the Rovers*
every week.
Adventure stories like
The Secret Seven,
marbles and **dominoes**,
    hide-and-seek.

'My **turn**'. 'I wasn't ready'
    'You **cheat**!' 'That's not fair!'
'You were looking!' 'No, I wasn't!'
        'I'm not playing any more!'

11 to 15
Life became slower. My friend Mary went off for hours:
knitting – huge **needles**, dropped **stitches**, uneven **rows**, 'Aren't I clever?'
sewing – I swear it took her half an hour to **thread the needle** every time.
doing **embroidery** – she managed one flower on a cushion cover in seven and a half
months.
doing **crochet** – 'Now I'm really grown-up!'
We got involved with:
chemistry sets – the smell of rotten eggs, the sound of breaking glass.
and flying my **kites** in the April winds.
I didn't see her so much after that, except for our **board games** together:
progressing from **Snakes and Ladders** – 'Your **go**.' 'Pass the **dice**.' – to **Monopoly**,
to **draughts**, to **backgammon**, to **chess**.
She never liked **card games**, but we did finally graduate from **snap** to **whist**, to
canasta, to **bridge**. We stopped short of **poker**; poker came later.

ace of spades   **king of hearts**   **queen of clubs**   **jack (knave) of diamonds**
'You **shuffle** the cards, she can **cut** them, and I'll **deal** them. Perhaps I can deal
myself a good **hand**. It's about time I won some **tricks**.'
She got bored by my **riddles** – 'What will go up a chimney down but won't come
down a chimney up?' 'Don't know.' 'An umbrella.' 'Huh!'
and made **paper aeroplanes** with my romantic poetry – 'You and the Daffodils,' to
Mary, love George.
She went to **ballet lessons** and then **tap-dancing classes**. I was sent to **ballroom
dancing lessons**. Does anyone know the difference between a **tango** and a
quickstep, a **waltz** and a **foxtrot**, a **samba** and a **cha-cha**? 'Take your partners for
a **military two-step**,' I hated every minute of it.

16 to 20
We got interested in **cookery** – 'The **recipe** said it would **rise** like bread, but it's as
flat as a pancake!'
I took up **photography** – expensive **camera**, **telephoto lens**, **light-meter** built in,
hours in the **darkroom**, **developing** and **printing**, **photos** of thumbs and backs of
heads.
Then came her **crosswords** – Clues: 1 **Across**: see 23 **Down**. (**Solution** below) –
and **word games** and **puzzles**.
And then, all of a sudden, **hi-fi**:
Mon: **check circuits** on **amplifier / tuner**.
Tue: **replace leads** and **jackplugs** on all **microphones**.
Wed: **overhaul cassette recorder**, **clean** and **demagnetise heads**.
Thurs: **fit new record deck** and **stylus**.
Fri: **sort out balance of speakers**; **correct distortion** on **left channel**.
Sat: **strip** and **check wires** leading to **phono input sockets**; **test all
              connections**.
Sun: play some music.
And nine months later, **motorcycle maintenance**:
oily rags and dungarees; **stripping engines**, **decoking**, **tuning**, **changing wheels**,
plugs, **pistons**, **oil**; sweating.

Then there were outdoor activities like:
skiing, skating,
surfing, canoeing,
horse-riding, wind-surfing,
parachuting, hang-gliding,
mountaineering, pot-holing,
roller-skating, skateboarding,
water-skiing, hiking,
camping and **shooting.**
My friends all told me they were great fun. I enjoyed the occasional **picnic** but my favourites were **indoor activities** like:
fruit machines and **pin-tables,**
table football and **video games,**
pool, darts,
skittles and **bowling.**
We can't all be outdoor types.

21 to 25
Once we went **hunting** together, all red and white –
red for the jacket, the fox, the blood,
white for the teeth, the trousers, her face.
That started her on a year or two of anger and **protest**:
meetings, demonstrations, placards and **posters**:
'**Down with** whatsisname,' '**Stop the** whatsit',
'**Hands off** thingummy,' 'Soandso **out!**'
Meanwhile, I began **gambling**:
£20 **bets** at fantastic **odds** of 10 to 1,
winnings of £200 plus my **stake money** back, if the horse that I'd **bet on** had won.
She then gave up **politics** for **dress-making** –
'You can't go wrong if you **follow the pattern**.'
I flirted with **gardening** – fun for a week –
'**Sow** in boxes, in moist **compost, plant out** carefully, **water** daily.'
Then I turned to alcohol, **brewing** my own beer,
distilling my own whisky, **making** my own wine.
She did **basket-weaving,** then **pottery** for a while:
handleless jugs and unusable vases,
while I tried my hand at **carpentry.**
I was in danger of becoming a **do-it-yourself** fanatic when,
suddenly and gloriously, I fell in love with **cars.**
After my love-affair with cars, what else was there left?
On and off, there was:
fishing – apparently the most popular outdoor pastime in Britain. Happiness for millions is a **rod** and a **line**, a good **catch** on the **hook**.
playing **bingo** – a strange phenomenon, a party game with gambling, and lots of prizes.
newspaper competitions – 'And this week, YOU can win any or All of the Prince's wedding presents!'
yoga, jogging and **keep-fit classes** – 'Touch your toes! Don't bend your knees!'
Cartwheels, forward rolls, somersaults, press-ups.
Anyone who can do all that must be made of rubber.
And, of course, **TV**
and **ante-natal classes**, and then:

Nursery Rhymes
with Mummy and Daddy
Humpty Dumpty
sat on a wall,
and *Once upon a time*
there was a boy called Hansel.
Fairy Tales
with Uncle Paul.

Practice

1 Note down the hobbies and activities you enjoyed from the age of five to the age of fifteen.

2 Write or discuss the answers to these questions.

1 What hobbies do you now regret not taking up when you were younger? Include any hobbies that you gave up too soon.
2 What activities will you encourage your children to enjoy? Are there any you will discourage them from?
3 Is there any reason why both girls and boys shouldn't be actively interested in any of the pastimes listed above?

3 Practise giving instructions on how to do your favourite hobby or at least three of activities **1 – 6**.

1 **play** a card-game
2 **dance** a dance
3 **look after** hi-fi equipment properly

4 **make wine**
5 **catch a** big **fish**
6 **develop photos**

4 Write a few paragraphs of a speech, in which you complain that girls and boys are treated very differently from an early age and therefore grow up with very different roles in society.

5 Write, in dialogue form, a conversation between a bored teenager and a parent who's trying to interest him or her in some worthwhile hobby.

6 Write a reply to a friend who has written asking for your advice on how to keep her six-year-old twins amused during the long summer holidays.

■ Add here any other activities that you know or hear of:

. . . .

. . . .

. . . .

. . . .

. . . .

. . . .

. . . .

. . . .

. . . .

. . . .

. . . .

. . . .

. . . .

Music and the Arts

Study

Arrange the **instruments** below so that they are in a more normal orchestral formation.

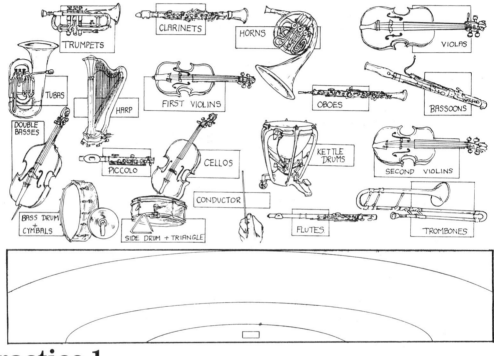

Practice 1

1 List the instruments in the orchestra that you would most like to play well. Also note down any that you would never like to learn and why.

2 Imagine that you are going to form your own **supergroup**, inviting famous **pop stars** and other **musicians** to join you. Choose the instrument that you would like to play from the list of instruments and types of singer below, in the line up for **the recording session** for this **pop group** or **rock band**. Then note down the instrument or **vocals** of your choice from each line and who you will invite to play them or to sing.

   1 **lead vocals**
   2 **lead guitar** (electric)
   3 **acoustic guitar, 12-string guitar, sitar**
   4 **bass guitar, backing vocals**
   5 **drums**
   6 **extra percussion, tambourine, maracas, bongos**
   7 **keyboards, organ, electric piano, synthesiser**
   8 **mandolin, steel guitar, electric fiddle (violin)**
   9 **harmonica, mouth organ, Jew's harp, kazoo**
 10 **saxophone, rhythm guitar, backing vocals**

3   The arrangements, production, sound engineering and mixing are still to be organised. Think of the **records** that you have got at home. Choose a **recording company** or **label** that you would write to, in the hope that they will help you to find a studio and market your record.

4   Now you've got your latest **single release** recorded, when are you going to go out **on the road** and do some **live concerts**? Note down the five **venues** that you would choose for a European tour.

Game

1   Look at some more instruments on the right that we can **strike, blow, shake, strum** or **pluck**. Which of each pair below is the one in the picture?
  1 banjo or **ukelele**?
  2 harpsichord or **spinet**?
  3 accordion or **bagpipes**?
  4 cornet or **bugle**?
  5 recorder or **xylophone**?
  6 castanets or **tom-tom**?

2   Now, a variation on a BBC radio game. You're being sent off to a desert island tomorrow with a toothbrush, bottle-opener and **record-player**. Make a list of the **pieces of music** that you are going to take with you. You're allowed some or all of the following:
2 **symphonies**
2 **concertos** or **sonatas**
1 **choral** or **orchestral work**: **oratorio, cantata**, etc.
1 **opera**: (**grand, light, comic** or **operetta**)
1 additional **piece** or **set** of **classical music**: a **rhapsody, overture, collection** of **nocturnes, serenades, studies**, etc.
1 **jazz LP**: (**modern** or **traditional**)
1 **album: folk, soul** or **blues**
1 LP by a **group**: (**pop** or **rock**)
1 **solo album**: male or female **vocalist**
1 other selection of your choice: **brass band** music, a **film score, nursery rhymes, electronic music**, pub **sing-songs**

3   In this short quiz, answer each of the questions.

   1 Which of these is not normally religious?
   a a **hymn**   **b** a **psalm**   **c** a **carol**   **d** a **ballad**
   2 Which of these would normally make the least noise?
   a a **round**   **b** a **lullaby**   **c** an **anthem**   **d** the **refrain** of a **madrigal**
   3 Which of these is the odd one out?
   a a **duet**   **b** a **triplet**   **c** a **quartet**   **d** a **quintet**
   4 Which order should these be in, starting from the top, that is to say the voice that can sing the highest notes?
   a baritone   **b bass**   **c tenor**   **d contralto (alto)**   **e soprano (treble)**
   5 In what order, chronologically, did these names become popular?
   a a **jukebox**   **b** a **record deck**   **c** a **phonograph**   **d** a **gramophone**
   e a **record-player**   **f** a **musical box**

Reading

1. Read through the text below and see how many of the **musical terms** contained in these reminiscences can be of use to you.

Try it again

I spent nearly six years **studying** and **practising** the piano at school; that's to say, four years playing **scales** and **arpeggios**, then eighteen months let loose on actual **pieces of music**.

My teacher, Mr Pearson, was the sort of person who thought that anyone who didn't have **perfect pitch** was educationally subnormal and as for pupils – like me – who had difficulty in **reading music** and never really began to master **sight-reading**, well, there was really no hope in life.

Looking back, I can see that he was not particularly modern or enlightened in his approach. There were weekly tests along the lines of:

'How many **flats** are there in the **key** of A flat **major**? '

'How were Bach's ideas on **melody**, **harmony** and **counterpoint** significant? '

'What was the **opus number** of Mozart's *Eine Kleine Nachtmusik?* '

and lots of unanswerable questions about **bass clefs** and **treble clefs**, etc.

Still, we persevered together for those six years, despite my numerous handicaps. For a start, my **sense of rhythm** – especially for anything **syncopated** – was virtually non-existent.

'How many **beats** in the **bar**, Haskins?'

'Three, sir.'

'Then kindly stop trying to squeeze in five.'

Then, being so small, neither of my hands could span a full **octave** which meant that **keys** were rarely **struck** by the finger recommended and that, particularly on the black **notes**, the little finger fell short of expectations.

'Is there normally a B flat in a B **major chord**, Haskins?'

'No, sir.'

'Right, then spare us it, will you?'

It wasn't that I didn't try. On the contrary, I had visions of one day performing in **concerts** and **recitals**, if not as a **soloist**, at least **accompanying** guest **singers** and **instrumentalists**. Somehow, the visions became fainter and fainter.

'I think if Beethoven had wanted a **minor chord** just there, Haskins, he would have **written one**. Don't you?'

So the years went on, endless **variations** on a single **theme**, dozens of **arrangements** of one basic **tune**, which I swear he **composed** himself.

I must admit there were times when I thought of changing **instruments** – going back to the **woodwind** class, where I had bitten through three **oboe reeds** in one session, or the **strings** department, where I kept dropping the viola **bow**, or the **percussion** wing, where I had snapped two **drumsticks** inside ten minutes, or the **brass** class, where I had nearly swallowed a trumpet **mouthpiece**. But I didn't. I stayed with Mr Pearson and his **finger exercises**, the **wrong notes**, the **missed entrances**, the 'Try it again's. I suppose I was lucky that you can't play the piano **out of tune**. I'm sure if it was possible to **play flat**, I would have done.

'What's the difference between an **F sharp** and an **F natural**, Haskins?'

'A **semitone**, sir.'

'Correct. Now, if you could remember that while you're playing, you might not make such a pig's ear out of one of the most beautiful melodies Brahms ever **composed**. Try it again.'

2 Read this contents page from a new book on the **visual arts**.

ART FOR BEGINNERS

Practice

1. Choose the part of the above book that you would like to read first. Give your reasons.

2. Describe two of your favourite paintings and why you like them. If possible, find them in a book so that you can refer to them or show them to other people. If you can't, then sit and look through a book of famous works of art and decide which ones you like and which ones you don't. Consider whether you would want all, any or some of them in your sitting room.

3. Describe your experience of learning to play a musical instrument or give the reasons why you never did so.

4. Discuss or write notes on the improvements in sound quality on records and tapes during your lifetime. Does the excellence of production nowadays disguise a lack of musical quality, technique or interest?

5. Choose a song or piece of music and explain what you like and don't like about it. Then compare it with a similar piece of music of your choice.

6. Describe how you would arrange a popular folk song for recording with the singers and instruments of your choice.

7. Write a magazine review of a recently released record you have heard – classical or modern.

8. Write, in dialogue form, a minute of conversation during one of Haskins's typical lessons with Mr Pearson.

9. You have been asked to speak at a discussion evening on the subject of 'Snobbery in Music'. Write the notes that will help you in your speech to express your opinions.

■ Add here any other words about music and the arts as you meet them.

. . . .

. . . .

. . . .

. . . .

. . . .

. . . .

. . . .

. . . .

. . . .

. . . .

. . . .

Cooking, eating and drinking

Reading

1 Look carefully below at the different things that can be made in the kitchen.
Why it should be me that goes out to work: an extract from the diary of a frustrated and indecisive housewife or -husband.

08.30 'Bye, bye. Have a nice day! ... Now what can I do for their dinner today? Something **simple** but **nourishing**, **tasty** but not too '**hot**' or **spicy**, not too **exotic** but not too **plain**. ... I've got a few **eggs**; I could give them to them **poached** – on **toast** – or **scramble** them, or **fry** them, or ... no, they don't like **boiled** eggs. I suppose I could make an **omelette** ... or a **soufflé** – they'd like that. The trouble is, my soufflés never **rise**. Besides, I'd really been planning to use those eggs in a **cake** – a nice **vanilla sponge**. I've got lots of **flour**, **butter**, **sugar**, **vanilla essence** and **icing sugar** to **dust** it; and for a **filling** I could use those blackcurrants from the garden. Lovely!

11.00 Then again, those blackcurrants are so nice and **fresh**, it seems a pity to put them in a cake. Better to have them **raw** after dinner. Or perhaps I ought to **stew** them; they'll probably need a bit of **sweetening**. I could put them into a **fruit salad**, or perhaps a **trifle** – we haven't had one for a long time. ... But I did say that I was going to **bottle** them this year, **preserve** them, or make **jam** with them; you can even make **chutney** from blackcurrants.

12.30 This is not helping towards dinner. Concentrate! ... How about a blackcurrant **tart** for **dessert**? The **pastry** would be no problem; **puff pastry**, perhaps, I can manage that. I could make a **flan** – that would make a nice change. And while I'm making pastry for the **base** of the flan, I might as well double the amounts and use the rest for a few **savoury vol-au-vents** and perhaps a **round of shortbread**. If there's any left over, I could always use it up on some **biscuits** or **macaroons** – the kids would love that. In fact, I could really go to town and make a **quiche** for all of us, or **fish and chips** – basic **pancake batter**, nothing to it, really.

14.30 No, I've got it! Forget the flan. A meat **pie**! A gigantic meat **pasty**, perhaps. I've got some beef in the freezer, and some kidneys. **Steak and kidney pie**. ... It's not their favourite, of course. They often say they prefer their meat **roast**. But that meat's no good for roasting. I could **braise** it, I suppose, but that takes such a long time. ... I could **mince** it and then ... No. Perhaps if I made it into a **stew** – a big **casserole**; that's easy enough. ... But if I don't do **pastry**, I'll have to **cook** some potatoes. **Roast** potatoes wouldn't go. **Jacket potatoe**s are easiest, but the ones I've got are so small. We've had them **boiled** for the past five nights. They can't stand them **mashed** or **creamed**. **Croquettes** would take me all afternoon. **Chips** don't really go with stew. ... Unless I change the stew to **kebabs**. ... No. Perhaps I'd better try and **bake** those little ones after all.

16.30   Come to think of it, I've got all I need to do some real **baking**: **flour**
         – **plain** and **self-raising** – and **yeast** for the **dough**. They'd
         appreciate some oven-warm bread. I could manage a few **buns**
         or **scones**, and they love those little **croissant**-type **rolls** I make for
         their birthdays. If they have some nice bread, they probably won't
         want more than a **soup** to go with it – a thick vegetable soup – that's
         it. I've got some carrots to go in and one or two other **ingredients.**
         Though I must say I prefer carrots **raw**, **shredded** in **a salad**... .
         In fact, a salad wouldn't be a bad idea. I've got **oil**, **vinegar**
         and **mustard** for a **dressing**. Talking of mustard, why don't I ...

17.30   Oh hello. Have a nice day? What would you say to a nice
         Chinese **takeaway** this evening?'

2 | Read the next entry from the diary and the menu that follows. Note down all that
you think needs to be done in order to serve the meal. Then read the list of things to
be done and amend or complete your notes.

The proof that cooking isn't for me: a further extract from the diary of a person who
is about to go out to work.
After several weeks of **Chicken Chow Mein** for dinner, I decided that things had
gone far enough. After all, there couldn't be that much to preparing a simple
four-course meal once a day. We sat down together to plan a **menu**, then a
programme of attack, adding a theatrical flavour for extra spice.

Our first menu
Asparagus Soup – for **starter**
Dover Sole
Roast Chicken, potatoes, carrots, peas – **main dish**
Peach Flan – for **dessert**

Our first performance

Act One   **scrub** asparagus stems
            strip away the base
            cut out woody parts
            scale the fish, **bone** and **fillet** it
            cut off head and tail
            peel and **wash** potatoes
            top and tail carrots
            shell peas
            thaw frozen chicken
            skin peaches and **remove** stones

Act Two   **chop up** asparagus or **shred** it
            place fish on **greased** foil
            slice potatoes
            dice carrots
            crack two eggs for the flan
            separate them

Act Three   **scald** marrow bones for **stock**
            brown them in oven
            put in large pan; **add** other **ingredients**
            bring to boil and **simmer** to **extract** juices
            strain through sieve or muslin
            brush fish with **melted** butter

stuff the chicken
cover the breast with bacon rashers
season and **rub** with lemon juice
cook in middle of **pre-heated** oven
sift flour and salt into bowl for pastry
cut up butter, **rub** into flour, **mix** or **blend**
add water, **sprinkling** evenly over surface
beat egg-whites and **fold** them into **mixture**
knead gently, then **chill** for 30 minutes

Act Four   **pour** stock over asparagus and **boil**
allow to bubble for an hour, **stirring** regularly
dress the fish
place in hot oven
steam vegetables
baste the chicken
roll out pastry
bake in oven
whip or **whisk** cream for topping

Act Five   **warm** the plates
skim the soup to **remove** fat, etc.
garnish the fish
coat with **pre-prepared** sauce (oh!)
drain vegetables
make gravy from stock
carve meat
grate nutmeg over flan
leave to cool

Finale   **Serve**

Epilogue   **freeze left-overs**

The next day I read the plan of action ... and went out to find a job. Chicken Chow Mein is OK, even though it has this rather strange **after-taste**.

Practice 1

Read the list of foodstuffs and the list of verbs. Note down what you can do to each of the foodstuffs by listing the appropriate verbs. Then take each verb and say which of the foodstuffs it can be used with.

1 eggs
2 potatoes
3 meat
4 pastry or dough
5 fish
6 cream
7 vegetables

roll	scale	whip	dice	braise
scramble	mince	stew	beat	chop
chip	knead	bone	stuff	poach
crack	blend	steam	baste	whisk
carve	grate	peel	mash	shred

Study and practice

To complete this unit, a look at **drinks** and the **drinking habit**. Note down the **beverages** below that you have tried. Beside each, put whether you like it or not and when you would normally drink it.

The cocktail you couldn't mix
It's funny, isn't it, how your friends never seem to get on well together? Let me introduce you to some of mine. They're nice people, all of them, but put them in a room together and the silence is shattering. I just don't understand it. I should have known they wouldn't get on, though, from their drinking habits.

Retired Colonel, William Smythe-Johnson, MBE:
　　double gins at his **club** with just a **dash of tonic** and a **slice of lemon**
　　claret at dinner and **brandy**, French **cognac**, after dinner
　　always has a cup of **tea** at four o'clock sharp

His wife, Wilhelmina:
　　dry martini most of the time
　　champagne cocktail when entertaining – **vintage champagne**

Will Smythe, bank manager:
　　scotch and **bourbon**, usually **with ice**, occasionally **soda**, mainly at home
　　goes mad with **duty-free schnapps** after annual skiing holiday
　　German light **white wine** with clients
　　sometimes treats himself to a **glass of port** after dinner

His wife, Helen:
　　Bacardi or other **white rums** with various **mixers**, most often **coke**
　　insists on a glass of **medium dry sherry** before evening meal
　　they share **freshly ground coffee** (never **instant**) at breakfast and offer the children **pure**, **natural**, **unsweetened**, nothing-added **whole fruit juice**

W. P. Smytheson, university professor:
　　a **teetotaller** – greatest love (after books) a **cup of cocoa** or **drinking chocolate** in the comfort of his rooms
　　drinks **mineral water** at the functions he has to attend

Helena Johnson, fashion designer:
　　occasionally a few **vodkas** in the **lounge bar**
　　vermouth – **Cinzano**, **Dubonnet**, etc. – at home
　　enjoys a good **sparkling wine** as an **aperitif**

Willy Johns, one of my best friends, a teacher:
　　Guinness (**draught**, not **bottled**) in the **saloon bar**
　　a lot of **orange squash** after cross-country runs with the boys

Billy Johns, unemployed at the moment:
　　either **lager** in the saloon bar or rough **cider** in the **public bar**; has had to cut down on drinking lately

Bill Smith, labourer:
　　drinks **mild** (dark beer) or **bitter** (brown beer) in the public bar
　　if he's won on the horses, he'll have a **bottle of light ale** and a **whisky**

His wife, Minny:
　　drinks **milk stout**, which makes her quite **tipsy**, or – less often – **shandy** (beer and **lemonade**), which doesn't.
　　keeps an undrinkable blackcurrant **cordial** (she calls it a **liqueur**) for when visitors come – visitors don't come very often

Practice 2

1 Write or discuss the answers to these questions.

1 What do you think a typical evening meal would be for each of the people in the text about drinking habits?
2 What are the pleasant and unpleasant aspects of cooking for you?
3 Do you think, with the growing popularity of fast food, convenience food, junk food etc., we are losing forever the art of fine cooking and good eating?
4 How serious would you say **alcohol(ism)** is in your country and/or any other countries you have visited?

2 Imagine you are an experienced barman or barmaid. You are showing a new employee around the bar. Write or act out your conversation, in which you talk about how the bar is run, the prices of drinks, what to give a customer if she/he asks for X, which glasses to use for what, where everything is, and so on.

3 Write a detailed **recipe** for a dish you know how to cook well, perhaps with a few personal tips.

4 Write a letter to a friend, describing the absolute disaster when you cooked dinner for your fiancé(e).

5 Write out the menu for the annual dinner dance of a club you belong to. It is quite a formal occasion, so choose a really nice four-course meal.

■ Add here any other words about food and drink that you may meet.

. . . .
. . . .
. . . .
. . . .
. . . .
. . . .
. . . .
. . . .
. . . .
. . . .
. . . .
. . . .
. . . .

Travelling

Reading

Read through this rather long text over the next day or so, noting some of the key words concerned with **trains**, **boats**, **cars**, **coaches** and **planes**. As you read, note down the details of each of the six journeys described.

Travel Broadens the Mind

June 29th ... June 30th ... July 1st. And **they're off**. **Suitcases packed**. Notes left for the milkman. **Arrangements made** for the budgerigar to be looked after. They're all off.

Uncle Bill and Auntie Jane are **on the quayside** at the **cross-channel port** of Dover – the first stage of their Mediterranean **cruise** – 'the **voyage** of a lifetime' their **travel agent** called it. They've been through **customs** (half an hour's delay while suitcases were emptied in search of missing **passports**) and they'll be **embarking** soon. When they **go aboard**, Bill will finally be allowed to take those **boarding cards** out of his mouth.

Granny's at **the coach station** armed with her special old-age pensioner's **season ticket** – a kind of **awayday**, **runabout**, **extended period**, **half-price ticket** rolled into one. Today she's off on a **one-day sightseeing excursion** to Stonehenge, Blackpool Tower and Canterbury Cathedral.

Julia's with her boyfriend **at the airport**, kicking their **cases** through the **departure lounge** of what they hope is **Terminal** 3 and the right place to be for the **package holiday charter flight** that their **tour operator** assured them would be leaving sometime this morning. To their right, the **1st class passengers** are sipping champagne cocktails; to their left, those in **economy** and **tourist class** are drinking coffee from the machine and, under their feet, those **on stand-by**, are looking hopefully up from their sandwiches.

Mum and Dad are already **on the open road**. They decided to make an early start on their **touring holiday** through the Loire valley. 'Your turn to **drive** now. Come on, let's get moving. **Switch on**, then. OK, it's **all clear**. **Pull out**, there's **nothing coming**. Well, **take the handbrake off**. Right, **indicate**. Come on, **drive away**. At last! Right, **keep over**. **Keep to the right**. **Change gear**, then. Come on, **accelerate**!'

'**Porter!**' 'Sir?' 'How much?' '50p.' 'No thanks; I'll manage my own **luggage**.' Uncle Mac is about to **board** the 10.40 **inter-city express** to Glasgow for a fortnight's holiday back in the homeland. 'Do I have to **change**?' 'No, it's a **through train**, sir, **non-stop** all the way.' It looks as if quite a few expatriates have had the same idea. The **compartments** all look full – especially the **non-smokers** – and the **buffet car** already sounds like Glasgow on the night of a Celtic-Rangers football match.

My brother's on the **slip road** of the M1 **motorway** at **Junction** 14, a **rucksack** on his back containing **sleeping bag**, biscuits and a change of underwear. He's been there for an hour and a half with his homemade sign saying 'Anywhere', trying to **thumb a lift**. There are no **hostels** or **transport cafés** in sight. The rucksack is getting heavier and the sky is getting darker. It's not much of a life sometimes, **hitch-hiking**.

Oh dear. Granny's coach has got **stuck** in a **traffic jam**, a **queue** of cars as far as the eye can see. OK, so central Birmingham is **on the direct route** from Blackpool to Canterbury. But during **the rush-hour**? With thousands of **commuters heading** for home? Not a good plan. After all, what are **bypasses** and **ringroads** for? 'Right, you can **overtake** this one. There's no **speed limit** here. Oh, a **diversion**. You'd better **turn off** the **main road**. **Pull across** to the middle. Now **keep in the right lane**. I mean the left lane. I mean ...'

Crashes at **take-off**, **mid-air collisions**, **flight recorders** never recovered, no **survivors** ... 'This is your **captain** speaking' wakes Julia's boyfriend up. Another nightmare over. The **stewardess** is smiling down at him. '**Fasten your seat-belts**, please.'

Uncle Bill and Auntie Jane have settled into their **cabin**, **unpacked** their things and have gone up **on deck**. The sea is calm, the sunset is out of this world, and Uncle Bill is beginning to feel just a little bit **seasick**. They are due to **set sail** in half an hour.

Traffic is still **crawling** along behind and in front of Granny's **coach**. You can see the casualties by the side of the road, in **lay-bys** and on the **grass verges** – **bonnets up**, **overheated engines**, **steaming radiators**. The **guide** is into his second hour on the history of Canterbury Cathedral. 'Toilets 1 mile!' the cry is heard. There is great happiness.

'Right, here's a **garage**. 'Essence' must mean **petrol station**. We'd better **pull in**. Come on, **slow down**. Now, what's French for '**fill up the tank**' and '**top up the battery**' and ... ?'

Brother got a **lift** half an hour ago – for five miles. He was dropped at the next **exit** off the motorway and is now trying his luck on a **minor road**. There's a **four-star hotel** on his left (**full board** £35 a night for a **single room**), a **guesthouse** on his right (£15 per person for **bed and breakfast**) and a long road ahead of him.

Granny's having her **packed dinner** and gazing at the silhouette of Canterbury Cathedral against the night sky. No matter. She can sleep on the **return journey** (**reclining seats** and **air-conditioning** on the coach), and tomorrow's another day. There's a **trip** to the local brewery; that sounds much better.

Uncle Mac is sitting on his cases in the **corridor** outside the **guard's van**, surrounded by a ring of miniature bottles of scotch.

Julia's plane has **landed**. Her boyfriend's wondering whether to try and save something from the bottles of **duty-free spirits** he's just dropped. Julia's more interested in the **connecting bus** that's supposed to take them to their final **destination**.

Uncle Bill is **on the bridge** with the **captain**, asking him if there's any chance of being **put ashore** before the sea gets any rougher.

'Well, it's about time we found a bed for the night, don't you think? You see that **motel** on the left? There! There, where I'm pointing! There, the one with the ... Hey, **pull up**! Pull up! Oh dear, **pull over**. I wonder what the French is for 'I'm sorry, we appear to have dented your bumper'.

Practice

1 Which form of transport – train, car, boat or plane – do you associate with each of the words and phrases below?

1 set sail	6 fast lane	11 quayside	16 charter flight
2 a cruise	7 to indicate	12 mid-air collision	17 to disembark
3 traffic jam	8 sundeck	13 departure lounge	18 express
4 compartment	9 commuter	14 buffet car	19 bypass
5 bonnet	10 take off	15 pull in	20 guard's van

2 Discuss or write the answers to these questions.

1 What, for you, are the pleasures and horrors of modern driving?
2 Look at the aspects of travel listed below. What are they like in your country? How are they different in any other country you have been to?
  a roads and **car-drivers**
  b airports
  c train services
  d hitch-hiking possibilities

3 What's the furthest you have travelled in one 24-hour period? Describe the journey.

4 Think of films or film sequences – **disaster** movies, **car chases**, **train adventures**, **sinking ships** – that involve travelling. Describe in detail the ones that impressed you most.

5 Write or act out a conversation in a car. A **driving instructor** is taking a **learner driver** out for their first lesson. The learner knows absolutely nothing about cars.

6 Write, in dialogue form, a conversation in which three friends argue about how they should travel to a distant city for a long weekend. One thinks it would be best to go by car, the second is for going by train, and the third would prefer to go by coach.

7 Write a circular letter to parents on the travel arrangements for a school's weekend excursion from London to the North of France, which you have organised.

8 Write a dramatic paragraph from your latest novel, as the hero tries desperately to get to the airport in time to catch his plane to Prague. It begins: *Jackson jumped into his waiting Porsche and ...*

■ Add here any other words or expressions that you meet on your travels.

. . . .

. . . .

. . . .

. . . .

. . . .

. . . .

. . . .

. . . .

Business, industry and agriculture

Study

See how many of the words and expressions highlighted below you can have ready for your future **economic** or **financial discussions**.

An A to Z of Economics: A Layman's Guide

A is for **automation**: bringing **widespread, full-scale unemployment** as the need for **manual labour** decreases.

B is for **balance of payments**: the discrepancy between the **amount of money** paid for **imports** and the amount of money received for **exports**.

C is for **cost of living index**: the system of measuring the **annual rate of inflation**. An **index-linked** pension scheme is not a bad thing to have on your side.

D is for **devaluation**: (The last resort? A panic measure?) an attempt, by reducing **the value of one's currency**, to increase the **volume of exports** compared to **imports**.

E is for **expansionist policy: reflationary, pumping money into the economy, boosting investment** and **employment**.

F is for **fiscal matters**: anything to do with the **Treasury**, particularly its **revenue**, especially through **taxation**.

G is for **GNP** or **gross national product**: the sum total of the money earned through a nation's **goods and services**.

H is for **health, hospitals, housing**: three **outlets for government expenditure** on **public services**. Other large items of **public expenditure** include **defence, roads and communications, industry and trade, environmental services** and **social security benefits**.

I is for **interest rates**: a weapon in the Government's armoury, used to **deflate, stimulate** or **stabilise the economy**.

J is for **jobs**: a key ball in the **economist's** juggling act. Are **full employment** and a **low inflation rate** mutually exclusive?
The **labour force** in Britain can be divided into three categories:
1 **primary industries (agriculture, fishing, mining, quarrying, forestry)**
2 **production industries (construction, gas, electricity, water, transport and manufacturing,** etc.)
3 **services (distributive trades, financial, business, professional and scientific, catering and tourism, national and local government).**

K is for **key industries**: those essential to the **economic welfare** of a nation, such as **oil** in **OPEC countries, precision engineering** in Germany, **grain** in Canada, **textiles** in South East Asia, **electronic goods** in Japan.

L is for **liquidity,**: **gold** and **foreign exchange reserves** are known as **international liquidity**, supervised to some extent by the **IMF (International Monetary Fund)**.

M is for **monetarism**: Professor Milton Friedman's brainchild, concentrating on the **control of money supply** to **conquer inflation**.

N is for **nationalised industries: state-owned corporations**, struggling in Britain to **break even** and **cover their costs**, often having to be **propped up** by the **Exchequer**. Though often **natural monopolies**, they sometimes **face competition** from the **private sector**. During the eighties, several nationalised industries in Britain were privatised.

O is for **output**: the **output per employee** multiplied by the number of employees gives a company or a nation's **productivity**. Britain's **low rate of increase** in this respect (often hardly any **growth**) used to be blamed on many things: poor **industrial relations**, the **Common Market (EEC)**, **world recession**, and, most of all, on old **capital equipment** that the too slowly **expanding workforce** had to use. There was some improvement in the eighties, however.

P is for **protectionism**: a **policy restricting free trade**, encouraging the **purchase** of **domestic products** by **imposing** some form of **import control** or **duty** (**tariffs**).

Q is for **import quotas**: **import restrictions**. This is one way to reduce the **deficit on current account**, and **regulating** the **volume of imports** allowed in.

R is for **pay restraint**: some kind of **incomes policy** attempting to **limit** the size of **wage increases** or, in a **wage freeze**, to stop them completely. Which is fairer: a **percentage increase across the board** or a **fixed sum** for everyone?

S is for the **Stock Exchange**: the source of most **long-term credit** in Britain, as it is the centre for the buying and selling of **stocks and shares**. Some of these are **fixed interest loans** with **dividends**, some are **gilt-edged securities**. This can be a risky way to save if there is a **stock market crash**.

T is for **taxation**: the Government's main means of **regulating its budget. Direct taxation** concerns people's **income**; **indirect taxes** are **levied** on **goods and services**.

U is for **underemployment**: the **overmanning** of a **plant**, the result of **restrictive labour practices** still common today. **Higher efficiency** means **fewer jobs**.

V is for **visible trade**, as opposed to **invisible trade. Visible exports** are **goods**; **invisible exports** are services which are the basis of an **international transaction**.

W is for: Why bother about X, Y and Z?

Practice 1

1 | *The Commercial See-saw*
Cover the column on the right. See if you can find the usual partner for each of the terms on the left.

buying	*selling*
export	import
supply	demand
revenue	expenditure
net	gross
profit	loss
in the red	in the black
borrowing	lending
credit	debit
wholesale	retail
stocks	shares
boom	slump, recession
the private sector	the public sector
stated-owned industry	private enterprise
management	workers, employees, staff
the boardroom	the shop floor
skilled labour	unskilled (or semi-skilled) labour
blue-collar workers	white-collar workers
take on new staff	lay off staff, make staff redundant

2 *A Businessman or Businesswoman's Day*

Note down the day-to-day business that is referred to in the diary below. You know he/she has to go to another meeting at 10.00. Rearrange his/her day, leaving one hour for lunch.

MON 24 OCT	
09.00	In-tray / Out-tray; Dictate correspondence Memo to staff re salary negotiations for 1990 Replies to Zurich re Consumer Association conference
10.00	Discuss finishing touches to next year's brochures with HJ from advertising agency
11.00	See Managing Director: check VAT figures with head of Accounts Department.
12.00	Meeting with Van Braun re Amsterdam deal. N.B Phone bank re delay on bridging loan for new plant transactions
13.00	Working lunch with Chief Buyer from Swan & Sons (J. White)(take catalogues, etc. and file)
14.00	
15.00	Conference with Marketing Division Executives (raise questions on expense accounts for Sept.) Telex Tokyo customers re latest order.
16.00	interview applicants for position of Personal Secretary – Miss Johnson, Ms Greer Issue Press Statement denying rumours of merger with J & J
17.00	Rocket for Smythe re disappointing sales figures – have ready latest balance sheets plus competitors' recent results: circular for all other sales reps.
18.00	Emergency Board Meeting on takeover bid by James & James – prepare agenda
19.30	Shareholders' annual cocktail party
20.00	

3 *A Farmer's Year*

Below are some of the jobs a British farmer has to do during the course of a year. Help him to plan his diary. Read the activities. Then look at the planning chart on the next page. Write beside each season the months of the year that apply in your country. Then match each activity with a season, or even a month if you can.

To be done this year

grape-picking	peak season for **milking**	**mating** of sheep and rams
reseeding	**rearing** of calves	lambs to **slaughter**
calving	**lambing**	**ploughing**
replanting	**feeding**	**sowing**
wood-collecting	**sheep-shearing**	**crop-spraying**
pruning, cutting back	and **dipping**	**fattening-up** of calves
bringing the sheep in	**silage-making**	**insemination** of cattle

putting cattle out for
    grazing
	harvesting, gathering in
	    the **crop**s, **reaping**
		haymaking

Season	Month	Activity
Spring		
Summer		
Autumn		
Winter		

Practice

1 Discuss or write the answers to these questions.
   1 What are the key industries in your country? Are they declining or growing?
   2 What are some of the good and bad aspects of **advertising:** on the screen, on paper and in the street?
   3 How do you imagine (or know) **farming methods** have changed over the past twenty-five years. How may they change in the next twenty-five years?

2 You are an **investment expert**. Write or act out a conversation in which you give a client advice on how he or she might invest £70,000 **redundancy money**.

3 Write a day's diary for either a bank manager or a farmer.

4 Write a letter to your MP, attacking the government's handling of either the current or a recent **economic crisis**.

5 An expert economist is giving a talk in your town this evening. Write down five questions you will want to ask him: five things you have never really understood about economics.

■ Add here any further expressions about business and employment you may meet.

. . . .

. . . .

. . . .

. . . .

. . . .

. . . .

. . . .

. . . .

Law and order, crime and punishment

Study and practice

Below you see the story of an extraordinary **case** in British **legal** history. The affair started in 1949 and was finally closed in 1966.
At the moment, there are a number of gaps in the story. Use the words below to complete it.

trial	confessed	court	custody	guilty
convicted	enquiry (x 2)	sentenced	jury	execution
arrested	innocent	charged	appeal	dropped
pardon	judges	plea	apprehended	hunt
suspect	tried	executed	statements	denied

The story began when a man called Timothy Evans was ... for the murder of his wife and baby. He was ... with the double murder, but a short time later one of the charges was ... and he was ... for the murder of his daughter only. During the ... Evans accused the man whose house he had been living in, John Christie, of the crimes, but no attention was paid to him. The ... found Evans ... and he was ... to death. An ... was turned down and and he was ... in 1950.
Some time later, more women's bodies were discovered in Christie's house: two, three, four, five, six. John Christie was the police's chief ... and they started a nationwide ... for him. He was soon ... . Alleged ... by Christie while he was in ... cast doubt on the Evans hanging. When he went to ... , Christie ... that he had murdered Mrs Evans, but in private it was said that he ... to that crime. His ... of insanity with regard to other murders was rejected and he was ... of killing his wife.
Soon afterwards there was an ... into the ... of Timothy Evans. The ... decided that justice had been done and Evans had been rightly hanged. It was only in 1966 that another ... was set up. This time it was decided that Evans had probably been ... and he was given a free ... . Better late than never, as they say.

Quiz

Now a quiz on some **points of law** – English style. The answers may well be different in your country. Simply answer the questions *Yes* or *No*. The answers according to English law are printed at the end of the quiz.

1 Is it a **crime** to try and kill yourself?
2 Is it **illegal** to help somebody to **commit suicide**?
3 Can you be **executed** for **murdering** a policeman?
4 If, after a murder, all the **victim**'s relatives plead: 'Please don't **prosecute**!' can **charges** against the **suspected culprit** be **dropped**?
5 If two **armed thieves break into** a house, guns in hand, and one of them shoots and kills the house-owner, is his **accomplice guilty of murder**?
6 If I surprise an **intruder** in my lounge at night stealing my millions, have I a **legal right** to **assault** him with a **weapon**?
7 If I **set a trap** – a fifty-kilo weight just above the front door – for any **burglars** who might try and enter the house, am I **breaking the law**?
8 After a **divorce** or **legal separation**, can a wife be required to pay **alimony** to her ex-husband?

9 If I promise to marry my girlfriend and then change my mind shortly before the wedding, can she **take** me to **court**?

10 If you said to your teacher in the middle of one of his lessons: 'You don't know the first thing about teaching!' could he **bring a civil action** against you?

11 Would I be in danger of **committing an offence** if I put an advertisement for my school in the paper saying: 'Male white teacher required'?

12 If, as a **defendant** (or **the accused**), I am not satisfied with the way my **barrister** has **handled my defence**, can I **sue** him?

13 If you were in my house – uninvited – and the ceiling, which had had a large crack in it for some time, caved in and broke your leg, would it be a good idea to **consult your solicitor**?

14 Can a person **suspected of** and **charged with rape** be allowed **bail**?

Answers

1 No, not any more.
2 Yes, even **mercy-killing** (**euthanasia**) is **against the law**.
3 No. **Capital punishment** was **abolished** in the 1960s.
4 No. Murder is a **crime against society** (this involves **criminal law**) and not just a **civil matter** between individuals.
5 Yes. **Joint guilt. In the eyes of the la**w, both are guilty.
6 No – at least, only in **self-defence**.
7 Yes.
8 Yes.
9 No, not now. Some years ago she could have **sued** me for **breach of promise**.
10 Yes, he could claim it was **slander** (or **libel**, if you wrote it in a newspaper). He probably wouldn't, though, because of the **legal costs**.
11 Yes, because of the **Sex Discrimination Act** and the **Race Relations Act**.
12 No.
13 Yes. You could sue me for **negligence** and I would probably have to **pay damages**.
14 Yes.

Practice 1

1 There are many **crimes** and **offences** apart from the few mentioned above. Explain, define or give examples of the offences listed below.

blackmail	driving without due care and attention
kidnapping	mugging – robbery with violence
arson	drug peddling
trespassing	espionage – spying
manslaughter	shoplifting
smuggling	treason
forgery	hijacking
bigamy	obscenity
baby- or wife-battering	bribery and corruption
conspiracy	petty theft
fraud	

Which of the above would or could involve the following?

1 counterfeit money 4 a ransom 7 state secrets
2 pornography 5 heroin 8 contraband
3 hostages 6 a traitor 9 a store detective

2 Here is the story of a very unfortunate, irresponsible man called Mr N.E. Body. Imagine that he was stopped by the police at each and every point of the drama. Read about what happened and, after each piece of information you receive, decide what **punishment** he deserves.
Here are some of the sentences you might wish to hand out:

You might feel the **death penalty** is in order, or **life imprisonment**, even **solitary confinement**. You could put him **on probation**, give him **community service** or **impose a fine** – anything from £10 to £1,000. You might consider **corporal punishment** (a short, sharp shock), a shortish **prison sentence** or, of course, you could make that a **suspended sentence**. You might make him pay **compensation**, or would you like to see him **banned from driving**? No? Well, his **licence** could be **endorsed**. Or would you **dismiss the case**, **find him not guilty** of any crime, **acquit** him, find the case **not proved**?

1 Mr Body drank five pints of beer and five single whiskies in a pub, got into his car and drove away.
2 He did not drive dangerously but **exceeded the speed limit** as he wanted to catch up with a friend who had left his wallet in the pub.
3 As he was driving along, a little girl ran into the road and he knocked her down.
4 There was no way he could have stopped, drunk or sober.
5 The little girl suffered only bruises and superficial injuries.
6 Mr Body's wife had left him two days before.
7 Six months later, it was clear that the little girl was to suffer from after-effects of the accident and would stutter for many years.
8 Mr Body had never previously received any **summons** for **traffic offences**.
9 The little girl admitted that it was all her fault.
10 The passenger in Mr Body's car was killed outright as he went through the windscreen.

3 Write or discuss the answers to these questions.
1 Which aspects of the law seem unsatisfactory to you?
2 What punishments would you, as a judge, give for the crimes in Practice 1? You may need to specify cases and give particular instances.
3 How have criminals been portayed in films you have seen recently? Were the criminals portrayed as heroes, idiots or evil individuals?
4 What – in detail – would happen to you in your country if you were caught:
   a **speeding** in your car?
   b **in possession of soft drugs**?
   c with a **gun** in your pocket?
   d **breaking into a house**?

4 Write a **judge's summing up** after a trial, reminding the **jury** of the **witnesses' testimony** and advising them on how to **reach their verdict**.

5 You have just read an article supporting corporal punishment with the headline 'A short, sharp shock is the only answer for most of today's criminals'. Write to the newspaper, putting the opposite view and criticising what was probably in the article.

■ Add here any other words or expressions about crime, punishment and the law that you may meet.

. . . .
. . . .
. . . .
. . . .

Quality

This unit is in the form of six passages, each of which deals with the **good**, the **bad** and the **ugly**; **complimentary** and **uncomplimentary** words, from the **unbelievably beautiful** to the **indescribably horrible**. Over 150 adjectives are included, so don't read all of them at once.

Reading 1

1 First, notice the contrasts in these excerpts from a letter.

Dear Helpful Hatti,
I am writing to you about my sister and all the problems I – .
She has got **exquisite** features – a **classic** profile – a **scintillating** smile – a
stunning figure – an **attractive** personality – and a **marvellous** sense of humour.
I have got a very **plain** face – very **ordinary** feature – (according to my friends)
a **rather ugly** smile – a **nondescript** figure – a **shallow** and **unappealing**
character – and a **coarse** sense of humour. What should I do?
She is a **sparkling** conversationalist – a **fabulous** dancer – a **graceful** mover –
super-efficient at her job – a **talented** sportswoman – and a **gifted** musician.
I am a very **dull** conversationalist – a **clumsy** dancer – an **awkward** mover – an
incompetent fool in the office – **useless** at sport – and **hopeless** at all musical
instruments. What advice would you give me?
She is always **well-dressed, smart, elegant** – extremely **ladylike** – very **refined** –
exceptionally **well-mannered** – and invariably **polite** to everyone.
I always look **shabby** and **scruffy** – **I tend to be rough** – **common** – **vulgar** – and
rude. What can I do about it?
She is very **cultured** – **well-educated** – well-read.
I was always **backward** at school – **semi-literate** – and am now very **ignorant**.
She is **bright** – **intelligent** – **witty** – and **clever**.
I am **slow** – **dim** – 'daft', my mother says – 'thick', says my father. Please help me.
I look forward to hearing from you.

2 Now read excerpts from two reviews of the same film.

– an **absorbing** film – a **fascinating** insight into – a **well thought-out** plot –
brilliant acting – **superb** photography – **delicate** direction by – many **dazzling**
moments – a **powerful** climax – **thoroughly enjoyable** – **totally satisfying** – a
memorable film.
– an **exceptionally tedious** film – an **excessively slow** and **boring** look at life in –
a **chaotic** story-line – **exceedingly poor** performance by – **awful, amateurish**
camerawork – under the **heavy-handed** direction of – **embarrassingly weak**
script – **horribly unnatural** dialogue – an **anti-climax** – an ending that was
ludicrous – **absurd** – **laughable** – **ridiculous** – **totally nonsensical** –
dreadfully disappointing – a **waste of time** – **absolutely worthless** – pointless
– **stupid**.

3 What do you think these two people are disagreeing about on this and the next page?

A '– a **spectacular** occasion
– **exciting** movements –
sensational colour –
thrilling speed – a **gripping**
climax – **tremendous** fun –

B '– a **senseless** 'sport'
– **mindless** violence – **brutal**
– **primitive** – **savage** and
degrading – **inhuman** –
a **disgraceful** exhibition –

an **enthralling** spectacle –
a **rewarding** experience!'

a **scandalous** abuse of innocent
animals – **revolting**!'

Practice 1

Choose the most suitable of the four given words to complete each of the sentences
below.

1 He's not only tedious, he's also ...
   a boring **b** incompetent **c** super-efficient **d** brilliant
2 Despite its director's high reputation, the film was ...
   a extraordinary **b** gripping **c** embarrassing **d** powerful
3 Can't always be elegant; sometimes I enjoy wearing ... clothes.
   a scintillating **b** scruffy **c** shallow **d** rude
4 Finally at the end, things hotted up; the ending was really ... .
   a gripping **b** delicate **c** chaotic **d** ludicrous
5 Not all film stars are beautiful; some are quite ... .
   a exquisite **b** stunning **c** vulgar **d** plain
6 We need someone well-educated and ... .
   a illiterate **b** dim **c** coarse **d** well-read
7 He's an extremely ... pianist.
   a graceful **b** gifted **c** exceptional **d** refined
8 It wasn't exactly exciting, but it was certainly ... .
   a enthralling **b** absorbing **c** thrilling **d** gripping

Reading 2

1 Read these two opinions of the same holiday resort.

Excerpts from the tour operator's brochure:
Come to sunny Sandshire ... **magnificent** views ... **unforgettable** scenery ... a
splendid cathedral, well worth visiting ... and many other **impressive** buildings ...
quaint little villages ... **picturesque** harbours ... **enchanting** bays ... **gorgeous**
beaches ... **pleasant** climate ... **colourful** night-life ... **stimulating** atmosphere ...
delightful for a holiday ... **ideal** for all the family ...

What George Grumbleweed had to say:
Well, the whole area's **rather drab** and **unwelcoming** ... the cathedral is **a
monstrosity, absolutely hideous** ... most of the other buildings are **pretty
grotesque**, too ... the villages are all **colourless** and **characterless** ... at night
they're **completely dead** ... by the sea it's **really ghastly** ... the water's **filthy** and
there's a **frightful** smell ... the coastline's very **bleak** ... it's a **horrible** place ...
totally unsuitable for holidays ...

2 And now two post cards from the same resort:

Dear Mum,
Hotel first class! Rooms luxurious, sumptuous! Food very tasty, delicious and ample! Service first-rate, outstanding. Organization excellent. Excursions absolutely breathtaking. Whole holiday out of this world, a dream! Wish you were here.
Love, Mervyn & Shirley

Dear Mum,
Hotel sub-standard. Rooms disgusting, inadequate hygiene defective plumbing. Food tasteless, often inedible, always insufficient. Service lamentable, third-rate. Organization shocking, unspeakably bad. Excursions ghastly. Whole holiday abysmal, a nightmare. Glad you aren't here.
Charles and Diana

Mrs. M.
21, Rosa
Old Wo
Oxfor
England

Mrs. E. Wi
21 Bucki
London w
ENGLANl

3 And, lastly, a musical disagreement:

A What a **lovely** song!
B Do you think so?
A Don't you think it's **beautiful**?
B I think it's **terrible**.
A Very **catchy**.
B **Monotonous**.
A **Tuneful**.
B **Repetitive**.
A **Original**.
B **Corny**.
A **Effective**
B **Idiotic**.
A Quite **moving**.
B **Rubbish**.
A I've heard worse.
B Have you? Poor you.

Practice 2

1 Act out or write a conversation in each of the situations below.

1 You are with a friend, on your way home from a cabaret that you have both enjoyed enormously.
2 You are with a friend, on your way home from a terribly boring conference that you have had to sit through for the past eight hours.
3 You have just seen a film which you thought was great and your friend hated.
4 You have just seen a TV programme that you thought was disgusting. You phone the BBC and speak to the Complaints Manager.

2 Think of a view that you used to love but now find really unattractive. Describe how what you can see has changed.

3 Write a description for one of your short stories of the most unpleasant person any of us are likely to have the misfortune to meet.

4 Write, in dialogue form, a conversation in which two people disagree about the merits of some paintings as they walk together around an art gallery.

■ Add here any other words or expressions about quality that you may meet.

. . . .
. . . .
. . . .
. . . .
. . . .
. . . .
. . . .
. . . .
. . . .
. . . .

Time

Reading

Let your eye run over the following lists over the next day or so, to remind you of a range of time expressions.

Life was hard

in prehistoric times
in olden times
back in the fifth Century
in the dim and distant past
before the Industrial Revolution
at the turn of the century
in those days
a few generations ago
between the wars
in the late forties
when I was little
in the early sixties
from 1960 **to** 1965
when I was **in my teens**
between 1965 **and** 1970
in the mid-eighties
this time last year
until this year.

Life has been hard

for as long as anyone can remember
ever since the war ended
over the past twenty years
from the late sixties **until** now
for the past few years
during the last couple of months
lately.

Life is hard

nowadays
these days
at present
as things stand
at the present time
at this moment in time
at this point in history.

Life is going to continue to be hard

from now on
for the next few months
during the next few years
over the next decade
until the present situation changes
for the foreseeable future
for the time being.

But things are bound to improve
> **in the coming years**
> **before long**
> **as time goes on**
> **sooner or later**
> **in years to come**
> **within the next** twenty years
> **in the 1990s.**

And life will be much better
> **one day**
> **this time next year**
> **when we're old and grey**
> **in another twenty years' time**
> **decades from now**
> **by the time** our children grow up
> **by the end of** this century
> **when we're all dead and gone**
> **in the far-distant future**
> **sometime in** the twenty-fifth century
> **light years from now.**

Reading

Now follow the adventures of a very busy lady.

Albert proposed to me	**ages and ages ago**.
Bernard asked me	**a long, long time ago**.
Colin did	**once, many** years **ago**.
David did his best	**a few** years **back**.
Edwin, too	**not so long ago**.
Freddy tried	**in the spring of** '82.
I think George did	**the year before last**.
I seem to remember Harry did	**at the end of** January.
Ian did it with roses	**a short time ago**.
Jock did it with chocolates	**a** month **or so ago**.
Kevin did it by letter	**one day quite recently**.
Larry sent a telegram	**a little while ago**.
Martin mentioned something about it	**the other day**.
Nevil thought we 'might make a go of it'	**about a** fortnight **ago**.
Oliver thought 'we'd make a good couple'	**the** Friday **before last**
	(or was it **the previous** Friday).
Peter did it on his knees	**one** afternoon **last week**.
Robert referred to the possibility	**earlier** today.
Sam has asked me	**within the last few** hours.
Thomas left a note on my desk	an hour **or so ago**.
Ulysses came out with it	**a couple of** minutes **ago**.
Valentine shouted through the window	**just now**.
William brought the subject up on the phone	**just a** moment **ago**.
And Zac popped the question	**a split-second ago**.
I'm thinking it all over	**now**.
I haven't got an answer	**at the moment**.
Zac obviously wants an answer	**here and now**.
He's standing in front of me	**at this very moment**.
I really can't give anyone an answer	**this minute**.
I know Zac's going to ask me again	**any moment now**.
And William's going to shout down the phone	**at any moment**.
I think I might give Valentine a shout	**in a** second **or two**.
I'll have to face Ulysses	**in a couple of** minutes.
I'm afraid Thomas will be back for a decision	**in** an hour**'s time**.

Sam will want an answer	**within the next few** hours.
I might phone Robert	**later** today.
I really must contact Peter	**one evening next** week.
I've promised to give Oliver an answer	**next** Friday
	(or was it **the following** Friday?)
	(or was it **the** Friday **after that?**)
I'll leave a message on Nevil's answer-phone	**the** week **after next**.
To Larry I'll send a telegram	**a fortnight tomorrow**.
I'll get in touch with Martin,	**but not in the immediate future**.
I'll have to reply to Kevin's letter	**some day soon**.
I'll inform Jack	**before too long**.
And I'll let Ian know	**one of these** days.
I'd better check whether Harry really did	**sometime**.
George will have to be told	**in the not too distant future**.
Freddy said he'd want an answer	**next** autumn.
I'll get round to telling Edwin	**but Heaven knows when**.
David can be told	**the** Christmas **after next**.
I'll probably drop Colin a line	**in a** year **or two**.
Eventually I'll have to say no to Bertie,	**but not for** ages yet.
And Albert? I might say yes to Albert,	**if I ever see him again**.

Brain teaser

Here's a little problem for you to solve. The answer is at the end of the book.

I always **set** my alarm-clock ten minutes **fast** – so that I have more time than I think in the mornings.
I keep my **grandfather clock** in the lounge, **set at the correct time – to the second**.
I set my **non-digital watch** fifteen minutes **slow** – so that I'm pleasantly surprised when it's time to finish work.
My alarm-clock **gains** fifteen minutes every twenty-four hours.
The grandfather clock **keeps perfect time**.
My watch **loses** fifteen minutes every day.
I set all three **timepieces** at midnight, by the BBC radio news, and **wind them up**.
At what time of day or night do all three **show the same time**?

Reading

Finally, have a look at this traditional rhyme and the text on the **time of day** and the **time of year**.

Thirty days has **September**,
April, June and **November**.
All the rest have thirty-one,
Excepting **February** alone
Which has twenty-eight days clear
And twenty-nine in each **leap year**.

The Ideal Day?
It would depend, of course, on the **season**. Endless days in **late summer**, in scorching **July** and baking **August**, cannot be compared with those short days in **mid-winter**, in frosty **January** and foggy **December**, in those weeks leading up to **Christmas**. Though the temperature in **autumn**, say **early October** when the **days are closing in**, may be similar to that in the middle of **March** and the rest of **spring**, their character is completely different. Now if you asked about **May**, well, ... I would get up well **before dawn**. **Daybreak**, just **before and after sunrise**, is a much-neglected **part of the day**. **By first light**, I would want to be on the terrace taking my first sip of coffee and second bite of toast. Everything is so peaceful **in the**

early morning, long before the horrors of the **rush-hour**. Newspapers at **breakfast-time**, then I would go inside and play the piano **for an hour or so. At about nine** I would take to my study and continue with the next chapter of my memoirs, taking a **mid-morning break** for 'elevenses'. **At half-past eleven sharp**, I would stroll down to the village pub for my first drink of the day and then follow that, **at about midday**, with cocktails at a club in the company of friends. That would bring me up to **lunchtime**.

After a modest luncheon and **during the hottest part of the day**, I would take a walk in the forest, then possibly go for a drive. **By mid-afternoon** I would no doubt be feeling rather tired, so **around teatime** I would go back to bed for **a couple of hours**. I would come down again **in time** to watch The News **at a quarter to six**, then in the early evening – with some **time on my hands** until **sundown** – I might play records and read. At dusk, to catch the colours of **the twilight hours**, I would go outside and paint.

At nightfall, I would go inside to eat. (If I had some **spare time beforehand**, I would have a swim in my indoor heated swimming pool.) **After dinner, towards ten o'clock**, I would go out to meet friends at a discotheque then, **at closing time –** or before, **around midnight** anyway – join a party going down to the beach. After a(nother) swim and a few glasses of wine, I would be driven home to bed **in the early hours**.

How about you? What would your day be like?

Practice

1. What – in full – is your answer to the question above: what would your ideal day be like?

2. How have your attitudes to the following changed over the past ten years?

   a work
   b relationships
   c family
   d happiness
   e the future
   f growing old

3. Choose five major inventions or events of the twentieth century. How has life been different since they were invented?

4. Write or act out three conversations with a friend in which you are telling him or her about three of the situations below:

   1 how an acquaintance of yours became more and more dependent on drugs.
   2 how a relationship of yours grew and grew and then went sour.
   3 how a car of yours went from being your pride and joy to a heap of useless metal.
   4 how your children went from being babies to secondary school pupils.
   5 how you went from beginner level to advanced in English.
   6 your ambition to reach the top in the company you've just started working for.

5. Write a passage from your political speech, in which you describe the state of the nation eight years ago, the events of the past eight years, the situation now and prospects for the future.

6 Write a paragraph from your latest novel, in which the heroine remembers autumn and looks forward to the spring. She's probably sitting looking out of the window, isn't she?

■ Add here any other words about time that you may meet.

....
....
....
....
....
....
....
....
....
....
....
....
....

Numerals and proportions

Reading

Read the dialogue below, paying attention to the words and expressions that refer to part, but not all, of something.

A Well, how did the meeting go?

B The meeting?

A Yes, the voting meeting.

B Oh, that meeting!

A Mm. **Full attendance**, was there?

B Yes, there was. **100 per cent turnout** and **not one empty seat.**

A Good. **What proportion** of them voted for me? **All of them**?

B No.

A Oh, **a few** went over to the other side, did they? Yes, you always get these **little splinter groups**, **exceptions to the rule**, people who want to be different from the masses. Still, an **overwhelming majority** for me, I suppose?

B Not really, no.

A Oh dear. Still, no doubt I got **the bulk of** the votes. What did they call the majority? **Large**?

B No.

A **Substantial**?

B No.

A It was closer than I expected. Only a **small majority** for me, then?

B Actually, no.

A Good Heavens! **Half and half**, was it? **Equally divided**? **Equal shares** of the votes? **50 – 50 split**? Incredible!

B No.

A You mean I didn't get elected? That's amazing! Oh well, I suppose I got a **very large minority**? A **reasonable percentage** of the votes?

B Not exactly that, no.

A Only a **small number**, eh? A **small** but loyal **section**. A **fraction of** the total but a **significant** fraction. It's a **partial success**, isn't it?

B They were **in complete agreement**.

A Complete agreement?

B They were **unanimous**.

A The **entire group**?

B **Every single one**.

A The **total population** of the school?

B **Each and every one**.

A But I got **the odd one or two** votes, surely?

B No.

A A **fair number of** abstentions, though. **Several** protest votes registered.

B **Not one**.

A **None**?

B **Zero**.

A You mean **nobody** ... ?

B **No-one**.

A **Not anybody**?

B **Not a soul**.

A Funny. I thought **everybody** liked me.

Practice

1. Which word or phrase is missing in each of the sequences below? Complete and continue each sequence.

    1 **one** **two** **three** **four** **five** **six** **seven** **nine** **ten**
    2 **first** **second** **third** **fourth** **sixth**
    3 **once** **three times** **four times** **five times**
    4 **one** a **half** a **third** a **fifth**
    5 **solo** **trio** **quartet** **quintet**
    6 a **baby** **twins** **quad(ruplet)s** **quin(tuplet)s**
    7 think of **a number** **double** it **quadruple** it
    8 a **double** whisky a **triple** (or **treble**) whisky

2. Now see how quickly you can find the answer to this rather long sum. The answer is at the back of the book.

    Four **add** two, **divide by** three, **subtract** one, **multiply by** eight, **take away** four, **times** three, **plus** two, **minus** four, **halved, equals** what?

3. Of all these numbers, 0 presents the most linguistic problems.
    Try to read out loud the following expressions including various words for the figure 0. Then work out the answer to questions 9 and 10. Look up the answers in the answer Key if you find this exercise difficult.

    1 Manchester City **0**, Manchester United **0**
    2 5, 4, 3, 2, 1, **0**!
    3 **0.1%** of the air
    4 Tel. **01 906 3002**
    5 H^2O
    6 $4 + 2 - 6 = 0$
    7 $6 - 0, 6 - 1, 6 - 0$
    8 the temperature is below **0°**
    9 What's left from £40 if you deduct four amounts of £5 and five sums of £4?
    10 How many fingers have you got on your feet?

4. Now think about the number 2. Read the text. How much of the language would change if Daniel found himself a third girlfriend?

    Well, take my friend, Daniel. He has **two** girlfriends. He likes **both** of them and they **both** like him. He plays tennis – mixed **doubles** – with **one of them**, and goes **pairs**-skating with **the other one**. They look very much like **each other**; **the one** could be **the other's double**. Obviously, he can't marry **both** of them but he could, he thinks, be happy with **either** of them. Unfortunately, **neither** of them knows about the other girl in his life. So far he hasn't proposed to **either** of them. I don't think he wants to be part of a married **couple** yet, anyway. Almost as a protest, he hasn't even got a matching **pair** of socks.

5. For further practice of expressions describing numbers, give an example of each item below.

    1 an **odd number**   5 an **even number**
    2 a **three-figure sum**   6 a **fraction**
    3 three **consecutive** numbers   7 a number with 5 **digits** after the **decimal point**
    4 a **multiple** of 49   8 an **equation**

6 There are several prefixes which indicate number in English. Try to find a word in the right-hand column which matches each definition **1 – 21**.

1 being able to speak two languages very well	**unification**
2 a period of **ten years**	**monologue**
3 a creature with about **a hundred legs**	**soliloquy**
4 a child's **three-wheeled** vehicle	**binary**
5 half **a pair of glasses**	**biannual**
6 to copy a document	**octet**
7 **one thousand** watts	**dioxide**
8 **a tenth** of a centimetre	**duodecimal**
9 the process of making a country completely one	**unilateral**
10 describing a decision that had 100% support	**unanimous**
11 a very large number of people as a crowd	**polygamy**
12 the state of having rather a lot of husbands or wives at once	**dual carriageway**
13 a system in which the only digits used are 1 and 0	**tricycle**
14 describing a system like: 12 inches in 1 foot	**millimetre**
15 the 0^2 in CO^2	**kilowatt**
16 a road consisting of two parts with traffic going in one direction only	**multitude**
17 **half-yearly**	**monocle**
18 a group of eight musicians	**duplicate**
19 **one-sided**, the sort of nuclear disarmament that pacifists would be happy with	**bilingual**
20 a longish passage spoken by one person	**decade**
21 a more romantic speech	**centipede**

7 There has been a survey of 300 people of both sexes and all ages in your town, in which they were asked the following questions. How do you think they responded? Remember how many ways you know of expressing proportions! If you are working in a group, then conduct a survey of your own and report your findings back to the group.

a What do you usually do in the evenings?
b What would you do with £100,000?
c Who is your favourite show business personality?
d Do you like Shakespeare?
e Which country would you emigrate to if you had to leave this one?
f Do you wish you had been born the other sex?

8 Have numbers any special associations for you? Have you got a lucky one? An unlucky one? What are some of the beliefs and superstitions about numbers in your country? Write a short paragraph answering these questions.

■ Add here any other words or expressions about numbers that you may come across.

. . . .

. . . .

. . . .

. . . .

. . . .

Rise and fall

Reading

Notice all the nouns here describing **change** in **quantity** and **quality**. When you have read the text, try to make similar comments about education in your country using the verbs given on the next page. Some of these verbs will be happy to operate intransitively; some will prefer a passive construction.

Twenty Years of British Education

We have seen:
a **dramatic increase** in the number of **comprehensive schools**
    a **steady decrease** in the number of **privately-owned secondary schools**
a **constant rise** in the number of **university students**
    a **sharp fall** in the number of **foreign students at universities**
a **general improvement** in **teaching standards**
    a **deterioration** in **pupil-teacher relationships**
the **growth** of **pupil-power**
    a **decline** in **discipline**
the **strengthening** of **parent-teacher organisations**
    the **weakening** of **teachers' authority**
a **tightening up** on **hygiene** and **safety regulations**
    a **relaxation** in terms of pupils' and teachers' dress
the **raising** of **minimum standards** and **qualifications** for **prospective careers**
    the **lowering** of the **school starting age**
the **build-up** of **technical and scientific departments**
    the **running-down** of **history and geography departments**
the **expansion** of **sociology faculties**
    the **contraction** of **modern language facilities**
the **extension** of **day-release schemes** from factories and offices
    the **shrinking** of **Classics departments**
a **widening of the gap** between **Further Education** and **Higher Education**
    a **narrowing of the gap** between **polytechnic colleges** and **universities**
the **introduction** of **Sixth Form Colleges**
    the **phasing out** of the eleven-plus **examination**
the **establishment** of **post-school opportunities schemes**
    a **reduction** in the number of **post-school jobs**
the **enlargement** of **physical education equipment and facilities**
    cuts in **amenities** like **free milk** and **school dinners**
marked progress in the development of **specialised skills**
    a **drop** in **ability level** relating to **traditional skills**
the **opening** of many new **nursery schools**
    the **closure** of numerous **primary** and **preparatory schools**
a **broadening** of pupils' **political awareness**
    a **lessening** of **interest in the arts**
an **upward trend** in terms of **physics, chemistry, biology** and **engineering**
    a **downward trend** in terms of **religious instruction** and **literature**
    and **countless changes – for the better and for the worse** – in terms of
    examinations, mathematics subjects – arithmetic, algebra, geometry etc. –
    degree courses, remedial studies for **slow learners, streaming, corporal
    punishment, correspondence courses, adult education**.

Verbs

> **increase   decrease**
> **rise   fall   improve   drop**
> **deteriorate   grow   relax   raise**
> **expand   contract   decline   strengthen**
> **weaken   tighten up   lower   build up   run down**
> **extend   widen   narrow   introduce   establish   close**
> **open   phase out   reduce   enlarge   cut   shrink   progress**
> **broaden   lessen   change**

Practice

1 Discuss or write the answers to these questions.

1 What do you feel were / have been the good and bad aspects of your own education?
2 What changes have you seen / did you see while at school yourself?
3 What significant changes have there been over the past twenty years in these areas

a work and jobs?
b love and marriage?
c transport and communications?
d entertainment?
e crime?

2 Write an elderly person's letter to a newspaper regretting the drop in moral standards he or she has witnessed in his or her lifetime.

■ Add here any other similar words that you may meet.

....
....
....
....
....
....
....
....
....
....
....
....
....
....

Normality and regularity

Game

Answer this questionnaire to see how young (or old) at heart you are. And note the expressions it contains relating to **frequency / infrequency**, **normality / abnormality.**
Cover the column on the right. Choose one answer to each question.

Are you middle-aged?

1 **How often** do you worry about money?
   a **daily, hourly** or **constantly**   3
   b **from time to time, once in a while**   2
   c **seldom** or **never**   1
2 Do you **tend to**
   a write short notes to friends?   2
   b write **exceptionally** long letters?   1
   c forget to write?   3
3 **How frequently** do you find yourself saying: 'They don't write songs like they used to'?
   a **every now and then**   2
   b **regularly**   3
   c **never**   1
4 Are you **inclined to** think that teenagers having green, orange or purple hair is
   a **perfectly normal**, nothing **out of the ordinary**?   1
   b **inexplicable, beyond belief, really weird**?   3
   c **slightly odd, a bit peculiar, rather strange**?   2
5 How often does it cross your mind that thirteen- and fourteen-year-olds should have the right to vote?
   a **occasionally**, but **generally** not for long   2
   b **hardly ever**   3
   c **repeatedly**, and **usually** for long periods   1
6 Are you **apt to** give dinner parties?
   a **once in a blue moon**   1
   b **on special occasions**   2
   c **as a regular habit, normally** on Fridays
     and Saturdays   3
7 **How regularly** do you watch the mid-evening News on TV?
   a **without fail**   3
   b **more often than not**   2
   c **rarely**   1
8 **How common** is it for you to ask your partner if she/he can see any 'new' grey hairs on your head?
   a **unheard of**   1
   b **not that common**   2
   c **a daily event** that's taken for granted   3

Now count up the numbers (on the right) that you scored. What's your total? Read the next page to see what your score tells you.

If you scored:

10 or under:	You have no worries; you're young, still a baby.
11 to 16:	You're pretty reasonable about the whole thing but you show **occasional** slight signs of ageing before your time.
17 to 22:	An average score, but you really ought to stop worrying. Enjoy yourself while you can.
23 or over:	You're showing the standard symptoms of middle-age; whether you're four, fourteen or twenty-four, you certainly think like a forty-year old. Oh dear!

Practice

1. Note down or tell a partner about ways in which you consider yourself to be:
   a average and normal.
   b unusual and rather eccentric.

2. Discuss with a partner or in writing whether it is boring to be normal.

3. Find out from your partners whether you are significantly different concerning the frequency with which you do each of the following.
   1 visit your dentist
   2 see your parents
   3 get very depressed
   4 go to the bank
   5 feel ashamed of yourself
   6 cry

4. Write a questionnaire similar to the one in this unit to focus on one of the following topics.
   1 whether the reader loves their partner or not
   2 whether the reader will be rich one day
   3 whether the reader is a good person to have as a friend or not

■ Add here any other words about the normal or the abnormal that you may meet.

. . . .

. . . .

. . . .

. . . .

. . . .

. . . .

. . . .

. . . .

. . . .

. . . .

. . . .

. . . .

Probability, necessity and free will

Reading

1 Notice the numerous variations on **must** and **needn't** in the following scene. Guess what they are talking about.

Mother	We're not going to **force** you, Luigi.
Father	Nobody's going to **compel** you to do it. Are we boys?
All	No. No. Of course not. No way.
Brother	No-one's going to **make** you do anything you don't want to.
Other Brother	Right. You tell him, dad.
Cousin	You **make up your own mind**.
Uncle	**The choice is yours**.
Other Uncle	**It's your decision**.
Mother	**It's up to you**.
All	Right.
Brother	You **don't have to** do it **if you'd rather not**.
Other Brother	**There's no need to** do it **if you'd prefer not to**.
Father	You're **under no obligation** at all.
Other Uncle	**It's a free country**.
Uncle	A man's **allowed to** change his mind, isn't he?
Brother	Sure. Breach of promise is not **prohibited by law** any more, is it?
Father	Oh no, not **forbidden by law**. On no.
Mother	No, **the law can't stop you** doing **whatever you like**.
Other Brother	That's right. The law **permits** you to **do as you see fit** ...
Cousin	To do what you feel your **duty** is ...
Uncle	As your **conscience** dictates.
Mother	So you **please yourself**.
Uncle	After all, you've got an **option**.
Father	You've got a **clear alternative**.
Luigi	I have?
All	Why yes. Sure. Of course. You bet you have.
Luigi	And if I don't?
Grandfather	We'll kill you.

2 This is the way job advertisements used to look.

PACKERS / SORTERS / SHELF-FILLERS **WANTED**
Owing to a **shortage of staff** in our Liverpool branch
following recent mergers, we are **looking for**:
10 packers
15 shelf-fillers
20 sorters
Previous experience **desirable**, but **not necessary**.
Lack of qualifications **not necessarily a disadvantage**.
References **optional**.
Applicants **should** be in good health.
Good salaries and prospects.
Apply: J. Mills and Son, Mersey Street, Liverpool 4.

3 How long will it be before we read adverts like this in our newspapers?

VACANCY OF XTJB/25 TYPE – LONDON

TLB plc are **in urgent need** of a button-pusher for their new AXK mobile hypermarket complex.
Minimum 10 years' experience with buttons vital.
M.Sc., Ph.D. plus two other post-graduate qualifications **essential, preferably** 1st Class.
15 good references **indispensable**.
Applications **must** be accompanied by a 10,000-word thesis on a subject of candidate's **choice**.
The successful candidate will **be required to** attend work between the hours of 09.00 and 09.10 and again between 17.55 and 18.00 two days a week.
He or she will **have to** write up full reports on each pushing.
Participation in in-service training schemes is **compulsory**, attendance at all lectures and seminars **obligatory**.
This position is **restricted to** those in the 35 to 38 age-group; **voluntary** redundancy **may** be taken at the age of 40, when the worker appointed will **be able to** draw a full pension – type Y2a.
Deadline for applications: 31.12.01

4 Finally, read this extract from the British news and note some of the degrees of **probability** it deals with.

'Good morning, and here is the 8 o'clock news, here on Radio Sunshine, for today, April 1st.

Hopes were fading last night of a peaceful settlement of the border dispute between North and South Wales. A long, bitter struggle now **looks inevitable** after the **predictable** breakdown of yesterday's talks.

Fears are growing for the lives of the fifteen people whose boat capsized and sank off the Isle of Wight early yesterday morning. A diver at the scene said: "There's really **not the remotest chance of** any of them being found alive now'. The accident was **almost certainly** caused by the **unexpected** change in weather conditions at that time and **may have happened** as close as twenty metres from the shore.

The safety of the 250 passengers hijacked late yesterday afternoon **was still in the balance** last night. The ten billion dollars had **definitely** not been paid by the midnight deadline, and it **seems unlikely** that it will be **in the foreseeable future**. What the hijackers' next move will be is **anybody's guess**.

Prospects of an end to the three-month-old strike of Public Service Employees still **look slim**. A union spokesman is quoted as saying: 'There's **no possibility of** any progress while the Government remain so stubborn. **There's no way** we'll accept two and a half per cent'. A Government Minister commented: 'An increased offer is absolutely **out of the question, certainly** this year and **most likely** for some years to come.'

It **looks as if** unemployment figures, interest rates and inflation are all **certain to** continue rising. Cabinet Misisters now admit there is very **little likelihood** of any improvement before the end of the decade. Meanwhile BP have announced that **in all probability** they will be forced to put up their petrol prices by 15% from next month. **It is thought** that their competitors **are bound to** follow suit. A further increase before the end of the year has not been **ruled out**, while heavier taxation on petrol is still very much **on the cards**.

Sport, and the eight-day cricket match between Canton Bern and Canton Zurich **seems set** to be a draw. After three days of heavy snow, it is **extremely doubtful whether** either side can force a result.

And finally, the weather: – today **is sure to** be wet and windy again; some areas **might** have thunderstorms and there **could** be some snow in the north. However, there is a **distinct possibility** that the sun will break through in some parts at tea-time, for a short period.

The time is five past eight. And now over to ...'

Practice

1 In what ways do you think the next few decades will bring the following to each individual?
   a less freedom
   b greater freedom

2 What do you think is the most likely future for each of the following items?
   a the Olympic Games
   b nuclear arms
   c marriage
   d books
   e the Aids virus
   f the ozone layer
   g the whale
   h space exploration

3 Write a letter to your local council complaining about the inconvenience you had to put up with while your road was dug up for new water pipes to be laid – and again for them to be laid properly – and for a third time while they were laid in the right place.

■ Add here any other words about the concepts discussed in this unit that you may come across.

. . . .

. . . .

. . . .

. . . .

. . . .

. . . .

. . . .

. . . .

. . . .

. . . .

. . . .

Cause and effect

Reading 1

Notice some of the ways in which the following single sentence can be added to and commented on.

I'm going to continue with my English,

because	I like the language.
because of	this book.
owing to	its importance in the world of business.
on account of	what my teachers have told me.
in case	I need it one day.
in order to	take Proficiency next year.
so as not to	forget what I've learnt.
so that	I can work in the States one day.
whether	you think it's a good idea or not.
wherever	I go.
whatever	happens.
whichever	country I go to next.
however	difficult the next stage is.
regardless	of my slow progress so far.
even if	I have to give up all my other interests.
whenever	I can.
if	it's possible.
providing	I can find a teacher.
provided that	someone agrees to teach me.
unless	you persuade me that Chinese is more useful.
although	I know I'm not the most gifted linguist.
even though	I'm a very busy person.
in spite of	the cost of these lessons.
despite	what you've said about my slow progress.
but	I think I'll give up Russian.
whereas	everyone else in the class is giving up.
unlike	the others, who are stopping.
as opposed to	my Japanese.
so	you'll see me again next term.
which	is a bit silly, I suppose,
considering	I live on a desert island.

Practice

What do you think of English now? Which of these statements apply to you? (Notice how cause and effect are expressed.)

1 A lot of my problems stem from trying to translate from my language.
2 My hesitation in speech is caused by a lack of vocabulary.
3 Some basic errors can be traced back to the way I learnt English at the beginning.
4 My large vocabulary is a direct consequence of knowing two other European languages.
5 Most of my problems have their roots in grammatical uncertainty.
6 Studying vocabulary has led to a better understanding of how English works.
7 More vocabulary means more fluency.
8 Learning a lot of words can result in confusion.

Reading 2

Notice, in this final and more difficult section, how a sentence can be added to, strengthened or balanced.

The illogical nature of much of English grammar makes it an unfortunate choice as a world language, **let alone** the leading one.

Consequently, many non-native speakers resent having English forced upon them. All possible attempts should be made, **therefore**, to further the cause of Esperanto. **For this reason**, we should all try to ensure that French is not lost as an international language.
In spite of this – or **because of** it, perhaps – English has been the vehicle for much of the world's greatest literature.
It does, **however**, prove to be a relatively easy language for most people to learn, **at least** in the early stages.
On the other hand, no other language can boast the richness and versatility that English has acquired over the centuries.
Furthermore, its vocabulary is impossibly imprecise, its preposition usage totally ridiculous, **not to mention** the absurdity of its spelling rules.
Moreover, it has lost so much of its charm over the past few decades that it no longer represents a satisfying subject for study.
What is more, the language has diversified into so many forms that most English speakers the world over would have difficulty in understanding each other.
Besides, who really wants a world language anyway? **In fact**, who needs language?

■ From now on, you will no doubt meet other ways of connecting two ideas. Make a note of them with examples below.

. . . .

. . . .

. . . .

. . . .

. . . .

. . . .

. . . .

. . . .

. . . .

. . . .

. . . .

. . . .

. . . .

. . . .

. . . .

. . . .

Index

Key

Age
Reading, page 11

The phrases marked with a star are usually used in conversation about a person who isn't there. They might be considered offensive if overheard by the person described or their family and friends.

Marital status
Practice, page 15

1   1 A b   B c   A c   B a   A c   B b

Build
Reading, page 25

The phrases marked with a star are usually used in conversation about a person who isn't there. They might be considered offensive if overheard by the person described or their family and friends.

Inside and outside the torso
Reading, page 32

The phrase marked with a star is usually used about a person who isn't there. It might be considered offensive if overheard by the person described or their family and friends.

Compound adjectives about the body
Study and practice, page 34

1 knock-kneed bow-legged   2 double-breasted pot-bellied   3 round-shouldered narrow-waisted   4 fair-haired slim-hipped   5 empty-handed right-footed   6 dark-skinned red-faced   7 cross-eyed strong-willed   8 sour-faced light-fingered   9 left-handed big-headed   10 broad-minded cold-blooded

Practice, page 34

1   1 hearty   2 leggy   3 chesty   4 handy   5 cheeky   6 nosey   7 skinny   8 hairy   9 bloody bloody   10 heady

The senses
Practice, page 37

2   1 sense   2 sensation   3 sensuous   4 sensible   5 sense   6 sensational   7 senseless   8 sensitive   9 sense   10 sensual

3   1 sense of power   2 sense of timing   3 sense of humour   4 sense of duty   5 sense of discipline   6 sense of adventure   7 sense of balance   8 sense of fairness   9 sense of fun

Character and personality

Game, page 39

ARIES: outgoing extrovert carefree light-hearted truthful open candid frank easy-going

TAURUS: strong-willed determined self-assured self-confident dominant ambitious demanding energetic competitive

GEMINI: proud arrogant pompous boastful selfish vain self-centred egocentric snobbish

CANCER: critical petty narrow-minded fussy stubborn obstinate materialistic mercenary possessive

LEO: unpredictable indecisive two-faced hypocritical dishonest changeable temperamental insincere unreliable

VIRGO: impressionable gullible weak-willed cowardly passive obedient secretive humble modest

LIBRA: sensible level-headed well-balanced practical calm fair-minded realistic rational logical

SCORPIO: aggressive violent brutal vicious ruthless unscrupulous malicious spiteful vindictive

SAGITTARIUS: passionate hot-blooded brave courageous adventurous lively dedicated devoted loyal

CAPRICORN: considerate tender gentle generous tolerant understanding protective affectionate thoughtful

AQUARIUS: impulsive impetuous impatient excitable rebellious revolutionary forgetful irresponsible uncontrollable

PISCES: shy self-conscious timid reserved sensitive imaginative creative emotional unstable

Attitudes and beliefs

Practice, page 44

1
1 l   2 b   3 e   4 h   5 t   6 q   7 d   8 j   9 p   10 c   11 g
12 m   13 k   14 s   15 n   16 a   17 o   18 i   19 u   20 r   21 f

Thinking, wanting and knowing

Practice, page 48

1
1 I'm looking forward to seeing him again.
   I'm dying to see him again.
   I can't wait to see him again.
   I'm longing to see him again.
2 I hadn't planned to spend so long there.
   I didn't mean to spend so long there.
   I wasn't planning to spend so long there.
   I had no intention of spending so long there.
3 I could do with a holiday.
   I feel like a holiday.
   I wouldn't mind a holiday.
   I wouldn't say no to a holiday.
4 I would rather go to London on Saturday, not Sunday.
   I would prefer to go to London on Saturday, not Sunday.
   For me, going to London on Saturday would be preferable to going on Sunday.
   My preference would be to go to London on Saturday, not Sunday.
5 I wouldn't be keen to move away from the coast.
   I'm reluctant to move away from the coast.
   I wouldn't fancy moving away from the coast.
   I don't like the idea of moving away from the coast.

Expressing oneself
Dialogue, page 57

1 greeting, greeting   **2** introducing, introduction   **3** inviting, invitations
4 accepted, acceptance   **5** decline   **6** suggesting, suggestion   **7** offering, offer
8 hesitant, hesitating, hesitation   **9** insisting, insistent   **10** agreed   **11** warning,
warning   **12** advising, advice   **13** apologising, apology, apologetic
14 reassuring   **15** sympathising, console, sympathetic, sympathy, consolation
16 enquiring, Enquiries   **17** complaining, complaints   **18** demanding, demand
19 threatening, threat   **20** insulting, insult   **21** complimenting, compliment
22 proposing, proposal   **23** congratulating, congratulations   **24** thanking, thanks
25 flattery, flattering   **26** praising, praise   **27** denouncing   **28** interrogation,
interrogating, questioning   **29** protesting, protest   **30** encouraging, encouragement
31 urging, urgent   **32** refused, refusal   **33** pleading, begging   **34** promising,
promise   **35** confiding, confidential, confidence   **36** heckling, hecklers
37 ignored   **38** blaming, blame   **39** admitting, admission   **40** confessing,
confession   **41** reproaching, reproachful, reproach   **42** mocking, making fun,
teasing, pulling leg   **43** boasting   **44** accusing, accusation   **45** denying, denial
46 reprimanding / scolding, telling   **47** ordering   **48** describing / condemning,
description / condemnation   **49** requesting, request   **50** reminding, reminder

Reacting to events
Practice, page 63

1   1 b   2 d   3 a   4 c   5 a   6 b   7 d   8 a

Sounds people make
Reading, page 65

1   a baby

2   a secretary

3   a magician's act

4   I had a bad cold, or 'flu.

Gesture, mannerism and body language
Practice 1, page 68

1   1 stared   2 peeped   3 peered   4 gazed   5 glanced

2   1 e   2 g   3 b   4 f   5 h   6 d   7 a   8 c

3   1 d   2 e   3 f   4 b   5 c   6 g   7 a

Practice 2, page 70

1   1 hugged   2 shook hands with   3 kissed   4 squeezed   5 embraced
       6 sat cuddling

Posture and movement

Reading, page 71

The plant world

Practice, page 81

[1] 1 willow   2 yew
     3 WILD: bluebell daisy orchid dandelion snowdrop primrose poppy
        GARDEN: iris carnation hyacinth marigold lily pansy rose narcissus crocus

[2] 1 waterlilies on the pond in the middle of the meadow   2 seaweed on pebbles in
     rock pools on the seashore   3 a ring of toadstools in a clearing in the forest
     4 heather and gorse on the heath and moorland   5 reeds in the marshland and
     swamps   6 coral all over the reef and the sea bed   7 long creepers among the
     undergrowth in the jungle   8 moss clinging to the bark of the trees of the wood
     9 ivy climbing the walls of the old house   10 cacti and palm trees near an oasis in
     the desert

The animal world
Practice, page 84

1.
Male:	stallion	fox	drake	gander
Female:	mare	vixen	duck	goose
Male:	buck	dog	bull	lion
Female:	doe	bitch	cow	lioness
Male:	ram	tiger	cock	tom(cat)
Female:	ewe	tigress	hen	cat

2.
dogs	puppies	sheep	lambs
cows	calves	pigs	piglets
horses	foals	butterflies	caterpillars
cats	kittens	goats	kids
hens	chicks	lions	cubs
insects	larvae		

3. cows: shed (or stall)   dogs: kennel   lions: den (or lair)   tame rabbits: hutch
canaries: cage   pigs: sty   bees: hive   horses: stable (or stall)
wild rabbits: hole (or burrow)   most birds: nest

4. 1 d   2 c   3 e   4 b   5 a

Food and drink
Practice, page 88

Poultry   1 c   Game   1 b
Fish 1 white fish: a b c e   oily: d f g h i   4 h
Cereals and grasses a 5 b 6 c 2 d 3 e 4 f 1

Furniture and household
Game 2, page 96

1. a rake   a pair of shears   a screw   a mop   a spanner   a pair of pliers
a corkscrew   a strainer   a cheese knife   a ladle   a mug   a pepper mill
a casserole dish   an ironing board

2. 1 a stethoscope   2 a tuning fork   3 a   opera glasses   b binoculars
c a telescope   d a microscope

3. b

Vehicles
Study and practice, page 102

2. 1 battery (sparking) plugs   2 boot tyres dashboard gear
3 bodywork bumper   4 accelerator (foot)brake clutch   5 choke carburettor

5. 1 A tandem is for two riders; a bicycle is for one rider.
2 A wheelchair is for someone who is ill; a push-chair is for a young child.
3 A scooter has small wide wheels; a moped has larger thin wheels.
4 A trolley is for carrying things in; a pram is for carrying a baby.

5 A sleigh is pulled by horses; you sit on a toboggan and slide down hill.
6 An estate car has a large boot; a hatchback does not.
7 A tricycle is a three-wheeled cycle; a three-wheeler is a car with three wheels.
8 In British English, a truck is a small lorry, often with an open area for carrying goods; a van is the smallest kind of commercial vehicle for carrying workmen and goods. In American English, a truck is what the British call a lorry.
9 A bus, either single- or double-decker, goes regularly throughout the day around a town or area; a tram runs on electricity and along rail around a town; a coach either goes on regular long-distance journeys or on special excursions.

Quiz 1, page 104

1 raft   2 houseboat   3 barge   4 ark   5 dinghy   6 lifeboat   7 trawler
8 yacht   9 ferry   10 paddle steamer   11 galleon   12 liner   13 punt
14 launch   15 canoe   16 powerboat   17 rowing boat   18 lightship
19 submarine   20 tug

Size, quantity, dimensions and measurements
Practice, page 112

1   1 branch   2 species   3 model   4 style   5 brand   6 group   7 race
8 family

2   1 part   2 breed   3 grade   4 bracket   5 department   6 make   7 form
8 category

Shapes
Practice, page 114

1   1 F   2 A   3 R

2   1 hollow cheeks   2 rough skin   3 pointed shoes   4 oval swimming pool
5 triangular roadsign   6 sloping roof   7 sharp blade   8 spiral staircase

Parts and components
Quiz, page 125

1   1 telephone   2 bicycle   3 bath / wash-basin   4 toilet   5 camera
6 television   7 electrical appliance   8 watch   9 shoes   10 skirt or dress
11 flower   12 vending machine   13 typewriter   14 tree   15 wine bottle
16 door   17 aeroplane   18 car   19 kettle or teapot   20 shirt or jacket

2   1 pair of compasses   2 hole punch   3 tent

What things do
Practice 1, page 128

1 b   2 b   3 a   4 c   5 b   6 d   7 a   8 b   9 b   10 d   11 c
12 b   13 b   14 b   15 a

Study and practice, page 129

The words occur in this order: stalling, overheating, breaking down, doing, veering, skidding, losing, letting, running out.

Practice 3, page 130

1 **1** a clock strikes **2** a volcano erupts **3** a kettle boils **4** a bell rings **5** a ball bounces **6** a violin string vibrates **7** a toilet flushes **8** a pendulum swings **9** a river flows **10** elastic stretches

2 **1** a bird hatches **2** an aeroplane takes off **3** a flower comes out **4** a plant takes root **5** a ship sets sail **6** day breaks **7** a problem arises **8** night falls **9** a war breaks out **10** the moon comes up

Births, marriages and deaths
Reading 1, page 135

In many legends, storks deliver babies by flying to the parents' house, carrying the baby in a shawl.

Practice 2, page 138

1 **1** assassin **2** mausoleum **3** asphyxiate(d) / suffocate(d) **4** strangle **5** martyr **6** malnutrition **7** cremate **8** wreath **9** will **10** requiem

Work
Game, page 140

1 dentist (dental surgeon) **2** optician **3** chiropodist **4** osteopath chiropractor masseur (masseuse) physiotherapist **5** hairdresser (hair stylist) **6** photographer **7** solicitor **8** travel agent **9** broker **10** piano tuner **11** antique dealer **12** vicar (priest) **13** (garage) mechanic **14** bookmaker **15** undertaker (funeral director) **16** driving instructor **17** (dog) breeder **18** estate agent **19** architect **20** building contractor (builder) **21** removal firm **22** scrap metal dealer (merchant) **23** glazier (and carpenter) **24** interior decorator **25** maintenance engineer **26** plumber **27** electrician **28** social worker **29** fire brigade (fireman) **30** psychiatrist

Health and illness
Practice 1, page 151

3 **1** d **2** e **3** a **4** b **5** c **6** f

4 **1** b **2** e **3** d **4** a **5** f **6** c

Practice 2, page 152

The words occur in this order: setting, performing, fitting, transplanting, saving, taking, giving, taking off, taking out, dressing, sterilising

Entertainment
Practice 1, page 160

1 **1** western **2** war film **3** romantic comedy **4** (Hollywood) musical **5** science fiction movie **6** horror film **7** documentary **8** disaster movie **9** cartoon **10** travelogue **11** historical film **12** thriller **13** blue movie

Game, page 161

1 d 2 a 3 c 4 b 5 e

Music and the arts
Game, page 169

 3 1 d 2 b 3 b 4 e d c a b 5 f c d a e b

Cooking, eating and drinking
Practice 1, page 175

1 scramble crack beat blend stuff poach whisk 2 chip peel mash 3 dice bone carve mince stew baste braise stuff chop 4 roll knead 5 scale bone steam poach 6 whip blend 7 grate steam peel dice chop shred

Travelling
Practice, page 180

1 1 boat 2 boat 3 car 4 train 5 car 6 car 7 car 8 boat
9 train 10 plane 11 boat 12 plane 13 plane 14 train 15 car
16 plane 17 boat 18 train 19 car 20 train

Law and order, crime and punishment
Study and practice, page 185

The words occur in the following order: arrested charged dropped tried trial jury guilty sentenced appeal executed suspect hunt apprehended statements custody court denied confessed plea convicted enquiry execution judges enquiry innocent pardon

Quality
Practice 1, page 189

1 b 2 c 3 b 4 a 5 d 6 d 7 b 8 a *or* b

Time
Brain teaser, page 193

The answer is never.

Numerals and proportions
Practice, page 197

1 1 eight 2 fifth 3 twice 4 a quarter 5 duet (duo) 6 triplets
7 treble it 8 a single whisky

2 The answer is 5.

3 9 nothing 10 none